CHRISTOPHER GILL
CRACKING
THE WHIP

Bretwalda Books Ltd

First Published 2012
Text Copyright © Christopher Gill 2012

All rights reserved. No reproduction of
any part of this publication is permitted
without the prior written permission of
the publisher:

Bretwalda Books
Unit 8, Fir Tree Close, Epsom,
Surrey KT17 3LD

info@BretwaldaBooks.com
www.BretwaldaBooks.com

To receive an e-catalogue of our complete
range of books send an email to
info@BretwaldaBooks.com

ISBN 978-1-909099-06-7

Bretwalda Books Ltd

Contents

Introduction
by Lord Tebbit

CHRISTOPHER GILL'S memoir of his times as a Member of the House of Commons is the story of a man unwilling to be swayed by political ambition or the herd instincts of political parties.

Gill's views about small businesses and European affairs were strongly held. He was of a dying breed of MPs who had experience in running a family business and little time for the political careerists of life.

To Gill the EU was a threat to all that he most admired about his country, its independence, history and constitution, which has been its guarantor of freedom. The collectivism and bureaucracy of the EU are anathema to his Conservative anti-collectivist conscience and belief.

These diaries record how those beliefs became incompatible with his membership of a Conservative Party increasingly obsessed with seeking office by compromising its values rather than persuading electors of them.

Two or three generations earlier there were many more like him. Men such as Harry Legge-Bourke, Derek Walker-Smith, Rear Admiral Morgan Giles who when gathered together were more likely by far to terrorise the Whips Office than to be terrorised by the Party Whips.

In Christopher Gill's time in the House, the careerists and compromisers had become easier meat for a leadership lacking the confidence and courage to campaign for what was right for fear it might be unpopular. He was one of the Maastricht "bastards" who have been proved right by events and his diaries record his unceasing efforts to persuade his follow back benchers to fight for those core values which have been undermined as the EU has extended its powers over this Kingdom.

He fought too against the changes to the constitution of the Conservative Party, which have subjugated local Conservative Associations to the power of the party leadership, making them no more than branches of Central Office and withering the grass roots, which once sustained the national organisation.

In the end Gill could take no more of it and concluded he could do more to uphold Conservative values through the Freedom Association than as a Conservative Member of Parliament and subsequently after resigning from the Conservative Party and declining to stand for re-election he joined UKIP. Any reader of these diaries will realise that Christopher Gill could be an uncomfortable colleague, but had there been more with the dogmatic courage of Christopher Gill, the Conservative Party could have been back in office by 2005.

Preface

On 1st May 1997 the Conservative Party suffered a most humiliating defeat at the hands of the British electorate and found itself in Opposition for the first time since Margaret Thatcher swept to power in 1979.

The author of this narrative, a Conservative Member of Parliament from 1987 to 2001, was surely not alone in hoping and trusting that the Party's time in opposition would be profitably spent analysing the reasons for its unprecedented defeat, formulating new policies for the future and, not least, replacing with fresh talent those members of the previous administration who had led the Party to such abject defeat.

The author's perspective as an implacable opponent of both European political union and economic and monetary union (EMU) predominates much of what follows but there can be no escaping the reality that European Union was a controversial and divisive issue. To this day it remains a powerful determinant of the Conservative Party's electoral prospects.

In 1997 the author had high hopes that the newly elected Leader, William Hague, would so stamp his authority upon the Conservative Party that these differences would be settled once and for all. For those Conservative MPs who believed in the paramount importance of European Union there was no lack of other homes to go to, as clearly evidenced by those of his colleagues who chose to abandon the Conservative Party in favour of either the Labour Party or the Liberal Democrats - even being rewarded with peerages for so doing!

For the so-called 'eurosceptics' the choice was much narrower. They could hardly 'cross the floor' to join either of the pro-EU (and socialist)

Parties, nor - because they journeyed on in the entirely mistaken belief that the Conservative Party could be persuaded to return to its roots - were they minded to throw in their lot with the nascent UK Independence Party. Having been elected as a Conservative MP by the electorate of the Ludlow constituency it was out of a keen sense of honour that the author, in spite of much speculation to the contrary, rejected the very idea of defecting although with the benefit of hindsight he can now see what an opportunity was missed in November 1994 when he was unceremoniously deprived of the Party Whip. To have then precipitated a by-election to either endorse or reject his strong and sincerely held belief that Britain would be better off out of the benighted EU might have changed the course of political history but, at that time, the prospect of convincing the Conservative Party to return to its roots still seemed a realistic possibility.

In 1997, although having originally intended to serve for only two terms, the author felt morally obliged to offer himself for re-election so as to give those who had first elected him in 1987 the opportunity to pass sentence on his 'rebellion' over the Treaty on European Union (Maastricht) and his subsequent refusal to vote in favour of sending more British taxpayers money to what he has described as 'that sink in Brussels' resulting in him, together with six others, having the Party Whip withdrawn.

That the author was returned with a substantial majority in 1997, when so many of his colleagues with bigger majorities lost their seats, is testimony to the almost certain fact that large swathes of the British electorate are wary of where European Union is leading them. Had the author not stood down as a matter of principle in 2001 the Ludlow seat would almost certainly not have fallen to the Liberal Democrats but, as became apparent, the Conservative Party was only too relieved to be rid of a 'rebel', even at the cost of losing a Parliamentary seat that they had previously held for well over a hundred years!

1997

1

" The leadership battle is not a beauty contest "

For the Conservative Party the General Election held on 1st May 1997 is cataclysmic. Colleagues with seemingly 'safe' seats, particularly in the London area, are cast out on their ear as majorities of 15,000 and more fall to Labour. It must be said, though, that due to boundary changes in some constituencies, direct comparisons with the results of the previous General Election in 1992 should not necessarily be taken at face value.

Perhaps the greatest shock of all is in the Enfield Southgate constituency where Secretary of State for Defence, Michael Portillo, sees his 15,545 majority overturned by Labour who are returned with a majority of 1433.

The swing against us is even more pronounced in Harrow West where Robert Hughes, Parliamentary Private Secretary (PPS) to Ted Heath, sitting on a majority of 17,890, is ousted by Labour who win the seat with a majority of 1240. Perhaps not surprisingly the biggest swing of all is in the Tatton constituency in Cheshire where the 22,365 majority of controversial former Minister for Corporate Affairs, Neil Hamilton, is converted into one of 11,077 by BBC reporter Martin Bell, standing as an Independent.

For the Group of Eight - so-called because of our having been deprived of the party Whip in the last Parliament for having dared to abstain on a motion to send more money to Brussels - the satisfaction of bucking the trend in terms of drastically reduced majorities is tempered by the loss of

Nick Budgen in Wolverhampton South West and Tony Marlow in Northampton North. Their relatively small majorities of 4966 and 4067 respectively are insufficient to withstand the tide of anti-Conservative feeling which sweeps the country resulting in the Party's Parliamentary representation being reduced from the 336 seats it had won in 1992 to a mere rump of 165.

The fact that the former 'whipless' Members fare relatively better than the majority of our colleagues gives the lie to accusations that we are unrepresentative of Conservative opinion in the country and that we are the cause of the Party's crushing defeat. The reality is that the seeds of the Conservative Party's defeat were sown way back in 1990 when the decision was taken to join the Exchange Rate Mechanism (ERM). As a direct consequence of this ill-fated decision, to adopt fixed exchange rates as a prelude to joining the Single Currency, the Conservative Party's reputation for economic competence had been utterly destroyed.

Between entry into the ERM in October 1990 and our ignominious ejection 23 months later this very un-Thatcherite attempt to 'buck the market' had created the conditions in which thousands of businesses had gone to the wall, tens of thousands of homeowners had seen their properties repossessed and hundreds of thousands had been thrown out of work – and apology came there none!

The Prime Minister, John Major, the Cabinet and indeed the whole Government, for there were no principled resignations, had sunk so much political capital into this ill-starred project that it seemed that the very last thing that they were prepared to do was to admit that they had made a mistake, to apologise for the consequences of their bad judgement and to undertake never again to repeat such a catastrophic exercise. None of these things were forthcoming and so on 1st May 1997 the electorate took their somewhat postponed revenge.

Major having resigned – the least he could do having led the previously almost unassailable Conservative Party to such an ignominious defeat – the first thing that we have to do in this new Parliament is to elect his successor.

First off the mark with a Press conference on May 13th is John Redwood (Wokingham). Given the opportunity by the 'reptiles' to knock fellow contender Ken Clarke (Rushcliffe) 'for six', John conspicuously fails to do so. This prompts me to say at a lunch in his campaign HQ two days later that the leadership battle is not a beauty contest and that he needs to be seen to be different to the other contenders, not least on the subject of Europe. John is reluctant to go down that particular road for fear of antagonising those of our colleagues who might otherwise be his supporters and whilst he tries hard to persuade me to declare my support for him, even offering the inducement of office in a shadow government, something inside me makes me reluctant to do so.

In the meantime, on May 14th, I have run the gauntlet of the TV cameras in Lord North Street to attend a champagne reception at the campaign HQ established by Michael Howard (Folkestone & Hythe) at the home of Jonathan Aitken (Thanet South). When we get down to business I invite Michael to give the assembled company a thumb-nail sketch of his policy on European Union. In his reply he rules out having a referendum on anything other than the outcome of the Amsterdam Inter-Governmental Conference (IGC), subsequently causing Norman Lamont (the recently deposed Member for Kingston-upon-Thames) to ask me if I was satisfied with the answer. When I put the ball back in Norman's court he confides that he himself, had he been able, would probably have stood as the 'Out of Europe' candidate, with, I understand, Jonathan Aitken as his campaign manager.

Another election that is pending is that for Chairman of the 1922 Committee (the '22) and members of its influential Executive. At its meeting on Monday 19th May members of the '92 Committee (a group of generally right of centre Conservative MPs) vote against having a 'slate' for the election to the chairmanship - i.e. a list of preferred candidates that colleagues would be under a moral obligation to vote for - because with no less than four of our group's own members in contention viz: John Butterfill (Bournemouth West), Archie Hamilton (Epsom & Ewell), Edward Leigh (Gainsborough) and John Townend (Bridlington), it is quite apparent that the group cannot be mandated.

In the event Archie Hamilton is elected Chairman and much to my surprise I find myself elected to the Executive, having allowed my name to go forward to test opinion within the Party following the dramatic events of the last Parliament in which, as previously related, the Party Whip had been withdrawn from myself and six others. That we seven came to be known as the 'Group of Eight' is explained by the fact that Sir Richard Body (Boston & Skegness) having actually voted for the European Finance Bill, in accordance with the Government's 3-Line whip, then went straightaway to the Whips office and resigned the Party whip in protest.

As a sad commentary on our times, Cornish fisherman, Mick Mahon, telephones me from Newlyn to say that he has met a couple of my constituents holidaying in Cornwall who tell him that they voted Liberal Democrat on May Day. They agreed with Mick that I was a good constituency MP, that I was 'sound' on Europe and that I had helped the fishing industry tremendously but they had not voted for me because of Conservative Party 'sleaze'!

At a meeting of the 'Group of Eight', sadly now only six, on 20th May the question of the Party leadership is the main topic of conversation. Dick Body is very much opposed to anybody in our group putting their name forward and is clearly on the point of declaring for Michael Howard. John Wilkinson (Ruislip-Northwood) has already declared for John Redwood, Teddy Taylor (Southend East) is being his inimitable self and Richard Shepherd (Aldridge Brownhills) is not able to be with us. That leaves Teresa Gorman (Billericay) and myself feeling somewhat disgruntled and afterwards, over a cup of tea, I suggest that if none of the now six leadership contestants is prepared to say what the public want to hear on the vexed question of Europe then one of us ought to stand. We agree to sleep on it.

The following day I meet Mike Penning, originally Teddy Taylor's research assistant and latterly PR man for the Group of Eight, to discuss the prospect of our group staging a Press conference tomorrow, ostensibly on the subject of the Dutch draft treaty to be put to the forthcoming IGC in Amsterdam but in reality to say that if none of the six leadership candidates viz: Ken Clarke, Stephen Dorrell, William Hague, Michael Howard, Peter Lilley and John Redwood are prepared to stand on an overtly anti-European Union ticket then one of us will. Subsequently I put this notion to a full meeting of our group, with the exception of Teddy Taylor who has gone to ground, but apart from Teresa there is no support and the idea is dropped.

By this time there is mounting pressure to change the rules for electing the Party Leader and bang on cue the irrepressible Jeffrey Archer (ennobled by John Major in 1992) is heard on the BBC 'Today' Programme sounding off about extending the franchise beyond the existing electorate of MPs only.

At 10.30 on 22nd May the Executive committee of the '22 meet and by noon have agreed, nem con, to recommend the status quo, tempered with an undertaking to subsequently carry out a root and branch review of the Party's structure, including the rules for the election of Leader. The Executive meets again at 16.30 to agree the final text of the statement to be made to the full '22 Committee meeting at 17.00. In the meantime the Chairman and the two Vice Chairmen, John Butterfill and Geoffrey Johnson-Smith (Wealdon), have lunched with the Chairman of the National Union Executive Committee (NUEC), Robin Hodgson, who is leading the charge for greater 'democracy' within the Party and whom the celebrated Alan Clark (Kensington & Chelsea) describes as being 'very left wing'.

Later in the day a colleague tells me that Robin Hodgson, whilst Conservative candidate for the Stratford-upon-Avon constituency, pulled out at the last minute due to circumstances surrounding his private life. This is confirmed to me the following day by an entirely different source who alleges that whilst Hodgson pulled out of Stratford 15 years ago, ostensibly for business reasons, the Party Chairman at the time, Cecil Parkinson, had been on to the constituency suggesting that there were other reasons why Hodgson's candidature should not be pursued.

My own involvement with the said Robin Hodgson, whose mother living in Astley Abbots is also my constituent, is about to intensify as a result of my volunteering to be the liaison officer between the '22 Executive and the NUEC. At our first encounter on June 5th I take the bull by the horns and insist upon addressing the assembled company on the subject of leadership contest rules. The NUEC is very hostile to what I have to say but nevertheless I feel that it is important to put the record straight, not least because it is apparent that chairman, Robin Hodgson, has no intention of reporting back to the committee on his various meetings with the officers of the '22 Executive. To cap it all, Party Chairman, Dr Brian Mawhinney – having successfully made the 'chicken run' from his old seat of Peterborough to Cambridgeshire NW in order to avoid the inevitable – instead of backing me and the unanimous decision of the '22, blathers on about how he doesn't agree with it and doesn't miss the opportunity of saying specifically that he 'doesn't agree with everything that Chris Gill has said' – just as he had disagreed with me four years previously when I had represented to him, in his then capacity as Health Minister, that the appointment of a rabid left wing socialist to the chairmanship of the Birmingham Health Authority should be resisted. "I should like to reassure you that I have every confidence in Bryan Stoten's ability to tackle this challenging role" he had replied. To this day the logic of appointing as one's agent a person who is implacably opposed to one's own declared principles and policies escapes me.

Not without some justification the NUEC are extremely angry about the way in which the Party is being run and not least about the perceived arrogance of its Members of Parliament. In the light of the disastrous General Election results their anger is particularly intense but few appreciate how that anger is being exploited by their Chairman for his own nefarious purposes. Personally I am of the opinion that they are barking up the wrong tree and that it would make much better sense if they were fighting to achieve 'one man, one vote' (OMOV) for the position of Party Chairman rather than Party Leader. When all said and done, none of the Party rank and file know the strengths and weaknesses of the leadership candidates better than the Parliamentarians with whom the successful contestant will inevitably have to work. By the same token it would seem not unreasonable to let the voluntary side of the Party have a very much bigger say in choosing the Party Chairman. The counter argument that the Leader must always be able to appoint to this important position someone that he or she is comfortable with has not always had the desired effect and in any case means that the voluntary side of the Party is kept at arms-length in terms of policy making.

It is no surprise when, early the following week, '22 Chairman, Archie Hamilton, tells me that he has had some reaction to my debut at the NUEC but it is left to his elder brother, Lord Hamilton of Dalzell, to really put the cat amongst the pigeons. Speaking at a Ludlow Constituency Conservative Association (LCCA) function at Robin Hodgson's home at Nash Court on 28th June his Lordship, in his capacity as Association President, tells the assembled company that he is opposed to OMOV in leadership elections. When subsequently I try to thank Robin and his wife Fiona for hosting our function he is incandescent with rage saying that Lord H. has abused their hospitality by expressing a view that is contrary to Robin's ! Not entirely undeservedly Robin Hodgson is known to a few as Enver Hodgson, after the former Albanian dictator Enver Hoxha.

The question of reform of the Party's constitution will run and run but in the meantime we have to get on with the urgent task of electing a new Leader. Word reaches me via Mike Penning that there is increasing frustration in the Redwood camp due to the antics of one Hywel Williams – shades of 1995! (see Whips Nightmare p. 158-166) – thus reinforcing my resolve not to get involved. In spite of that decision, on 3rd June, in company with Teddy Taylor and Teresa Gorman, I attend John Redwood's press conference in the Grand Committee Room. JR's delivery is frankly wooden but he loosens up during the Question and Answer session where I express the opinion that saying 'NO' to the Single Currency six months ago might have prevented the mass defections that we suffered at the polls on 1st May but that to get those people back onboard it will now be necessary to go much further and offer the electorate the prospect of getting out of the collectivist EU altogether.

Earlier in the day Jonathan Collett, Campaign Director of the Bruges Group, who very generously gave several days of his time to help me during the election campaign, has told me that they are backing Peter Lilley but feels sure that they would switch to anyone who was prepared to stand on an 'Out of the EU' ticket. For my part I say that I haven't ruled out the possibility of doing just that and Jonathan rings back the following morning to say that his chairman, Dr Martin Holmes, is enthusiastic that I should.

In conversation with ITN's Political Editor, Michael Brunson, he expresses the opinion that if an 'Out of Europe' candidate stands for the leadership it will indicate a total lack of unity within the Conservative Party although he recognises the strength of the arguments in favour of the idea, not the least of which are the millions of voters who are currently disenfranchised on this issue.

On the morning of June 4th Stephen Dorrell (Charnwood) pulls out of the leadership race and later in the day holds a joint press conference with Ken Clarke (Rushcliffe). The following day the five remaining candidates are invited to make their case in front of the '92 Group. In the event, Ken Clarke's presentation is appalling, Wm. Hague (Richmond) and Peter Lilley (Hitchen & Harpenden) are unconvincing and so the choice appears to be between Michael Howard and John Redwood who excels himself by making by far and away the best presentation of them all. Earlier in the day he has attended a meeting of the 'Group of Eight' where, in vino veritas after a most agreeable Livery & Court Luncheon at Butchers Hall, I tell him that if I had his intellect I would also be a contender simply because of the absence of any other candidate saying what the voters want to hear us say. As a result of this meeting Teddy Taylor pledges his support to JR, leaving only Teresa Gorman, Richard Shepherd and myself as yet uncommitted. At the lunch one of my fellow Liverymen tells me that he didn't vote for Rupert Allason in Torbay because of his arrogance – Rupert lost by 12 votes!

Back in the Ludlow constituency at the weekend the opinion, as represented to me by each of the LCCA's three area committees - viz: Bridgnorth, Bishops Castle and Ludlow – is that Ken Clarke should be our next Leader but there is no way that I can possibly vote for that man. As Secretary of State for Health, Education Secretary and Home Secretary he has successively alienated NHS workers, doctors, nurses, teachers and policemen, not to mention the guilt he shares for having been one of the assassins who did for one of the most successful leaders the Conservative Party has ever had, Margaret Thatcher.

Ironically, Ken Clarke is credited with having been a successful Chancellor of the Exchequer. In point of fact, in that role, he could do no more than follow the only course left open to us once we had been forced to abandon the Exchange Rate Mechanism (ERM) of which he himself had been such a passionate advocate. It is barely credible that this man whom I regard as the principal architect of our misfortunes should now be enjoying such popular appeal. His one redeeming feature is his complete frankness about his support for the concept of 'ever closer union' within the EU. Whilst I entirely reject that concept myself and believe that the majority of my Parliamentary colleagues have similar feelings and will not therefore elect him Leader, one cannot but respect him for sticking to his principles – principles which, incidentally, might perhaps be more easily accommodated in one of the socialist parties.

Whilst there is no fear of me declaring for Ken Clarke I am still reluctant to declare for any of the other candidates either. Doing so is going to put me in bad odour with some of my constituents whichever way I jump and having taken a relatively high profile in the contest to oust John Major in 1995 I am content to leave it to others to make the running in this one. John Redwood is anxious for me to declare for him but notwithstanding that I had managed his campaign office two years ago I am reluctant to go beyond promising him my vote which is, in any case, more than I had intended to do until hearing him speak at the '92 Group meeting last Thursday.

On the eve of the first leadership ballot Peter Lilley attends a meeting of

15

the 'Group of Eight' and is asked some searching questions including one from Teresa who questions whether he really wants to be Leader. In reply Peter says that coming from William Pitt's home town it has been his lifelong ambition to emulate him! In the event Peter attracts 24 votes, one more than Michael Howard, JR gets 27, Wm. Hague 41 and Ken Clarke, the beneficiary of the votes of all 17 Conservative MEPs, tops the poll with 49. Immediately after the result is announced the Executive of the '92 Committee meet in John Townend's office where the decision is taken to bring maximum pressure to bear upon Howard and Lilley to throw in their lot with Redwood. When I telephone Howard shortly after our meeting (at 18.50 to be precise), urging him to throw his weight behind JR and to recommend his supporters to do likewise, the only response that I get is "I hear what you say".

After the 10 o'clock vote I tell a small group of colleagues, at a meeting convened by Bill Cash (Stone), that instead of trying to finesse the outcome of the next ballot it would be better if they all voted in accordance with their own first preferences. In my opinion Clarke cannot win and therefore there is no need to go for a compromise candidate.

Incensed at the refusal of Howard and Lilley to back Redwood I subsequently find myself at a meeting in JR's office also attended by my Shropshire colleague, Owen Paterson (Shropshire North), who is equally annoyed. The upshot of the meeting is that we are all given lists comprising the names of those colleagues we need to contact to maximise the Redwood vote in the next ballot.

When the Redwood team meet again the following morning (June 11th) I suggest that he should write to all those of our colleagues who were listed in the Daily Mail on 30th April as being opposed to the adoption of the single currency, pointing out that he is the only candidate positively articulating this particular point of view. Later in the day there is a long debate at a meeting of the '92 Group where Nick Hawkins (latterly Blackpool South but now representing Surrey Heath), Nigel Evans (Ribble Valley) and others try to justify voting for Wm. Hague rather than their fellow group member, John Redwood. There is nothing in our rules to say that colleagues must at all times follow the group line and in any case, in a secret ballot, it is of course quite impossible to know whether they do or not. On the other hand I do suggest to our Chairman, John Townend, that when members like Peter Lilley, having failed to make the cut themselves, conspicuously refuse to throw their weight behind another group member, their membership of our group really ought to be terminated. This is certainly my view in the case of the two colleagues who are reputed to have voted for Ken Clarke.

An interesting comment on yesterday's events is provided by James Cran (Beverley & Holderness) who tells me that Howard's decision to transfer his support to Hague was made at 17.45, in other words immediately after the result of the ballot was declared and a good hour before I was able to speak to him myself.

Having spent every spare moment of the previous day canvassing support for JR I am able to report back to his campaign team meeting on June 12th the result of the conversations that I have had with no less than fourteen of our colleagues. I also, contrary to my original intentions, volunteer to declare publicly for JR and am instrumental in persuading Ann Winterton (Congleton) to do the same. Sir Richard Body, having supported Howard in the first round, rings and when asked if he will declare for Redwood says that he has already done so – in the Times newspaper and on the BBC's 'World at One' programme.

Roger Knapman (Stroud) expresses the opinion that the Party's National Union ought to have regular meetings with the '22 Committee which to me seems to be an entirely sensible proposition, not least because Sir Anthony Grant, who had preceded me as the liaison officer between the '22 Executive and the NUEC, volunteered the information at a lunch at the Carlton Club yesterday that the National Union had been very angry for a very long time. Notwithstanding its obvious merit I doubt that Roger's suggestion will make any progress because I suspect that it suits the chairmen of both committees to conduct their business on a one-to-one basis without the hazard of their members actually being privy to their discussions. Continuing with this practice is hardly likely to defuse the present tension between the Parliamentary Party on the one hand and the voluntary side of the Party on the other but then, hey, what do I know!

At a hustings in Committee Room 10 on 16th June, organised by Bill Cash, the three remaining leadership candidates set out to sell their respective merits to the assembled company. Redwood, in spite of the Division bell starting to ring whilst he is in mid flow, performs better than either Clarke or Hague who are soon at each other's throats on account of Hague saying that anyone joining his Shadow Cabinet will have to toe the line – something that Clarke is not renowned for doing!

On the morning of the second ballot, 17th June, there are discussions in JR's campaign HQ in Wilfred Street about the day ahead. I agree to go on the BBC's 'PM' programme to comment on the outcome of the vote, where I will be joined by Tim Yeo (Suffolk South) representing Wm. Hague and John MacGregor (Norfolk South) representing Ken Clarke. In the event I get very little time on air because JR gets only 38 votes, compared with Hague's 62 and Clarke's 64. Returning to the Redwood campaign HQ later that evening we hear JR say that 'you cannot trust a word that Hague says and I couldn't possibly deal with him'. Support for JR's idea of joining forces with Ken Clarke comes mainly from the newly elected Members and one or two more senior Members such as Andrew Robathan (Blaby) and Julian Brazier (Canterbury). For my part I gently warn that if in these circumstances Clarke doesn't win then JR will be sunk and, furthermore, his team will all be seen not to have held together. I am not the only one to say that they would have to consider abstaining if JR proceeds to form an alliance with Clarke. Angela Browning (Tiverton &Honiton) is adamant that this is what she would do. Regardless of any feelings of solidarity with JR we are simply not prepared to transfer our votes to the arch Europhile former Chancellor of the Exchequer.

Waking up the following morning I am more than a little concerned about the prospect of a Clarke/Redwood pact and before 8 o'clock put in a call to Ian Duncan-Smith (Chingford & Woodford Green) to tell him so. Ian is JR's campaign manager and suggests that I attend a meeting at the Wilfred Street campaign HQ scheduled to start at 10.00. It so happens that I am unable to get to Wilfred Street on time but in any case I need hardly have bothered because walking there along Buckingham Gate I bump into John Townend coming the other way. 'It's all over – finished – Redwood's gone over to Clarke' says John. Together we repair to the nearby St James Hotel where over a cup of coffee John and I discuss the future of the '92 Group in the light of the events of the past few weeks.

Later in the day JR tells me that he didn't go public on his deal with Ken Clarke until 10.30 in which case I should perhaps have gone on to the meeting. On the other hand I am not sorry to have fortuitously avoided being associated with any deal with Ken Clarke.

Much later in the day JR says that I must stick by him in tomorrow's vote but I am obliged to tell him that I cannot possibly, under any circumstances, vote for KC. Fortunately this is the message that I have been giving out all day, oblivious of a report in the Times newspaper saying that Dick Body and I are likely to support KC! This explains the indignant letters received from Sir Roger Moate, formerly the Member for Faversham, and also from my former research assistant, Adrian Lee, who will, coincidentally, go on to fight that seat at the next General Election. It also explains the conversation with Dr Michael Clark (Rochford) who reminds me that I had urged him to vote for Redwood in the second ballot and to worry about stopping KC in the third round.

The day of the final ballot arrives (June 19th) and Norman Lamont, formerly the Member for Kingston-upon-Thames, telephones to say 'vote Hague'. Even at this late stage I am undecided. Had William given me a better answer a few days ago when I asked him what his policy on European Union would be I would not now be thinking in terms of abstaining, but the fact remains that what he told me was that his policy was the same as that of all the other candidates – whatever that might be! In other words he didn't answer the question and therefore didn't give me any reason to vote for him.

Eventually, and more than a little reluctantly, I drag myself off to Committee Room 14 to vote for, figuratively speaking, the lesser of the two evils and subsequently find myself on the winning side. Wm. Hague attracts 92 votes to Ken Clarke's 70 votes although for inexplicable reasons the count takes nearly twice as long as last Tuesday's when there were, of course, three contestants.

When David Wilshire (Spelthorne) says what a mistake it was to expand the Redwood campaign team I cannot but agree with him. He tells me that the original nucleus of the team viz: himself, Ian Duncan-Smith and Angela Browning were not in favour of the Redwood/Clarke electoral pact, the rationale for which will continue to elude me for a very long time to come.

The Ludlow Constituency Conservative Association (LCCA) AGM on Friday 20th June is attended by West Midlands Area President, Michael Price, who declares his support for OMOV in future leadership contests. Notwithstanding that Cecil Parkinson, a man of similar vintage, has just been appointed Party Chairman, Michael Price has been told that there are no other jobs for him in the Conservative Party because of his age! He also tells me that as a member of the panel interviewing prospective Parliamentary candidates he was reprimanded for asking them if they were in fact members of the Party on an occasion when it transpired that only two out of a group of eight aspirants actually were!

At the '22 Executive meeting on June 25th vice Chairman John Butterfill reports back on meetings with National Union (NU) President, John Taylor, and NU Chairman, Robin Hodgson, concerning the electoral college for future leadership elections. Whilst conceding that a 'primary' could be held exclusively within the Parliamentary party they are looking for anything between 25 and 40 per cent representation in the subsequent ballots. A fortnight passes without any apparent further progress and on July 9th I feel obliged to express my concern at the '22 Executive that time is running out in terms of reaching agreement with the rest of the Party regarding re-organisation before the impending Summer recess. Chairman, Archie Hamilton, sidesteps my questions regarding the Party Leader's views on this subject and what he feels should be the subject heading in the ongoing debate. Whilst OMOV is the subject of many informal conversations I have to remind Archie of my previous request that we should discuss this matter formally within the Executive.

Whilst our new Leader's views on this and other subjects have yet to emerge, at a private meeting with him on 7th July I am given the assurance that the Conservative Party will, in the event of a referendum on the Single Currency, campaign for a 'NO' vote. Compared with his predecessor's policy on this vexed question this is a distinct improvement but William's subsequent refusal to rule out entry into the Euro beyond the next Parliament, or for the duration of his leadership, will prove to be a disappointment and evidence of the continuing malign influence upon him of the Europhile rump. At the next General Election these same 'wreckers' will accuse Hague of losing because of his being too 'eurosceptic'. The reality is that his policy would have had much greater credibility and popular appeal had he gone the whole hog instead of allowing himself to be hamstrung by the fudge foisted upon him by the likes of Ken Clarke whom he had, when all said and done, fairly and squarely beaten in the leadership contest.

On the same day as my meeting with William I have no compunction in telling our Chief Whip, James Arbuthnot (now NE Hampshire but previously Wanstead & Woodford) how absolutely fed-up I am with Jeffrey Archer, Leon Brittan, Ted Heath, Geoffrey Howe et al shouting the odds when the rest of us, who actually have to submit ourselves to the public for re-election, are having to exercise much greater self-control and restraint.

The sequel to what the Leader has told me about his policy regarding the Euro is that two days later Bill Cash tells his Amsterdam (EU Treaty) study group that he has heard that Wm. Hague will campaign for a 'NO' vote in any Single Currency referendum. Because the only person that I have spoken to on this subject since meeting William is Lord Stoddart of Swindon I can only conclude that his Lordship has been busy, since last evening, passing on the news. Just over a week later, on 18th July, at a British Council colloquium in Paris, I hear David Curry (Skipton &Ripon) tell the assembled company that Wm. Hague has given him an undertaking that "the policy on the Single Currency would be settled by collective discussion" and that he, David Curry, "would not have accepted a place in the Shadow Cabinet on any other basis".

Charles Lewington, also attending the colloquium and latterly Director of Communications at Conservative Central Office (CCO), is equally appalled at what we have both heard David Curry say but it is nearly another fortnight before I get the opportunity to challenge the Leader about this apparent contradiction in his position. Meeting him privately on 30th July he is just a shade less than convincing when I tax him with the difference between what he has told me and what he is alleged to have told David Curry. On another subject, that of the fishing industry, he promises to read my recent speeches on the subject of the Common Fisheries Policy (CFP) in advance of his planned visit to the West Country next week. In this connection I stress the importance of winning back the fishing community's trust by making sure that his actions match his rhetoric. Similarly I suggest that he needs to be careful how he treats his Parliamentary colleagues because the reality is that we are not his employees and cannot therefore be forced to swallow the 'party line' if it varies according to whom he is speaking to – shades of John Major!

Whilst in Paris for the British Council colloquium I had quite by chance found myself sitting next to BBC Chief Political Adviser, Anne Sloman, at breakfast one morning. In the course of our conversation she tells me about what she regards as bad behaviour on the part of my Parliamentary colleagues. She cites jeering at Question Time, wanting to engage in Yah Boo politics and not turning up to lunches when invited! She says that she intends to give CCO a second chance to field someone senior to represent the Party on these occasions but goes on to say how she regards ex-Party Chairman, Brian Mawhinney, as being absolutely appalling – a sentiment with which secretly I am bound to agree.

Before Parliament breaks up for the Summer recess I am flattered to receive compliments from such a diverse range of people as Labour MP Roger Godsiff (Birmingham Sparkbrook), Paul Keetch, the newly elected Liberal Democrat Member for Hereford, Channel 4 News presenter Jon Snow and BBC Head of Current Affairs, Mark Damazer, for my principled stand against European Union. This is mirrored in my constituency where several of those attending an LCCA function in Worthen say that whilst they couldn't bring themselves to vote for the Party, they had voted for me. Peter Barclay, who has chipped in £600 towards the cost of election expenses, says much the same thing when he states that whilst he doesn't support the Conservative Party, he does support me!

To demonstrate their support for country pursuits, on 10th July, 100,000 people descend on Hyde Park in an endeavour to persuade the new Government that imposing a ban on hunting with hounds is something that they really should not be doing. Journeying to Hyde Park on London Underground I accost a fellow passenger who is happy to tell me that whilst he doesn't himself hunt, shoot or fish he is intent upon attending the rally to defend the right of those who do. Like so many others beating a path to Hyde Park that day he is not a countryman but nevertheless recognises the significance of the principle that is at stake.

Unfinished business at the time Parliament goes into recess at the end of July is the question of the future rules and structure of the Conservative Party. After I have attended the General Purposes Committee of the National Union on 29th Archie Hamilton asks me if I think Robin Hodgson realises that the NU is going to be axed. The following day great anger is expressed at the '22 Executive about Party Chairman Archie Norman's questionnaire addressed to constituency Chairmen and Agents regarding Party 'democracy'. I tell the Executive that as far as I am concerned I am a private individual who stands in the Conservative interest and takes the

Conservative Whip. I go on to say how monstrous it would be to enfranchise Party members who may be paying only a minimum subscription and who might only have done so for the sole purpose of skewing the outcome of a leadership contest. Meanwhile, back in the West Midlands, former LCCA Chairman, Michael Wood, is disappointed in the ballot to elect a new chairman of the Area Council which goes to future West Midlands MEP, Philip Bradbourn, with Michael being re-elected to represent the Area on the National Union.

1997

2

" There is no future in appeasement "

When Parliament resumes on 27th October I am in the House early in the hope of catching the Speaker's eye to speak in a debate on Defence but, in spite of being one of only a tiny handful of Members to have actually served in the Armed Forces, I am not called.

The big issue is still the Single Currency and my constituency neighbour, Peter Temple-Morris (Leominster) and others are playing up about the Conservative Party's new stance on this crucial topic. In a statement to the House the Chancellor of the Exchequer, Gordon Brown (Dunfermline East), pledges the Government's support, in principle, for the Single Currency and goes on to signal the possibility of a national referendum on the subject early in the next Parliament. As events unfold this will be seen to have been a rash statement which Labour will be reluctant to honour. As public opinion against the Euro increases and the Government's prospect of winning a referendum correspondingly decreases, the idea will be kicked into the long grass even before this Parliament ends in mid-2001.

From the dispatch box Peter Lilley's response to the Chancellor's statement is feeble and the Conservative benches are left looking pathetic. So incensed am I by the failure of either the Shadow Chancellor or the Leader of Her Majesty's Loyal Opposition to seize the opportunity to say that the Conservative Party is now, under its new Leader, opposed to the Single

Currency that I feel obliged to collar James Arbuthnot to request a meeting. At that meeting I tell our Chief Whip that it is far better, as far as the Party is concerned, to have all the blood on the carpet at the beginning of the Parliament rather than later. The Chief assures me that Wm. Hague is not going to give in to the Europhiles and that under his leadership there will be no fear of compromising with those who do not support his policies. As well as venting my anger on the Chief Whip I also pen a letter to Peter Lilley urging him to be very much more forthright on the question of the Single Currency when he speaks at the LCCA Annual Dinner at the end of the week.

Ironically, Peter Temple-Morris has, in the meantime, announced that he will remain in the Conservative Party now that Michael Heseltine (Henley) and Ken Clarke (Rushcliffe) have made it clear that they will be actively working to co-ordinate a 'YES to the Single Currency' campaign. In respect of two other arch-Europhiles there is better news., On 29th October Ian Taylor (Esher & Walton) announces his resignation as front bench spokesman on Northern Ireland and three days later David Curry emulates him by resigning as Shadow Agriculture Minister. Not to be outdone, on Remembrance Sunday (9th November), Ted Heath (Old Bexley & Sidcup) will tell the world that he will not be voting with the rest of the Party against the Amsterdam Treaty and that he intends to abstain. This reminds me that, when he was our guest speaker at a highly successful '92 Group dinner on 4th November, Wm. Hague had made it quite clear that he would be absolutely consistent in what he told different wings of the Party. Called upon to ask the first question I first of all remind William of my experience of having had the Party whip withdrawn in 1994 for failing to respond to a 3-line Whip on the European Communities (Finance) Bill and then go on to invite him to assure the meeting that the Party's code of discipline had not changed. Notwithstanding Alan Clark (Kensington & Chelsea) thinking that was a "brilliant" question I remain unconvinced that the 'wreckers' in the Party will be treated similarly although it has to be said that before the month is out the Whip has been withdrawn from Temple-Morris who has promptly resigned his membership of the Party. Next June he will 'cross the floor' and after a decent interval his new-found friends in the Labour Party will elevate him to the House of Lords.

On the day after Ted Heath's outburst my Whip, Oliver Heald (Hertfordshire North), seeks my opinion on a number of issues such as whether the Conservative Party should abandon Unionism in favour of nationalism; whether England should have its own Parliament; what I think about Proportional Representation (PR) and not least whether I am happy about the imposition of a 3-line Whip for the vote on the Amsterdam Treaty in two days time. With regard to the latter I tell Oliver that the same should happen to Ted Heath as happened to me three years ago when I abstained on the EC Finance Bill. Such a course of action would demonstrate Wm. Hague's mastery of the Party; would be helpful to the Party Whips in terms of maintaining discipline and might go down extremely well with the millions of our Party's supporters who now see Ted Heath as a spoiler.

Although Wm. Hague's policy on the Single Currency is hardly likely to appeal to the relatively few remaining committed Europhiles within the Parliamentary Party these political dinosaurs, who have the effrontery to call themselves the 'Mainstream Group', will continue to have a disproportionate influence upon Party policy for a long time yet to come, as evidenced by Hague's subsequent announcement that his opposition to the Single Currency is limited to the duration of the next Parliament. If he felt that he had to qualify his original position then the most natural qualification would have been to say that it was ruled out for at least the duration of his leadership. Meanwhile, at a meeting of the Shropshire branch of the Confederation of British Industry (CBI) one of the members goes out of his way to say that the West Midlands CBI backs Hague's current policy on the single currency and wants us Shropshire MPs to make sure that he knows it.

When , on 3rd November, I find myself dining with '22 Committee Vice Chairman, Geoffrey Johnson-Smith (Wealdon) he is seething about the way in which the seminar which the Mainstream Group plan to hold on November 6th is being portrayed as a rallying point for dissidents. More to the point he is angry about the potential this initiative has to create 'a party within a party', something which we so-called rebels had been so careful to eschew back in 1994.

With the prospect of a referendum on the single currency now looming large I am anxious to persuade my colleagues of the importance of avoiding the 'NO' campaign becoming too closely associated with individual politicians, or, for that matter, with the hugely discredited Conservative Party, for fear that it is seen to be partisan rather than an organisation which transcends everyday party politics. At a breakfast meeting of the European Research Group (ERG) I try hard to persuade the assembled company, particularly Lord Pearson of Rannoch, that to win a referendum it is essential that the campaign is strongly identified with the issue rather than with the personalities of those leading the charge. Our message has to be sold like a commercial product, soap powder or whatever, where prominence is invariably given to the brand name rather than to the name of the manufacturer or its directors. Malcolm Pearson is clearly not convinced and when he goes on to say that Yorkshire millionaire, Paul Sykes, recently resigned from the Conservative Party due to the Shadow Cabinet's pusillanimity on the single currency issue, is in town, I ask him if he would involve me in his meeting with him. Not convinced that Malcolm will do this I put my secretary, Vicki, on to tracking Paul Sykes down, the upshot of which is a 'phone call from him the following morning and an appointment to meet him at lunch time.

My advice to Paul Sykes, for which he expresses himself grateful, is firstly that the 'NO' campaign has to be non-attributable and must avoid giving prominence to individual politicians which would be counter-productive. Secondly, the campaign needs to be essentially populist, in contrast to the corporatist 'YES' campaign. Thirdly, no time or effort should be wasted in trying to build up a mass membership which would require a sizeable administrative organisation. Finally, there is a need to establish a 'mission control' capable of representing and co-ordinating the campaign as well as being able to issue instant rebuttals as and when necessary.

As well as directing my fire at the ERG I also try to influence Bill Cash's Amsterdam Group (formerly the IGC Group) by telling them that there is only one game in town and that is a 'NO' campaign against the single currency and how important it is that the campaign be kept anonymous – Bill Cash being in most peoples' eyes the most likely politician to hijack the campaign for his own glorification! I also urge the group to use whatever opportunities arise to persuade Wm. Hague to stop qualifying his opposition to the single currency by relating it to a time scale. As a matter of principle one is either for it or against it - putting time limits on his opposition is simply making his stance look barely credible.

Meanwhile the Norwegian Ambassador who, unlike the majority of his fellow countrymen is an unreconstructed Europhile of the first order, tells me and the other officers of the Anglo Norwegian All Party Parliamentary Group that Britain's failure to join the single currency is an act of cowardice! For sheer silliness this remark rivals that of Adair Turner, who, in his capacity as Director General of the CBI, responds to my question about the effect of fixed exchange rates upon unemployment levels by saying that the problem with the Gold Standard was that, as with the ERM, 'we went in at the wrong rate'. Whereas it is a matter of opinion as to what the correct entry rate should be, history demonstrates that the result of fixed exchange rates is almost invariably an increase in unemployment. On entry into the ERM in October 1990 unemployment in the UK stood at 1.67 millions but by the time of our unceremonious exit in September 1992 it had risen to 2.85 millions, just as between 1923 and September 1931 the fixed exchange rate imposed by our adherence to the Gold Standard had driven unemployment up from 1.25 millions to 2.9 millions. This is an argument that I shall use again and again whenever the subject of the single currency arises and whenever I hear people make the wholly unsubstantiated assertion that joining the single currency will 'bring down interest rates, lower inflation and reduce the level of unemployment'. This is what the dreamers said before the UK joined the ill-fated ERM, the forerunner of the single currency, and five years later they are still saying it, as though the leap in unemployment, the rash of bankruptcies and the tidal wave of repossessions between 1990 and 1992 had never happened.

On 18th November it is the turn of the Engineering Employers Federation to have the benefit of my views on the single currency and the following day I stage a repeat performance at a meeting between the Midlands Industrialists Council (MIC) and Conservative MPs representing Midlands constituencies. The MIC is a significant source of Conservative Party funding but, unbelievably, some of their members still hanker after joining the single currency just as the farmers, as represented by the National Farmers Union (NFU), do too. On 15th December, at a meeting with their Director General, Richard Macdonald, I get him to agree that NFU President, David Naish, should not have stated that "we remain convinced that a single currency would be in the best interests of the country". He is perfectly entitled to express the opinion that it would be in the best interest of his members but the consequent disenfranchisement of the Westminster Parliament as a result of surrendering control over interest rates and exchange rates is a matter upon which other sections of our society might well take a different view to that of David Naish and the top brass at the NFU.

During the long Summer recess, in my capacity as Secretary of the All Party British Gibraltar Group, I have written to Foreign Secretary, Robin Cook, drawing his attention to the colony's concern about border controls arising from the terms of the EU Amsterdam Treaty. Although I fail to get in at Prime Minister's Questions (PMQs) on 5th November to rubbish the PM's assertion that the UK got a good deal at Amsterdam, I am pleased to hear Robin Cook concede that on the subject of Gibraltarian border controls he had blundered. Such an admission from such a senior Minister is almost without precedent and, love him or hate him, one is bound to admire Robin Cook's frankness.

Meeting his shadow, Michael Howard, on 2nd December is a different kettle of fish altogether. After explaining the Gibraltarian problem to him we go on to talk about other matters European at the end of which he asks me what I conclude. I tell him that my conclusion is that we should get out of the European Union – that was not my starting position but rather it is the conclusion that I am inevitably led to by the logic of all my arguments. I instance how Welsh farmers, even as we speak, feel driven to take action at Fishguard and Holyhead in respect of meat imports. Having concluded that they cannot get satisfaction through the normal democratic process because neither their own elected representatives nor, collectively, the Westminster Parliament, can alter the terms of the Common Agriculture Policy (CAP) they have taken matters into their own hands and have resorted to the Gallic solution i. e. direct action. When I say to MH that perhaps this should be my theme for any contribution that I might make to this week's debate on the European Community (EC) he urges me not to talk about repatriation of Agriculture policy, having already urged me not to talk about leaving the EU altogether for fear of upsetting 'people like Ray Whitney (Wycombe) who are desperately unhappy with things as they are'. MH is at pains to say that the new line on the single currency is an enormous achievement in itself and that we should sing small for fear of, on the one hand upsetting some of our own colleagues and also, on the other hand, for fear of giving the Government the opportunity to draw attention to splits in the Conservative Party. He is also keen for me to use my best offices to get an amendment to the motion for Thursday's EC debate withdrawn. The amendment in question seeks to prevent the European Communities (Amendment) Bill coming into force until the Treaty on European Union has been amended so as to re-establish national sovereignty.

On a similar subject I had already, on 11th November, had a private meeting with the Party Leader to talk about the CFP. Wm. Hague's reaction is to play for time, telling me that he needs to think things through before responding. On the eve of my meeting with William I had dined with Manuel Monteiro and Salvador Correa de Sa, respectively the President and Treasurer of the Portugese Partido Popular who are keen to broker a pan-European grouping to oppose Socialists and Democrats who, in the context of the EU, represent broadly similar views. Having encouraged the Portugese to try to persuade Wm. Hague that he could become the leader of such a grouping, in the same way that Prime Minister, Tony Blair, apparently wants to become leader of the EU Socialists, I am naturally interested to hear his reaction on this front too. He tells me that his meeting with the Portugese went well and appears to be receptive to the idea that he might take the lead in Europe against the massed ranks of Socialists and Christian/Social Democrats whose views are often synonymous. When I mention Tony Blair's aspirations to become leader of the EU Socialists he grasps the point that I am trying to make, although subsequent events will throw some doubt on this conclusion.

Quite apart from the single currency, the CAP and the CFP, there are several other areas in which EU policies are cause for concern. One of them is the policy to create a 'Europe of the Regions' and so it is depressing to hear Shadow Constitutional Affairs Minister, Michael Ancram, confess that regionalisation within the UK is playing straight into the EU's hands. What a pity it is that he didn't appreciate this point when, in the last Parliament, he helped to push the Maastricht Treaty through the House and when the then Conservative Government set up Government Offices in each of the EU inspired and, especially in the case of England, contrived British regions.

Reverting to the question of Agriculture, a stormy meeting of European Standing Committee 'A' on 10th December has to be adjourned to a bigger room when the attendance of 49 MPs far exceeds the number that usually attend this particular committee. The subject under discussion is 'Reform of the Common Agriculture Policy'. Prominent amongst the Conservatives present at this meeting are Messrs David Curry (Skipton & Ripon), Tony Baldry (Banbury) and Michael Jack (Fylde), all former MAFF Ministers and all, certainly in the eyes of Owen Paterson (Shropshire North) and myself, who are there as permanent members of the committee, largely discredited – there is certainly no love lost for them in the fishing industry. The fact that so few of my colleagues will come to terms with is that any fundamental reform of the CAP requires unanimity within the EU Council of Ministers and that, in terms of amending the policy to the advantage of British farmers, such unanimity is simply not forthcoming because what suits us will almost certainly not suit others.

The following day John Townend accompanies me to a meeting with the aforesaid Michael Jack, now Shadow MAFF Minister, which proves to be a total waste of time. He studiously avoids answering any of our questions about the CFP but repeatedly tells us that he 'is totally flexible' – whatever that means! He implies that if we want to know what the Party policy is on Fisheries we will have to talk to Peter Lilley who will doubtless say 'and what does Michael Jack think'. Jack agrees that we can tell Peter Lilley that he is flexible! This totally unsatisfactory encounter makes me more determined than ever to see the Chief Whip so as to sort things out before we break for Christmas.

At that meeting, on 16th December, the Chief Whip is, as ever, courteous and listens attentively whilst I give him the benefit of my advice and experience. Principal amongst the points I make is that even with the best policies in the world we cannot succeed unless we also have the right people. I instance my less than satisfactory meetings with Michael Howard and Michael Jack and the procession of discredited former Agriculture Ministers who turned up at last week's European Committee 'A'. I tell him that there is no future in appeasement and that we simply cannot go back to where we were in the last Parliament – we have to move on. Finally I repeat my call to give the Party a fresh image by bringing into the Shadow Government team some new younger talent in place of the old has-beens.

As far as the Party constitution is concerned nothing is yet decided in spite of the many meetings which have been held to consider the matter. At the end of October the '22 Executive discussed proposed new rules for leadership elections and agreed to hold an open-ended meeting the following week to thrash the matter out, although I suspect that behind the scenes the principle of giving the voluntary side of the Party a say in these matters has already been conceded. There is a lot of bad blood concerning the perceived poor performance of Conservative MPs, much of it whipped up by the NUEC Chairman, Robin Hodgson, who, prompted by a question from the floor at a meeting of the West Midlands Area Council on 1st November, doesn't miss the opportunity to bad mouth them. At its meeting on 5th November I try yet again to persuade the '22 Executive that giving the voluntary Party a vote in future leadership elections is fraught with hazard and invite them to recognise where all the pressure to do so is coming from – my constituent, Robin Hodgson! Notwithstanding my best efforts to quash the idea, the pass is effectively sold when '22 Chairman, Archie Hamilton, in a brief appearance at the NUEC meeting in CCO on 6th November, tells the assembled company that the '22 is prepared to give a 'significant share' of the votes in future leadership contests to the voluntary side of the party. In an amazing display of sheer hypocrisy Robin Hodgson encourages those present to press their demands for an even bigger say but argues strongly against making the elections to the proposed new Party Convention and Board subject to OMOV - 'One Man, One Vote'. In the next breath he deftly converts a growl of opposition to the idea of the Party having the right to deselect a sitting MP whose Constituency Association membership is at an unsatisfactorily low level into a majority show of hands in favour of taking such powers. Before the five hour long meeting ends at 16.30 Hodgson has taken yet another swipe at MPs by allowing those MEPs present the opportunity of joining in the general denigration of their Westminster colleagues.

Subsequently, when on 11th November I tell Archie Hamilton about the way in which Hodgson had finessed the vote on deselecting MPs, Archie says that that is not how Hodgson presented it at the meeting he had had with him this morning. He then goes on to say that this proposition is only floating around because of two words – Teresa Gorman, who, incidentally, has written to Wm. Hague telling him to make me Shadow Agriculture Minister! Archie expresses his confidence that the proposed Party reforms will not make matters worse for the Parliamentary Party. Not sharing his confidence about that I instance how 'democracy' is being forced upon the Parliamentary Party by the voluntary Party – for which read Robin Hodgson –whilst it has itself set its face against the very idea that its own upper echelons should themselves be elected by the Party membership.

The following day the '22 Executive flags up three sticking points in relation to the proposed Party reforms. Firstly, the proposition that low constituency Association membership numbers should trigger an automatic reselection process for the sitting MP is totally unacceptable. Secondly, the representation of MPs on the new Party Board has to be strengthened and finally, that there must be no change to the leadership contest rules without the agreement of the full '22 Committee.

Robin Hodgson's success in putting down the poison against MPs is demonstrated yet again on 25th November when West Midland MPs attend a meeting with West Midland Area Council officers, The meeting gets off to a bad start with Chairman, Philip Bradbourn, accusing the MPs of being generally useless. With other meetings to attend I leave after only 15 minutes by which time Michael Spicer (Worcestershire West) is in full cry after him.

As a long standing member of the Party and one who had an active involvement in the voluntary side of the Party before being elected to Parliament, a background which is not typical of many of my Parliamentary colleagues, I am determined to make my voice heard in all matters affecting Party reform. The Party is intent upon setting a minimum membership fee which it has never had before and at a meeting in CCO on 3rd December I try to interest Vice Chairman, Archie Norman, in the idea that it would be better to create two classes of membership with Full members paying the agreed minimum subscription or more and Associate members paying whatever they can afford, the reality being that many existing members regard their subscription more as a donation to a cause that they wish to support than as a means of obtaining the privileges that go with full membership.

Similarly, I ask Party Chairman, Cecil Parkinson, to consider whether the cause of Party democracy would not be better served by allowing the voluntary side of the Party to elect the Party Chairman, Deputy Chairman, Treasurer and a majority on the proposed Board and to leave the election of Leader in the hands of the duly elected MPs. In reply Cecil tells the meeting that he is absolutely on side with Wm. Hague on these matters and that there would be enormous risks in allowing the voluntary side of the Party to elect the Party Chairman – we shall see!

There is encouragement from Paul Sykes when he telephones on 10th December to say that he has finished meeting all the people that he felt he wanted to see and that in future there is only one person that he will want to meet when he comes to London and that that person is myself!

The last word as far as 1997 is concerned must however be reserved for our erstwhile Leader, the Member of Parliament for Huntingdon. On 17th November, at the Parliamentary Party's weekly 'Forward Look Group' meeting at which the week's business of the House and other matters are discussed, I raise the question of a replacement for the Royal Yacht BRITANNIA. There is no support forthcoming from those present and the Chief Whip suggests that I leave matters as they are for a while, not least because we don't know what the Royal family themselves think and in the meantime to talk to Shadow Defence Secretary, George Young (Hampshire NW). The following day I am able to introduce the Chairman of the All Party Parliamentary Royal Yacht Group, Lord Ashbourne, to George Young as we travel back to Westminster by river ferry after attending an event onboard HMY BRITANNIA laid on by the Royal Navy Presentation Team. George appears to be only moderately interested in the question of a replacement Royal Yacht and seems to be more focussed on settling the fate of the existing one before giving any consideration to the provision of a new one. He says that opinion polls carried out by the last Government demonstrated that the idea was not a sure-fire vote winner, to which I feel bound to point out that had the survey been taken of exclusively Conservative voters it might well have told a very different story.

Be that as it may I am not inclined to let the matter drop and a few weeks later I table an Early Day Motion (EDM) to mark the end of BRITANNIA's illustrious service. No less than 81 MPs sign my EDM but when I invite John Major to add his signature he dithers and then declines, saying that if it hadn't been for one or two in the Cabinet "I would have done something about this"!

The EDM read "That this House, whilst much regretting the decommissioning of HMY BRITANNIA, wishes to place on record its sincere thanks to all past and present members of her ship's company, several of whom have served aboard the Royal Yacht for very many years; pays tribute on this her final decommissioning date, to all Royal Navy and Royal Marine personnel who have served aboard 'BRITANNIA' during the past 44 years; and commends them for their service and dedication to a much loved British institution".

1998

1

" Seldom do things go entirely according to plan "

As the new year opens the question of Party rules is still not resolved and Michael Spicer, for one, is not best pleased by the letter that Chairman, Archie Hamilton, has sent to all members of the '22 Committee saying that all the Officers and the majority of the Executive are in favour of 25% or 45 Members, whichever is the lesser, being the number necessary to trigger a vote of no confidence in the Leader when clearly the majority of the Executive do not support this view. Archie says that this is what the Leader, Wm. Hague, would like but in reply I make the point that it is not the function of the '22 Chairman or the Executive to reflect the views of the Leader but rather to represent the views of the backbenchers.

The following day, 14th January, a ballot of Members is heavily in support of abandoning the annual re-election of Leader in favour of a 'no confidence' procedure and in any future leadership contest giving 'one man, one vote' (OMOV) to all Party members, after the Members of Parliament have conducted a 'primary' to produce a shortlist of two or three candidates.

At a subsequent meeting of the '22 Executive Michael Mates (Hampshire East) indicates that the recommendation of the Officers was not unanimous, not least because he, as Joint Secretary, wasn't even present when the decision was taken!

Meeting again the following day the Executive works hard to try and agree what questions to put to the full committee to implement the result of yesterday's ballot. Subsequently Michael Mates assures me that we will not be determining the outcome of the ballot on leadership election rules using the median of the votes cast but will look at the results and then decide the best way forward. In the meantime, at a meeting of the NUEC held on Saturday 17th January, as if we haven't got problems enough already, it is proposed that Shropshire should be lumped together with Herefordshire to form one of the new smaller areas to replace the former West Midlands area.

Arriving at the House in time for Agriculture Questions time at 1430 on 22nd January I am told by Michael Spicer that in my absence a meeting of the '22 Executive has been held at midday and that it has been decided that 15% of the Parliamentary Party, without any stated minimum number, will be the threshold required to trigger a vote of 'no confidence' in the Leader and that any Leader thus defeated would not be eligible to stand again.

This proposition is put to a full meeting of the '22 that afternoon when Archie announces that it is the recommendation of the Officers and most of the Executive. The Leader, who is present, then makes a short address in which he explains why we have to get on with it – to suit the reform and renewal timetable – and why it would be quite wrong for a defeated Leader to stand again.

After the meeting, in my capacity as the '22 committee liaison officer to the NUEC, I feel obliged to tell Hague's PPS, David Lidington, that it would be inadvisable for the Leader to repeat that the NUEC had completed their deliberations last Saturday because clearly that is not the opinion of the NUEC who intend to have another run at it on February 27th.

There are some protests about the way in which the final decision is being imposed but, when put to the meeting, the motion is carried by an overwhelming majority. Whilst I am personally not unhappy with the outcome I am obliged to tell Archie that he really ought not to have sent out his recommendation on 8th January and that I am cross about not having been contacted about the meeting of the Executive at noon.

Three weeks later an extraordinary meeting of the '22 Executive is convened to agree final amendments to the new rules before they are published in the form of a 'White Paper'. Whilst I am not able to attend the launch of the 'White Paper' by Wm. Hague at 09.45 on Monday 16th

February I do have to warn Archie Hamilton that the voluntary side of the Party are not going to be best pleased at being bounced into the final solution because they thought that they would get another chance to debate it at the NUEC meeting on 27th February.

When the '22 Executive next meets on Wednesday 18th February I suggest that, given that the new rules envisage greater participation by the voluntary side of the Party in policy making, it might not be inappropriate for the '22 Committee itself to get involved in this area. I get immediate support from Bowen Wells (Hertford & Stortford) and, following some discussion, Michael Colvin (Romsey & Waterside) says that he thinks that it is 'a good hare to have set running'.

The consensus amongst the Executive is that Shadow Ministers might be invited to attend the Executive and that corresponding debates could be held, perhaps monthly, at the regular '22 Committee meetings. When I subsequently discuss my proposition with Chairman Archie we agree that inviting outsiders with relevant experience to address the full '22 would be beneficial and would have the added advantage of allowing shadow Ministers to sum up the discussions without boxing themselves in prior to further deliberation and the eventual formulation of policy. In the meantime, as judged by an article appearing in the Daily Telegraph on Saturday 21st February, the idea appears to have got off the ground.

A long and tedious meeting of the NUEC on Friday 27th February is punctuated by Chairman Robin Hodgson's last ditch attempts to get his own way. His proposition, to reselect former MPs who lost their seats last May only if 85% of the constituency membership agree, is defeated – but only after the forceful objection of my own constituency chairman, Michael Wood. But for Michael's timely intervention the motion would almost certainly have been carried. Archie Hamilton is given a rough ride on the question of whether sitting MPs should be reselected by secret ballot which is an issue to which Hodgson repeatedly returns. Like a dog with a bone he simply will not let it go and even in his summing up of the day's proceedings, mentions it yet again. The fact that Archie was given such a hard time at the meeting had obviously been orchestrated and rehearsed.

According to Michael Spicer, who was present at the '22 Executive on 4th March which I missed, there were ructions about the matters relating to the NUEC which I had reported on to Archie Hamilton the day after their meeting. I had told Archie that Robin Hodgson had behaved most disgracefully, that Archie had been well and truly set up and that RH had no business re-opening issues which had, presumably, been decided at meetings of the Steering Committee which RH had attended as the representative of the voluntary side of the Party.

A month later, following the Party's half-yearly gathering, Archie tells the '22 Executive that Robin Hodgson took full advantage of his time on the platform in Harrogate to, once again, vilify Conservative MPs. This is my cue to tell the committee how RH had shamelessly orchestrated the NUEC in advance of Archie's appearance on 27th February. There is general agreement that RH needs to be warned off!

During the Christmas recess several of our Europhile colleagues – all the usual suspects – have signed a letter to the 'Independent' newspaper advocating membership of the single currency. On returning to Westminster one of my first tasks is to tell my area Whip, Oliver Heald (Hertfordshire North) that since Wm. Hague has got the endorsement of the Party for his policy on the single currency the wreckers must be told to shut up or do the other thing, in which case we'll be well rid of them. In reply Oliver says that he doesn't know why I'm worrying so much – 'you've won the argument' he says, to which I retort that whilst it is very magnanimous of him to say so the fact of the matter is that I haven't yet won the war. The problem, I tell him, is that the Party does not have a strategy and that until it does it will not be possible to devise credible policies. In terms of sorting out our strategy we need to decide whether we are going to allow ourselves to be subsumed by the European Union or whether we believe that the freedom and independence of our country is what really matters.

Still on the subject of the single currency shadow Foreign Secretary Michael Howard tells me that he has been sent a copy of a letter that National Farmers Union President, Sir David Naish, had written to me on that very subject. Much to my delight Michael has told the farmers in his constituency that he couldn't possibly support adoption of the single currency. When he attends a meeting of the '92 Group on 2nd February Michael makes a very eurosceptic, anti-single currency speech but when, after the meeting, I tackle him and ask him whether I can assume that what he has said is now Party policy he says that 'it isn't yet'. My response to that is that it had better be, and soon! The following day I urge the secretary of our European Research Group, Daniel Hannan, to use his best endeavours to persuade Lord Pearson to secure the name 'Patriotic Alliance' as an umbrella for a single currency 'NO' campaign, the sequel to which is that at the weekend I receive a telephone call from his Lordship who is full of apologies for having forgotten to make contact with the former 'Whipless' MPs in connection with his plans (for opposing the single currency).

One of the interesting features of political life is that seldom do things go entirely according to plan. On 10th February I prepare for one speech that I don't actually make because of not being called to speak in the debate on the Government's 'Beef Bones Regulation' and haven't prepared for a speech that I do make. Nevertheless my off the cuff address to the London Swinton Circle is extremely well received. To my utter amazement the Procedure Committee meeting the following day has, according to my informant Richard Shepherd (Aldridge-Brownhills), noted that I was not called to speak in the previous night's debate. They apparently take the view that with my particular expertise I should have been called but I tell Richard that I am less concerned about that than the fact that former Conservative Agriculture Ministers, of whom there seem to be far too many, parachute themselves into committees and are, understandably, called to speak with the result that we backbenchers – the poor bloody infantry – are squeezed out.

The quite ridiculous regulations banning the sale of beef on the bone will come and go but other topics such as the single currency and the Common Fisheries Policy go on forever! It is in connection with the latter that on 11th February John Townend (Yorkshire East) and I go to meet our Leader. Wm. Hague appears to be very receptive of our views and recalls that I have been to see him twice before on this topic. He hints that he may find 'coastal state control' acceptable in a way that the existing CFP is not. He goes on to tell us that Fisheries will be discussed by a sub-committee of the Shadow Cabinet and when asked agrees that it will be in order for us to obtain the names of the members of the sub-committee from either his PPS, David Lidington, or his Chief of Staff, Seb Coe (Falmouth), who are both sitting in on our meeting. I conclude that unless William is doing a John Major number on us – telling one group one thing and another group the opposite – our meeting with him is most encouraging. That John and I have made some sort of impact is evidenced the very next day by Wm. Hague telling retired Fleetwood trawler skipper, Mark Hamer, that he discussed Fisheries with us only last evening. The hoped for names of the Shadow Cabinet fisheries sub-committee do not appear to be forthcoming and practically a fortnight later I am obliged to remind David Lidington that I am still waiting. As well as providing David with more information I also take the opportunity of updating Agriculture Whip, Stephen Day (Cheadle), drawing his attention to the significance of the fact that Fisheries Minister, Elliot Morley, has felt constrained to write to the industry newspaper, Fishing News, challenging what I had said to the assembled company at the recent 'Crabbers Ball' in Torquay where I had been the Guest speaker.

Through the good offices of his excellent secretary, Shana Hole, I also ensure that the Chief Whip receives my latest propaganda on the Fisheries issue and two days later I meet him in his office where he tells me that he is anxious to make European Committee 'A', where matters relating to the CFP and the benighted Common Agriculture Policy (CAP) are debated, more effective. In that case the very first thing that he needs to do is to stop former Agriculture Ministers parachuting themselves into meetings of that committee, notwithstanding that they and any other backbenchers are perfectly entitled to do so, for the sole purpose of speaking on popular issues. I am also at pains to explain that unlike former Ministers the appointed members of the committee - Owen Paterson, Keith Simpson and myself - are not carrying any baggage from the previous Parliament. When I point out that our differing views on European Union are an added complication the Chief says that he would prefer to talk to me about that separately. As we walk out of his office I tell him that I am ready to do that just as soon as he is but he says that he needs more time to study the information that I have already given him. As we part I tell him that I have not come to my opinion out of blind prejudice but as a result of seeing what the CFP and the CAP have done to two of Britain's basic industries.

On a similar theme, when, later in the day, the '22 Executive rehearses what it might say at its evening meeting with the Leader I say that my interest is to convince him of the need for a strategy and that, at the risk of being contentious, that means deciding whether the Conservative Party stands for the freedom and independence of the nation or whether, conversely, it believes in moving incrementally towards 'ever closer union' within the EU. When I put this question to Wm. Hague he answers by saying that he will be making an important speech on this subject soon and that he will be doing so on the continent. I have already said that as Captain of the ship he must make the decision and that the rest of us must fall in behind that decision. Mine is the final question and he comes only slowly to it after answering the preceding questions at length. To his credit, in answer to an earlier question, he tells Peter Emery (East Devon) that he is not going to give different people different answers to the same question, an assurance that he will repeat when he attends a lunchtime meeting of the European Research Group on March 2nd.

When he attends a meeting of the '92 Group Executive on March 3rd William Hague has to hear me again when I make the point that we have to play to our natural constituency, most of which we upset in the last Parliament, and that there is a plethora of organisations like, for example, the National Lottery, which we ourselves established that are inimical to our interests and which are staffed largely by people who are positively anti-Conservative. William reminds us that the Lottery was Michael Heseltine's idea which I say perfectly illustrates the point that I am trying to make.

As we walk together to cast our votes in the Division Lobby William says that he agrees that there is, as I have described, a problem and that it is a fact that we didn't do anything about it when we had the chance. He also assures me that he isn't going to go back on any of his commitments. This is all very re-assuring although not entirely consistent with his having last month rebuked John Redwood (Wokingham) for his critical comments about the German Chancellor, Helmut Kohl, being granted the Freedom of the City of London. Interestingly, John Redwood assures me that everything that he had had to say on that subject had been cleared by CCO in advance. The problem he thinks was caused by Hague's press secretary getting carried away. On the strength of this information I go off in search of my own Whip and the Chief Whip but in their absence Deputy Chief Whip, Peter Ainsworth (Surrey East) gets both barrels – how Hague's reaction to Redwood's comments is a PR disaster of the first order and, not least, a turn-off for all those voters we need to win back from UKIP and the Referendum Party.

As February draws to a close I yet again remind David Lidington that I am still waiting for the list of names on the Shadow Cabinet fisheries sub-committee. Two days later, after remonstrating with the Chief Whip and telling him that I have no means of knowing whether failure to provide me with the names is because the Leader has changed his mind or because the apparatchiks are being obstructive, the list finally turns up in the next day's mail, albeit without attribution. Although it will take until the end of the year to achieve, my objective is to persuade the Conservative Party that it simply has to take a stand against the iniquitous CFP. On 5th March, over a drink in the Smoking Room, I take the opportunity of broaching the subject with our Constitutional Affairs spokesman, Michael Ancram (Devizes). He appears to be on-side saying that at the General Election the two big issues were coal mines and fisheries. A few days later I have a very satisfactory chat with Francis Maude (Horsham) who appears to take the point that there is a political imperative involved in getting our fisheries policy sorted out. At the risk of labouring the point I tell him that it is important that we reach the right conclusion before the Labour Party beat us to it. In the event it will be the Scottish National Party (SNP) who will steal our thunder although even they must surely recognise the contradiction in terms of on the one hand being a pro-EU party and on the other hand saying that they will dissociate themselves from such an important EU policy i.e. the CFP.

Apart from fisheries and our Party re-organisation the other issue which rumbles on is the question of the single currency. Rumour has it that Bruce Udale, a substantial farmer in the adjoining constituency of Telford, has resigned office in the NFU in protest against their policy on this specific issue and although nothing comes of it I am prompted to suggest to Michael Spicer that the ERG might be interested in trying to launch an initiative to focus the attention of farmers on alternatives to the received wisdom of the NFU. On Friday 20th March I get secretary Vicki to speak to CCO to obtain an explanation of the headlines in both the Times and Daily Telegraph newspapers proclaiming a climb-down by Hague on Economic and Monetary Union (EMU). CCO say that there is absolutely no truth in the reports and that they don't know where they came from. By Monday it will be apparent that they resulted from a meeting between an unidentified journalist and one Ken Clarke!

Hard on the heels of this revelation there is, at a highly successful ERG dinner held the following day, spontaneous support for the idea of putting the question of the single currency to a ballot of Party members, an idea which within 24 hours, is put to a meeting of the '22 Executive. In that particular forum, opinion is divided and the point is made that the cost of a ballot at something like £150,000 cannot be ignored. The Executive concludes that a ballot of the full '22 Committee would not serve any useful purpose and on a show of hands in which Nick Winterton (Macclesfield) and John Butterfill (Bournemouth West) who, in John Townend's words, 'never takes our part' in spite of being a member of the '92 Group, vote with the Europhiles to effectively quash the idea.

Later in the week Christopher Story, editor of the International Currency Review, poses the not unreasonable question as to why we should be putting so much effort into completing the single currency, which could so easily be postponed, at a time when there are other problems such as the 'millenium bug' which cannot – a question which I put to Niall Fitzgerald, Chairman of Unilever plc when he addresses the Conservative European Affairs backbench committee on 30th March.

Fitzgerald says that he will approach the subject of Europe from the standpoint of a 'practical and pragmatic businessman' on the strength of which I ask him whether a practical, pragmatic businessman, faced with two king-sized decisions, one of which he could postpone and the other which he could not, would not choose to put off, in this case the single currency until the other, the 'millenium bug', had been resolved'. He replies to the effect that whilst that might have been a reasonable question 18 months ago there can be no turning back now because the political decision has been made and in any case his own company will be ready for the single currency at the end of this year. When I ask him whether he recognises that the strength of the Pound Sterling is, because of the weakness of continental currencies as they struggle to achieve the convergence criteria, only relative, he starts to waffle. When further challenged by my instancing how unemployment increased massively following our entry into the fixed exchange rates of the Exchange Rate Mechanism (ERM) in 1990 he trots out the old mantra about going in at the wrong rate whereupon I draw his attention to the effect upon unemployment rates of our previous experience of fixed exchange rates, on the Gold Standard between 1923 and 1931. Unbelievably his answer is the same – we went in at the wrong rate!

At the backbench Agriculture Committee meeting the following day I make another attempt to persuade my colleagues to make an objective judgement on the CAP. Shadow Agriculture Minister Michael Jack (Fylde) says that he is on the lookout for distinctly Conservative policies which provokes me into telling the committee that far from being Conservative policies both the CAP and the CFP are collectivist policies i.e. communist policies. Sadly nobody is willing to take me on although after the meeting is ended Peter Luff (Mid Worcestershire) says that he agrees with me and that the CAP should be scrapped. I tell him that it might have been more helpful if he had spoken up in my support during the course of the meeting, whereupon he refers me to the Agriculture Select Committee report on CAP reform published last month.

A further straw in the wind is provided by Douglas Hogg (Sleaford & N. Hykeham) who tells me over dinner in the Members Dining Room how, following the Danish 'No' vote in their referendum in June 1992, he had written to the PM, John Major, saying that it was his considered opinion that we should no longer proceed with the Maastricht Treaty.

All of this encourages me to believe that, with the notable exception of the serial 'wreckers' within the Parliamentary Party, there is a softening of the Europhiles position. Wm. Hague's commitment to 'lead not plead' is possibly starting to have an effect.

On the eve of the Easter recess and as we approach the anniversary of our crushing defeat at the polls I go round the metaphorical track with the Chief Whip saying that now that the Party reforms are at long last behind us Hague must stamp his mark upon the Party and tell us in which direction we are going to go. Giving the Chief the benefit of my own experience I tell him that William will not be able to achieve much unless and until he has the right people around him and that as a matter of priority he should replace the old guard with new faces, giving them the opportunity to shine or otherwise be replaced, before the beginning of the next General Election campaign. I warn about the potential hazard of 'screening committees' selecting predominantly Europhile candidates for next year's European Parliament elections which would, I believe, result in a low turnout at the polls leading to accusations that this was because the Leader was pursuing the wrong policies. In that case Hague would be well advised to carry out his promise to ballot the Party membership on his policy regarding the single currency so that the 'party line' is quite clear and having regard to all the circumstances, as far as the Party's European Policy is concerned, he might just as well be hung for a sheep as a lamb. In that context, sorting out our Fisheries policy as an earnest of our intent was an important priority and that, to be more specific, we couldn't afford to have our Fisheries spokesman, Michael Jack, refusing to meet the mainly Conservative 'Save Britain's Fish' campaigners in favour of meeting the Scottish Fishermens Federation who are definitely not of our political persuasion. On the strength of this the Chief asks me to leave him a copy of the catalogue of events surrounding Jack's visit to the important fishing port of Peterhead in Aberdeenshire drawn up by SBF Chairman, Tom Hay. As a parting shot I tell the Chief that I confidently predict that there will soon be a 'Save Britain's Farming' campaign to match SBF and that the majority of the farmers involved will be disillusioned Conservatives. Having got all that off my chest and recalling all my other efforts over the past 12 months I feel that there is little more that I can do short of direct action!

1998

2

" The EU juggernaut continues to flatten every obstacle in its path "

On April 20th the single currency pot is given another stir when the Daily Telegraph reports Newt Gingrich, Speaker of the US House of Representatives, as saying that it is an 'extraordinary experiment ... and an extraordinary gamble'. Using this quote in my maiden speech in the Council of Europe I attract the only applause in the whole of a debate entitled 'Democratic functioning of National Parliaments'. After I have spoken, Norwegian Christian Democrat, Anita Saele, comes over to ask me for a copy of my speech saying that there are many people in Norway believing as I do but that she has never heard a politician express that opinion so clearly! Ironically, two days later, another Norwegian, this time a so-called Conservative, attempts to undermine the recommendation that David Atkinson (Bournemouth East), the leader of the British Conservative delegation, is making in his capacity as leader of the European Democratic Group to the European Democratic Union. This provokes me into making some blunt comments about the EPP to which we are, in my opinion, quite wrongly allied. This in turn makes my British Conservative colleagues inexplicably nervous. I am at pains to point out that the EPP are federalists and therefore in favour of EU collectivism. After the meeting I explain to

David and others that in Norway it is the Conservatives, unlike ourselves, who are federalist and the Christian Democrats who are anti-federalist. It seems to me that they are all in the wrong groupings but to avoid any future misunderstanding I must be careful to refer to the collectivists as integrationists rather than federalists because of the different interpretations that different people put upon the latter.

Meanwhile in 'la belle France' the National Assembly has today voted 334 to 49 in favour of the single currency and tomorrow the Bundestag will defy opinion polls showing that a majority of Germans are opposed to single currency by voting 575 to 35 in its favour.

Back at Westminster I hammer away at the weekly meeting of the '22 Executive saying that the Party must buck up on the question of electoral reform in the light of Lord Jenkins stomping round the country with his electoral reform team, the so-called 'Independent Commission on the Voting System' to which, in due course I shall be making my own submission. (see appendix A). I also repeat my call for the old has-beens in Shadow Cabinet to be put out to grass. When the discussion turns to policy matters I remind the committee of what I had said several weeks ago to the effect that we first of all need to agree the strategy – is it to carry on down the road towards European integration or, alternatively, does the Party believe in Britain being a free and independent nation? That being said I tell them that whilst they may not like having to face up to this reality, sooner or later they will simply have to. Given the difficulty that the Party appears to be experiencing with anything to do with policy it is hardly surprising when Party Vice Chairman, Archie Norman (Tunbridge Wells) tells me how absolutely fed up he is. The problem is, he says, that nobody will make a decision! How very depressing to find talented new Members so totally demoralised after less than a year in Parliament. Personally I haven't stopped trying and am scheduled to have yet another meeting with the Chief Whip early next month. Being such a nuisance to all concerned it is somewhat surprising when Lord Freeman, previously Roger Freeman, the Member for Kettering, expresses the opinion that I would be a good person to have in the House of Lords. He is curious to know whether I will be standing at the next General Election and when I say that I very much doubt it, that is his response.

At our 25 minute long meeting on May 6th I can't help telling the Chief how depressed I am about the way things are going, in reply to which he says, 'do you want to talk about fisheries – I have your letter here with me in my pocket'. No, I say, I want to talk more generally, about how Wm. Hague and deputy Party Leader, Peter Lilley (Hitchen & Harpenden) are both talking about the nuts and bolts, the mechanics, of EMU when they should be talking about the principle. The Party, I say for the umpteenth time, has got to make up its mind as to whether it is going to go on down the road towards European integration or whether it is going to stand up for freedom and national independence. I am pleased when James seems to register interest at my mention of the word 'freedom' but I go on to make the point that because the European treaties are so tightly drawn there can be no halfway stages, nor indeed any compromises. What an irony I say, that the Party can apparently make up its mind on the question of a Mayor and an Assembly for London or on the Belfast Agreement affecting Northern Ireland but not on the most important issue of them all. I go on to tell him that notwithstanding the fact that the Party cannot make a decision, I have made mine – I intend taking a sabbatical whilst they sort themselves out. The Chief says that he has no powers to keep me in Westminster. I respond by saying that 'I know that' and he goes on to say that I will not be doing myself or my cause any good by taking such action. On the contrary, I say, I will be lending strength to his own arm in explaining to the leadership how dire things are becoming. James urges me to wait for Hague's impending speech to INSEAD in reply to which I tell him that I'll think about it but, by the same token, he must answer the question – integration or freedom. (INSEAD, founded in 1957, just three months after the Treaty of Rome, prides itself on being the Business School for the World.)

To his credit he appears to accept that the proliferation of pressure groups is symptomatic of the failure of the Conservative Party to reflect the aspirations of the its activists and that the same people, once having left the Party, are not going to be inclined to return. I conclude by suggesting that our Leader should not attend Bilderberg meetings, the next one of which is scheduled for 14th, 15th and 16th of this month at Turnberry in Ayrshire, because it sends out quite the wrong signal to our potential supporters - advice that will also fall on deaf ears.

Also on May 6th I am called at Prime Minister's Questions. My question, "is the Prime Minister aware that the Italian gross domestic product, as published by the International Monetary Fund, incorporates the underground economy, which is by definition unmeasurable, so Italy's debt to GDP ratio is false, misleading and grossly understated"? receives the answer that "the matter was investigated by the European Commission and the European Monetary Institute, which both found in favour of Italy being allowed to join monetary union". The rest of the PM's answer is good knock-about political stuff about differences of opinion within the Conservative Party and how criticisms by people such as myself "who are in truth viscerally opposed to everything European, do not carry a great deal of weight with me or anyone else". In other words he isn't going to let a few inconvenient facts stand in the way of 'le projet' which is far more concerned about achieving its political goal than with any evidence that certain aspects of it are fundamentally flawed. (Seven years will elapse before the chickens come home to roost. By 2005 Italy's economy will be in dire straits, because of the European Central Bank's 'one interest rate fits all' policy, and the clamour to revert to the lira will be mounting as both politicians and financiers come to realise how the Italian economy is being crucified by Italy's membership of the Eurozone.)

There will be elections to the European Parliament (EP) next year but attention within the Conservative Party is almost entirely focussed upon the selection of candidates rather than upon policy. In 1999 the EP election will, for the first time, be on the basis of PR (proportional representation), multi Member constituencies and Party lists. The single Member constituency and the 'first past the post' system of election is yet another casualty of the EU juggernaut which continues to flatten every obstacle in its path. In order to preserve a semblance of local democracy Conservative candidates will be chosen by a convention of all Party members belonging to the Westminster Parliament constituencies within the new EP constituencies, which themselves replicate the 12 EU inspired UK regions. To reach the point at which candidates appear before the regional conventions they must first of all seek and obtain the blessing of so-called 'screening committees'. The hazard is that the screening committees will, as certainly proves to be the case in the West Midlands, embody a pro-EU bias and therefore tend to favour pro-integrationist applicants In those circumstances I make it my business to warn those closest to the Leader, such as Alan Duncan and David Lidington and anyone else who will listen, that fielding integrationist candidates will simply invite a low turnout of Conservative voters at election time, leading to a bad result for the Conservative Party which, in turn, will reflect badly on Wm. Hague's leadership. In the event I am proved entirely wrong and the swing to the Conservatives at the EP election proves to be the highpoint of William's incumbency. In the meantime, having explained my fears at a working breakfast of the European Research Group (ERG), such luminaries as Francis Maude (Horsham), David Heathcoat-Amory (Wells) and Viscount Cranborne undertake to speak to the Leader to make him aware of my concerns. At the same meeting I suggest that Robert Cranborne, as Leader of the Conservatives in the House of Lords is best placed to tell William that it is not in his best interests to continue to allow his name to be used in support of the pro-EU London Europe Society where it appears alongside the names of well known Europhiles. Reverting to the candidate selection process, as I explain to the Chief Whip and the Chairman of the '22 Committee, the problem at local level is that the very people who should be getting involved with the selection process are not prepared to give their time to something that they don't believe in, thus leaving the field wide open to those that do. When on 26th March I happen to bump into the leader of the Conservatives in the EP, Edward Macmillan-Scott, I am naturally somewhat surprised when he tells me that he has been to see the Leader and that William has told him about our fears that the selection process gives them, the Europhiles, an advantage.

Two casualties of the process are former colleagues Charles Goodson-Wickes and Nick Budgen. Over lunch at the beginning of May, Charles expresses regret that he didn't make a stand with the rest of us in the last Parliament and I know that he is in for a further disappointment at the weekend when he learns that he hasn't got onto the list of EP election candidates for the West Midlands region. When Budgie telephones me on 9th May, having heard that he too has not made the cut, I tell him bluntly that, according to my information, his CV, as submitted to the screening committee, was a mess to which he responds by saying that he hasn't got a secretary! I tell him how I have been remonstrating with the powers that be about the constitution of the screening committees but I am actually rather annoyed that this is apparently the first time that Budgie has felt moved to show any interest in the voluntary side of the Party and it is because of that there is no fund of goodwill for him to fall back on.

On 11th May he telephones me again, wanting help. I agree to discuss the matter with Richard Shepherd which I do over dinner that evening in the Members Dining Room. Our discussion, which includes Bill Cash, is fairly inconclusive except that Richard 'phones Budgie to tell him to crank up the Press about the way in which the Conservative Party in the West Midlands have sifted the candidates. The following day Budgie is on the telephone yet again and we agree to tackle West Midland regional Party Agent, Tim Statham, about substitutes for constituency chairmen who are unable to attend the candidate selection meetings this coming weekend. Budgie tells me that he will have an article in tomorrow's Press but my own efforts to speak to Acting Area Chairman, Anthea McIntyre, Party Chairman, Cecil Parkinson, as well as his deputy, are all to no avail. Later in the day Anthea McIntyre contacts my secretary, Vicki, to say that whilst she agrees with the substance of my complaint she feels that she has no alternative other than to stick to the agreed rules. Whilst sitting in the Chamber at Question Time I am able to broach the burning question with Party Vice Chairman, Archie Norman (Tunbridge Wells) and we adjourn to the Tea Room where I tell him that I am not at all happy about the European Parliament candidate selection procedure and that discontent within the Party on this issue is likely to hit the Press. This prospect becomes ever more likely when Budgie telephones before 8 o'clock the following morning asking me to write a letter to the 'Daily Telegraph'. After much to-ing- and fro-ing, during which time the letters editor claims that my 385 word letter is nearly 500 words and needs to be condensed, he finally rings back at 19.37 to say that it is going in tomorrow's edition – but in an amended form! Reaction to this letter which duly appears in the DT on 15th May is limited to a single letter of protest from the Chairman of the Worcestershire and South Warwickshire European Constituency Council whose sitting MEP is the arch-federalist John Corrie. In the meantime an attempt by Julie Kirkbride (Bromsgrove) to raise the question of EP candidates at the weekly meeting of the '22 Committee attracts no support. There seems to be almost a conspiracy of silence on these matters.

With the new Party rules now firmly in place I am anxious to know what the newly constituted Board has been up to and so in advance of the meeting of the '22 Executive committee on 19th May I give Archie Hamilton's secretary notice that it is my intention to call upon him to make a report. In the event the Executive is yet again content to concentrate on domestic issues, such as the Members' Fund, Members' pensions, Members' interests etc. rather than on topics of a more political nature with the consequence that the meeting is nearly out of time before I manage to ask my question about the activities of the Party Board. In reply Archie reels off a list of appointments to various sub-committees and concludes by warning that the Party's financial situation is desperate.

Before Parliament breaks for Whitsuntide there is another opportunity for me to hammer away at the iniquities of the CFP when European Standing Committee 'A' meets on 20th May. Whilst I regret not having taken the opportunity to have a frank exchange of views with Shadow MAFF Minister Michael Jack when we met at the previous day's briefing meeting I do have the satisfaction of having seen him, his sidekick James Paice (Cambridgeshire South) and my namesake, Ben Gill, President of the National Farmers Union (NFU) all looking extremely sheepish at the weekly meeting of the Conservative backbench Agriculture Committee. I get the impression that the nails that they have all been sitting on for so long, in the shape of the CAP and the single currency, are at long last beginning to make them feel somewhat uncomfortable, but sadly any prospect of them abandoning these collectivist policies still looks highly improbable.

Returning to Westminster for the Summer sitting my main preoccupation is to establish whether Wm. Hague will hold to the views that he has expressed on the EU and, not least, his stated opposition to the single currency. Over an agreeable lunch at Rules restaurant I ask Shadow Social Security Secretary of State, Iain Duncan-Smith (Chingford &Woodford Green) if Hague really believes what he says about the European question. Iain says that he believes that he does and goes on to say that as far as he is personally concerned it is the only thing that is keeping him in politics. He says that he has given up all outside interests to concentrate on the job in hand but that he cannot afford to go on eating into capital for much longer – the time is fast approaching, he says, when he will have to put wife and family first.

Later that day when I pose the same question at a meeting with the Chief Whip, James Arbuthnot asks me how well I know Wm. Hague. When I say 'hardly at all' he says that if I knew him better I would know that he definitely means what he says. Having ploughed through the rest of my agenda I come away from my meeting with the Chief feeling well pleased that I am making progress – a mood which continues until I hear William speaking on radio the following Monday morning. Interviewed on the BBC 'Today' programme William refuses to say that he rules out the single currency as a matter of principle. Later, when I bump into Bill Cash he is in high dudgeon and on his way to deliver a letter to the Leader expressing his dissatisfaction at what he has heard on the radio and also reminding Hague about the statement that he made to the 'European Journal' during the course of the leadership contest.

Incensed by this latest development I tackle Archie Norman about Hague's real position on the European question. Archie, who is now the Conservative Party's Chief Executive, says that I must talk to the Leader himself on the strength of which I ask PPS David Lidington to arrange a meeting. Iain Duncan-Smith is curious to know what I have been discussing with Archie and when I tell him he repeats what he told me last week saying that the European question is the only one that matters to him and that it is the only thing that is keeping him in politics.

In the meantime, in his new capacity as Shadow Health Minister, Alan Duncan has visited the Ludlow constituency which provides me with the opportunity to ask him too about Hague's views on Europe. Alan assures me that Hague means what he says and if anything would be inclined to go further than he has already gone – an opinion that is somewhat negated by Hague's interview on the following Monday's 'Today' programme.

On 10th June Chairman Archie Hamilton tells the '22 Executive that the Conservative Party is 'skint' and that we are not going to like the drastic measures that are going to be taken to balance the books. As far as the Ludlow constituency is concerned I express the opinion that if the whole of Conservative Central Office were to be closed down it really would not be missed!

After the meeting of the full '22 Committee Teresa Gorman (Billericay) berates Archie Norman about the Party Whips spending too much time in useless meetings and too little time organising effective opposition. When I try to talk to Archie Hamilton about the Party's financial crisis he refers me to Archie Norman who has apparently been told that he isn't going to achieve any of his political ambitions unless he first sorts out Central Office! I surmise that being made Chief Executive of the Conservative Party is probably not part of Archie's personal career plan anyway. Being the boss of a supermarket chain where he is justifiably credited with having turned the fortunes of Asda from failure to success is a far cry from running a voluntary organisation, not least a voluntary organisation engaged in politics. Archie has been handed the proverbial poisoned chalice and although no doubt flattered to have been propelled into this senior position barely 12 months after being first elected to Parliament one wonders at the naivety of those who believe that the skills of running a commercial operation are necessarily those that will produce the best results in the voluntary sector. As luck would have it Archie happens to be the guest speaker at the LCCA Annual Dinner this coming Friday where he describes me to my supporters as being 'direct'. When, privately, I take him up on this description he says that being 'direct' is what my people like about me!

The same cannot be said about the Prime Minister who, in answer to my question about the outcome of the Council of Ministers meeting in Cardiff at the weekend, says that "I am afraid that we just disagree". My question is about the collectivist nature of the EU Agriculture and Fisheries policies which also forms the basis of my keynote speech to the meeting of the Anti-Maastricht Alliance 'Congress for a Europe of Free Nations' held in Cardiff to coincide with the Council of Ministers meeting. At Cardiff station, waiting for a train home, a railwayman, upon seeing my lapel badge 'No Euro, Keep Our Pound' says 'too bloody right, my Dad didn't lose a leg in the war for us to be ruled by the French'!

The upshot of my question to the PM is a rare invitation from the BBC to be interviewed tomorrow morning when I am mildly surprised to be given nearly four minutes air time on the 'Farming Today' programme to articulate my views. In spite of being the only Member of Parliament with practical experience on both sides of the meat and livestock industry the BBC, because of my strong views in opposition to the EU and all its works, is generally reluctant to feature me on any of its programmes and even when it does the arrangements for doing so are often made as difficult for me as possible.

At the weekly meeting of the '22 Executive I get a lot of support for my suggestion about getting rid of the regional structure in the Party organisation whilst at the same time making it clear to the new Areas that if they want Conservative MPs and Conservative Councillors then it's down to them to do something about it rather than sit back thinking that CCO or the Region are going to do it for them.

At the same meeting I am only too pleased to support John Townend (Yorkshire East) when he points out that many pressure groups, half of which he and I have previously agreed would not even exist if the Conservative Party came down firmly on one side or other of the European argument, are attracting quite significant funds which might otherwise be coming to the Party. Whilst on the subject of funding I tell the committee that the Party could save itself a considerable amount of money if instead of scrapping the existing logo it simply took more trouble to explain that the current emblem is the 'Torch of Freedom'! The Party is clutching at straws if it believes that a change of logo, along with rule changes, is going to be an adequate substitute for tackling the all important question of policy. Its almost pathological aversion to taking a stand on anything is illustrated by the reaction of Shadow Culture Secretary, Peter Ainsworth (Surrey East), when I question the propriety of the Arts Council using taxpayers money to sponsor 'Queerfest'. Peter's opinion is that we have to be careful because Chris Smith, the Secretary of State, is one of them!

One of the remits of the Secretary of State for Culture, Media and Sport is, of course, the BBC and on 30th June when the Chairman of Governors, Christopher Bland, attends the All Party BBC Group I am there to ventilate a few frustrations such as the BBC's recent decision to alter, yet again, the timing of the 'Farming Today' programme; their platitudinous justifications for doing exactly what they themselves want to do, regardless of the licence paying viewers and listeners, and not least, their serious lack of political balance.

Another organisation of which I am equally suspicious is the so-called 'Independent Commission on the Voting System' chaired by former Labour Home Secretary and European Commission President Lord (Roy) Jenkins of Hillhead. When members of the 'Independent Commission' attend the Grand Committee Room, also on 30th June, for the expressed purpose of listening to the views of Parliamentarians I am one of the MPs who feels obliged to let them have the benefit of my own thoughts on this controversial subject. The essential point that I seek to make is that as one of that rare breed of MPs who have had their Party Whip withdrawn I have a particular perspective on these matters which, though I say it myself, illustrates one of the essential strengths of the present arrangements which make it possible for an individual MP to represent their constituents, even to the point of defying the Party Whip, in a way that simply would not be possible under a 'party list' system. Mercifully, thanks to the fact that the present system has delivered a Labour Government with a massive majority, we shall hear little more from the Jenkins commission. Even the arch proponents of proportional representation, the Liberal Democrats, will become less and less vociferous on that account as their electoral success under the 'first past the post' system begins to significantly improve.

In the final month before the long Summer recess the European Union and Economic & Monetary Union (EMU) continue to be the major pre-occupation. Lunching with Yorkshire's one and only Paul Sykes on 1st July he tells me that he is determined to run his own campaign against the Single Currency. He plans to start on 1st January and given the continued ambivalence of the Conservative Party on this subject I tell him that in my opinion he is absolutely right to do so. Indeed I go so far as to suggest that if CCO simply runs out of money it will probably be a blessing in disguise in that they might then have to accept what the Party rank and file would like to see happen. The following evening we meet again at a drinks party thrown by Sir Peter Tapsell (Louth & Horncastle) at his apartment in the Albany. All the eurosceptics are there, including Richard and Sarah Smith who tell me how much they agree with what I had to say at their home last month when they hosted the inaugural meeting of the Leominster Constituency Conservative Association's Patrons Club. The only person to disagree with the contents of my speech on that occasion was a man whose wife had been Julie Kirkbride's constituency chairman at the time of the last election. One person who sticks out like a sore thumb at Peter's party is Anthony Steen (Totnes) who in spite of all his Delphic protestations is not 'one of us', he being a supporter of the arch-europhile Ken Clarke (Rushcliffe). Another person present, who most definitely is 'one of us', is Margaret Thatcher herself who, in spite of increasing frailty, insists upon standing on an upturned wooden box to address the assembled company. Afterwards I am rash enough to give her a copy of the speech which I intend to deliver this coming weekend at County Hall, Truro, on the subject of EMU.

At Truro I find myself pitted against, amongst others, Bill Newton-Dunn, a former Conservative MEP, who is appearing on behalf of the European Commission. When Newton-Dunn challenges another speaker, Lord

Stoddart of Swindon, asking him if he's never heard of competition, his Lordship instantly responds with a spontaneous put-down – "competitors? I thought you told me that they were our partners"!

Before catching the train to Truro I attend a highly successful businessmens' conference at the Cafe Royal sponsored by the European Research Group (ERG). Thanks to Michael Spicer's superb networking skills the conference is attended by an impressive number of the great and the good from the world of trade, industry and commerce. Out of this meeting will spring 'Business for Sterling' which, in its turn, will sponsor the successful 'No to the Single Currency' campaign. Speaking at the conference on behalf of the 'Federation of Small Businesses' (FSB) Donald Martin makes reference to the Marxist origins of the EU ethos and I, for my part, feel obliged to underscore what he has said by saying a word or two about the collectivist nature of its policies.

Someone who most definitely does not share my opinions on the EU is the Norwegian Ambassador. On 6th July, in my capacity as one of the two Vice Chairmen of the All Party Anglo Norwegian Group, I attend a dinner at the ambassador's residence in honour of the Norwegian Prime Minister. I am somewhat surprised when the ambassador says that he very much hopes that I will continue to serve on the group. This leaves me wondering whether this is a covert signal that the Norwegian PM might just be 'one of us' and that the Ambassador is simply trimming to the prevailing wind or whether the Ambassador has said something derogatory about me that he needs to neutralise.

On 8th July I am obliged to leave the debating Chamber before being called to speak in a debate about the Strategic Defence Review in order to be at the Leader's office in time for our meeting at 16.40. The meeting goes well and I am able to make all the points on my agenda except the one about urging William to grasp the nettle before it is too late. Nevertheless I am encouraged by the fact that he has seen me on only his third day back after two weeks sick leave, sandwiching me in between an earlier meeting with Cecil Parkinson and Archie Norman and Shadow Cabinet at 17.00.

At the '22 Executive meeting it is decided to refer the matter of Mr Peter Samuel's appointment to the staff at CCO to Archie Norman when he attends our meeting next week. Unbelievably, Mr Samuel, who stood as a Liberal Democrat against Crispin Blunt in Reigate at the General Election and is reputedly chairman of the mid-Surrey branch of the European Movement, has been engaged to mastermind economy measures at CCO – further evidence that you don't need to be a believer to prosper in the modern Conservative Party!

When Archie Norman attends the Executive Committee meeting the following week to brief members on the action that he is taking to balance the books at CCO I express the opinion that the only way to make worthwhile savings is by cutting out whole functions such as the network of regional offices. I go on to say that the real problem is on the income side because money that might otherwise be coming to the Party is going to various pressure groups, especially those on either side of the EMU argument, due to the Party's failure to promote more acceptable policies. This causes slight uproar notwithstanding which I tell the committee that whilst they may not agree with me now, sooner or later they will have to come round to my way of thinking.

In terms of policy I have, two days previously, told Shadow Chancellor, Francis Maude, how necessary it is that the Party's 'top brass' spell out the dangers of the Single Currency for the simple reason that the public are far more likely to be persuaded if the message is coming from the top of the Party than if it comes from the likes of myself. When I go on to tell him that somebody has told me how much they admire him for having had the courage to say that he had made a mistake in signing the Maastricht Treaty, he says not so – he only signed the treaty because, with the Single Currency 'opt-out', 'it was a good treaty for Britain'!

Barely a week later, during the course of a debate in the name of the Liberal Democrat Party entitled 'European Single Currency', Francis Maude's contribution so incenses me that I am tempted to walk out of the Chamber whilst he is still speaking. Walking home after the 10 o'clock vote I tell James Cran that for two pins I would have resigned the Party Whip there and then but settle instead for penning a strong letter to the Chief Whip expressing my utter disgust at Maude's failure to oppose the Single Currency as a matter of principle.

A private meeting on 23rd July with Shadow Foreign Secretary, Michael Howard, is equally depressing. He doesn't agree that it is a prerequisite of electoral success to spell out the Party's policy on Europe very much more clearly. He refuses to say where competence for Fisheries should lie –

Westminster or Brussels – and he is very much against making any policy commitments beyond ruling out the Single Currency for the duration of this Parliament and the next. Having regard to the fact that during last year's leadership contest he produced a series of eurosceptic pamphlets, each one more robust than the last, it is all rather frustrating and so on the last day of the Summer sitting (30th July) I am glad to have the opportunity of waylaying the Leader's PPS, David Lidington (Aylesbury) in the Members Lobby. The gist of what I have to say to David is that, with more than a year gone since his election as Leader, Wm. Hague's window of opportunity is beginning to close and that he really needs to make up his mind, by the time of the Party Conference in October at the latest, which side of the European argument he really is on and that the longer he leaves it the harder it will get to make that fundamental choice. For good measure I repeat the message that we're heading for a poor turnout in the European Parliament Election next year and that the sooner William gets on with the ballot of Party members on the question of the Single Currency the better. Finally I point out to David that the voters don't trust us on the European question and that it will take more than a few well chosen words in the next election manifesto to bring them back into the Conservative fold. With only three years to go before the next General Election we need to start work now and unless we prevent the Single Currency from being adopted and the Political Union which will surely follow, the whole raison d'etre for a conservative Party will disappear. As a parting shot I tell David that I'm getting tired of playing the white man and not getting anywhere and will soon be forced to adopt another tactic!

When or if David reports this conversation to his master it will hardly come as a surprise given that I had already said to William at his meeting with the '22 Executive on 13th July that he should not underestimate the electoral appeal of traditional Conservative policies and principles, the abandonment of which in the last Parliament had cost us so dear in the General Election. In response to those comments William had assured me that his 'Listening to Britain' exercise did not mean that basic principles were being forgotten.

Never one to miss an opportunity, at the annual meeting of the Centre for Policy Studies (CPS), addressed by Press baron Conrad Black, I am giving the wife of the United States Ambassador the benefit of my views on the

European issue when we are joined by Ambassador Lader himself. Whether he appreciates me telling him that the USA should stop trying to propel Britain into the EU I shall never know but maybe upon reflection he will come to recognise the logic of my argument which is that, in the circumstances in which the UK became fully subsumed by the EU, America would one day find herself standing alone, with their trusted and long-standing ally formally prevented from taking their part by dint of the EU Common Foreign and Security policy. At the same gathering I am able to tease former Defence Secretary, Tom King (Bridgwater) by saying that I hope he agrees with what we have both heard Conrad Black say. Tom replies by drawing my attention to the magnificence of the room in which the illustrious company is gathered. This includes Margaret Thatcher with whom I have a brief chat which confirms that she definitely hasn't read my Truro speech, but then again I would have been more than surprised if she had.

Before the Summer sitting ends Wm. Hague addresses the full '22 Committee and whilst he does well he certainly doesn't look it. In the previous week he has addressed the 800 people who sat down to dinner at Peplow Hall in Owen Paterson's constituency on 16th July. Having taken questions after his speech the general impression is that people think more highly of him now than they did previously but he still has a long way to go in terms of convincing the Party that he is going to be a successful Leader.

Meanwhile, back in the Ludlow constituency, all is not well. On 21st June, for whatever reason, I had felt constrained to give the members of the LCCA Finance & General Purposes Committee a pep talk when we all met at the Chairman's Whitton Court home. Subsequent events make me glad that I have done so. Trying to explain to Association Vice Chairman, Justin Caldwell why immediate past Chairman Michael Wood is feeling aggrieved about recent developments is averagely a waste of time because it seems doubtful that he really understands the issue and probably sees it in terms of personalities rather than politics.

On 30th June the F&GP Committee have appointed Alan Screen and Katherine Lumsden to be the LCCA representatives on the Party's new Area Council . This causes me to telephone Association President, Lord Hamilton of Dalzell, the very next day to warn him that there is trouble on the line. He quickly grasps the situation and recognises that Michael Wood has to be supported. A couple of days later, on 3rd July, I telephone Justin Caldwell to suggest that he should contact the LCCA Chairman to offer her his support in her hour of need. During the course of a long conversation I have to keep bringing Justin back to the point that the Association rules have been broken and that personalities and differences of opinion do not enter into it. Later that day, whilst on a train to my speaking engagement in Truro, I learn that there is to be an LCCA Executive Council at the end of the month. That was on Friday but by Monday the situation is different because the chosen date, according to LCCA Chairman, Pam Twitchell, does not suit former Treasurer, Anthony Thompson, and the ambitious Alan Screen. By nightfall on Tuesday the news is even worse when I hear from Michael Wood that Area Council have elected one Martin Sheldon as their Chairman. When Chairman Pam telephones me the next morning to tell me what I already know about last night's Area Council meeting she refuses to tell me how she herself has voted, from which I deduce that she hasn't supported Michael. Once again the Ludlow constituency, which she keeps saying is Shropshire's premier constituency, finds itself effectively disenfranchised and whilst I go into some detail with her about the political significance of what is going on I get the distinct impression that it is all simply water off the proverbial duck's back. On 28th July I hold a meeting with LCCA President, Lord Hamilton, regarding all these local difficulties. He says that he agrees with Michael Wood and that he will write to the Chairman requesting an Executive Council meeting. Ironically, the following day, Lord Hamilton's younger brother, 1922 Committee Chairman Archie Hamilton, reports that on the national scene things are no better. Robin Hodgson, Chairman of the NUEC, is still pushing for the automatic reselection of MPs and I remind Archie that as Hodgson was party to the deal regarding the new Party rules he must be told to stick to the bargain struck at that time.

For my debate in the Summer Adjournment about the state of the British pig industry the Public Gallery is full of farmers and the NFU's 'top brass'. On the floor of the House the whole of the Government Agriculture team is in attendance, including the new Agriculture Minister Nick Brown, the Member for the not so rural constituency of Newcastle-upon-Tyne East & Wallsend! Even the BBC shows interest by broadcasting excerpts from the debate on the following morning's edition of the 'Farming Today' programme and on that happy note I head off for the long awaited Summer recess.

At its first meeting of the Michaelmas sitting the ERG rejects the idea of a county by county ballot on the question of the Single Currency but, with a view to sponsoring ongoing opinion polls, agrees to commission a survey to establish what questions are most likely to resonate with voters. The following day – Trafalgar Day – I try to persuade the AGM of the Freedom Association that getting the Conservative Party onside is vital if we are to stand any chance of winning a referendum on the Single Currency.

At the '22 Executive meeting held on the same day I express some frank views about the so-called 'bonding session' for Conservative MPs held in Eastbourne during the recess. I argue that this was a missed opportunity to hammer out a strategy as a prelude to making policy. I contend that each shadow team should have been put in a separate room so as to give backbenchers an opportunity to input into the thinking of whichever subject area they had a particular interest or expertise in. I then instance the failure of our Press Office to act professionally and to get a better press for us at the time of the Party Conference. Conducting press conferences in physically uncomfortable premises and allowing the vexed question of Europe to spill over into four days had not been conducive to winning the Press over to our side which was always going to be difficult anyway, without us creating unnecessary obstacles.

In the area in which I am particularly interested a meeting with our new Shadow Agriculture Minister, Tim Yeo (Suffolk South), on 22nd October is most encouraging. On the question of the Common Fisheries Policy I suggest that the 'get out of jail free card' for the Conservative Party is Conservation – surely nobody can argue about the desirability of conserving fish stocks which the appalling CFP is hazarding in a most reckless and irresponsible manner.

The following week, at the regular Conservative backbench Agriculture Committee, I am disappointed not to be able to get a clear run on Fisheries but the committee decides to invite me to make a presentation at next week's meeting. This will be an opportunity to put the record straight on the CFP but, when I suggest that the problems in the Agriculture industry are not the result of what has occurred in recent years but are ones that have been coming as an inevitable consequence of joining the CAP, the Europhiles present, such as Tom King (Bridgwater) and John MacGregor (Norfolk South), would clearly prefer to change the subject!

When I come to make my presentation to the committee a week later these people are, not surprisingly, conspicuous by their absence and I am obliged to tell my friendly Whip, James Cran, how appalling it is that 'the enemy' will never engage on these matters. The committee, with the exception of Shadow Agriculture Minister, Tim Yeo, and Party Whip, Caroline Spelman, agrees with what I have to say and subsequently Eric Forth (Bromley & Chislehurst) is kind enough to compliment me on using the committee system in an absolutely proper way to bring about change in Party policy. Notwithstanding James Cran's undertaking to raise the issue at the daily Whips' meeting I make it my business to personally tackle Chief Whip, James Arbuthnot, about the continuing and craven refusal of the Europhiles to fight their corner, not even amongst their colleagues in the privacy of a committee room! The Chief responds by saying that he doesn't know why I am worrying about it if I am winning the argument to which I reply that I'm worried because Party policy is being made to reflect the views of those who won't even argue their case in private, let alone in public. When he says again that he can't see why I'm worrying I tell him that I don't want to win the argument by default – I want to have the debate and I want to be seen to have won the argument on the merits of my case. The situation is amply demonstrated at a public meeting at Sutton Coldfield Town Hall on 6th November when Robert Coppinger, the West Midlands area organiser for the pro-EMU European Movement, utters not a word throughout the course of a debate about the Single Currency.

1998

3

" I am On the Warpath "

That we are winning the argument on the EU is evidenced by the result of the debate organised by the NFU which takes place on 20th November at the Three Counties Showground at Malvern. The topic under discussion is Economic & Monetary Union (EMU). Before the debate begins 57 of those people present declare themselves as being in favour of the Single Currency, 36 are against and 10 abstain. In spite of some rather ill-judged comments on his part, Rodney Atkinson and I, opposed by a Bank of England representative and a Labour MEP, manage to convert some of the protagonists and at the conclusion of the proceedings only 43 remain in favour with 59 against and only 6 abstentions.

On 11th November Teresa Gorman gives me advance notice of a letter she has written to the Chairman of the '22 complaining about the Party's failure to get its act together. When I ask Archie Hamilton if he will raise the matter at the '22 Executive he describes Teresa's letter as 'outrageous' and so it is left to her to speak up for herself at the full meeting which follows. Speaking in support of Teresa I instance how we threw away a golden opportunity at Eastbourne to have a proper debate about strategy instead of being talked at by outsiders; how the Party, as well as heeding the results of the 'Listening to Britain' campaign, also ought to be listening to its own MPs; how a robust debate about policy would be good for the Members and also good for the Party and finally, how embarrassing it was that when challenged about the future of the Bank of England we didn't have an answer. John Townend (Yorkshire East) weighs in to support, as does Douglas Hogg (Sleaford & Hykeham) who says that he doesn't often agree with Teresa but that on this occasion she is right.

Subsequently Douglas Hogg joins me at dinner in the Members Dining Room and expresses himself as being mildly excited at the prospect of a 'peasants revolt' on the backbenches and even goes so far as to aver that he is a bit of a rebel himself! He is really pleased that the principle has been established whereby in future the '22 Committee will be able to summon Shadow Ministers to appear before it but whether the backbenchers will be forceful enough to hold them to account remains to be seen. Perhaps for this reason Douglas subsequently tells me that at the election of Members to serve on the '22 Executive at which, incidentally, John Townend and Andrew Hunter (Basingstoke) were voted off, he voted for me to remain on.

An innovation of this Parliament, in which the Conservative Party has had to come to terms with being in opposition, is the 'Forward Look Committee' which meets every Monday afternoon to note the business of the House for the forthcoming week and to make plans accordingly. As an additional forum in which to express opinions and make constructive comments about policy I welcome this new development and at its meeting on 16th November suggest that as a matter of principle the Party should oppose any measure which threatens to impose additional cost burdens upon Trade, Industry and Commerce. Establishing some basic principles is, I believe, a necessary part of trying to mount a coherent opposition and a necessary prelude to formulating a sensible manifesto for the next General Election. Later in the week concern is expressed at the '22 Executive that the Leader's intention to attend the Forward Look committee on a regular basis bodes ill for the future of the '22 itself. The prospect of the centre of gravity within the Party shifting is a distinct possibility but the '22 Committee will surely retain its importance as the focus of backbench opinion (and discussion!).

Perhaps due to an excellent lunch at the Portugese Embassy, Teresa's further broadside at the 18th November meeting of the '22 is long and rambling and, willing as I am to support her, provides nothing that I can latch onto.

Back on the subject of Fisheries, on 11th November Shadow Fisheries Minister, Patrick Nicholls (Teignbridge) rings to say that he hopes to ask a leading question at Question Time tomorrow. This encourages me to believe that we may finally have hooked this particular fish in which case we are well on the way towards getting the Party to adopt a more sensible Fisheries policy.

One week later I make a final attempt to persuade Shadow Foreign Secretary, Michael Howard, of the importance of the decision that he and Shadow Agriculture Minister, Tim Yeo, Shadow Minister for Constitutional Affairs, Liam Fox and Patrick Nicholls will make next week regarding Fisheries policy. Disappointingly, on 24th November, Liam Fox tells me that the meeting which should have taken place tomorrow has been postponed. Michael Howard assures me that they really are taking the matter very seriously and that the reason for the postponement is because of an Adjournment Debate on Foreign Affairs. Not content to let the matter rest I buttonhole Tim Yeo on 25th saying that I do appreciate that he has a different perspective on European Union to myself, in response to which he says that, on the contrary, he has a very open mind on the issue!

Perhaps sensing that I am on the warpath and not likely to give up on the Fisheries question Hague's PPS assures me that I will get the appointment with his boss that I had requested earlier in the month. David Lidington tells me that I will definitely get to see the Leader before Christmas. In the event the meeting takes place on 3rd December, the day after William has sacked the Conservative Leader in the House of Lords, Lord Cranborne, for doing deals with Tony Blair and Blair's Press Secretary, Alistair Campbell, behind William's back. Robert Cranborne has effectively given away the Party's principal bargaining counter, in terms of House of Lords reform, by backing down on the policy of 'no stage 1 without stage 2'. Given the obvious difficulty of finding a satisfactory alternative to the existing composition of the Upper House the Conservative Party had, until Robert's capitulation, held the moral high ground by not unreasonably saying that until Blair announces the total package we could not possibly agree to its first phase. The deal now is that whilst the hereditary Peers will be allowed to elect 92 of their own number to stay on as full Members of the Lords, all other hereditary peers will be automatically disqualified. What happens after that is left hanging in the wind.

My meeting with Wm. Hague is very satisfactory. Given the events of the past 24 hours I am more than a little surprised that my appointment has not been cancelled and that he sees me at the time previously agreed. He says that he will instruct the Fisheries team to tell me what their policy is in advance of the annual Fisheries debate on 15th December. I tell him that this will be a defining moment. He knows that people are going to go on asking where competence for Fisheries should lie – in Westminster or in Brussels - and he also recognises that the CFP is inconsistent with his mantra of being 'in Europe but not run by Europe'.

Wonders never cease – on 9th December there is a message on my pager asking if I would like to speak in the forthcoming Fisheries debate. When I tell the MAFF Whip, Caroline Spelman, that the answer is 'yes' she asks me who else I think would like to take part in the debate. That the 'management' at last appear to be sitting up and taking notice of what I have been saying on this subject is most encouraging although, as evidenced by a conversation with Tim Yeo later in the day, there is still a long way to go. When I tackle him about the impending Fisheries debate and ask him which side of the fence the Shadow Fisheries team are going to come down on he recommends that I continue to lobby those concerned. In which case, I say, I might as well start with you! Does he not understand that to talk of renegotiation is a cop out for the very good and simple reason that to achieve any fundamental reform of the CFP requires unanimity amongst the Member States and at least one of them, i.e. Spain, is almost certain to exercise the veto in order to protect the very advantageous terms that the CFP, as presently constituted, gives them. On this theme I am able to tell Tim that I believe that Shadow Foreign Secretary, Michael Howard, will be advocating renegotiation which is in stark contrast to what he was saying at the time of the leadership contest when he talked about repatriation. Tim says that he didn't know that, so I promise to let him have the evidence.

On the eve of the Fisheries debate I meet with Shadow Minister for Constitutional Affairs, Liam Fox, who will be winding up the debate for the Opposition. He says that he would much prefer that the Party keep its powder dry until mid-February. In response I tell Liam that continued procrastination will only serve to convince the public that our assertion that we want to be 'in Europe but not run by Europe' is just empty rhetoric. He seems to sit up and take note when I say that the outcome of the next

General Election could be even worse than 1997 if people like me, who have hung on in there out of a sense of loyalty, conclude that the Tories are never going to defend the things that they believe in. To illustrate the way things are moving our way I hand him an extract from Michael Heseltine's contribution to the debate on the Queen's Speech in which Hezza is recorded in the Hansard for 26th November as saying:

"My final point is a chilling one. I am a European. I believe that this country's best interest is served by our playing a leading role in the European Community as it is now emerging. I have believed that for 40 years, and I believe it today as profoundly as ever. We have to fight within Europe for the United Kingdom. However, there is another European agenda, which is a federalist one. It wants to bypass the nation state.

Federalists want to bypass the nation state because they realise that, if they can regionalise Europe, they can exercise a much more pervasive influence from Brussels and through the European Parliament than they will ever be able to do if the nation states are the building blocks of Europe. What the Government are doing – I doubt whether they have even thought that this is what they are doing – is creating a blueprint that brings this country into line with a potentially regionally governed Europe"

I also make sure to give Liam a copy of the article that Michael Howard had written for the European Journal in May last year about repatriating Fisheries policy.

In spite of the fact that Liam has been burgled at home and lost most of his day as a consequence, he affords me a good hour of his time and by the time we have finished I am satisfied that I have covered all the necessary points.

On the day in question the time spent in the morning preparing my speech is entirely wasted as John Townend is the only backbencher on our side called to speak. Much of my speech would in any case have been superfluous in the light of Fisheries spokesman, Patrick Nicholls' brave and excellent contribution to the debate. I am scarcely able to believe what I am hearing and will have to read Hansard to confirm that Patrick really is saying that we have to bring Fisheries policy back under national control.

On 17th December I am obliged to telephone the BBC to complain about the story they are running on the 'Farming Today' and the 'Today' programmes about fishing quotas. Quite apart from them not having presented a balanced picture by having an Opposition spokesman on air they have conveniently failed to mention the fact that, as a consequence of quotas, huge quantities of perfectly fresh, saleable fish are being dumped back dead into the sea. The BBC's explanation is the crisis in Iraq which is, of course, a totally spurious excuse and so I call Patrick Nicholls and suggest that he speaks to them himself to see if they will have him on air.

Later in the day the news breaks that the RAF and the USAF are bombing Baghdad but nevertheless on the following day's 'Today' programme the pro-Brussels Broadcasting Corporation interviews Fisheries Minister, Eliott Morley (Scunthorpe), and yet again make no attempt to balance the report by also interviewing an Opposition fisheries spokesman. Nor indeed do they make any mention of discards i.e. the above quota fish thrown overboard to rot on the seabed.

Quite apart from the amorality of catching fish that will never be eaten and the affront to the sensible conservation of fish stocks that this represents, the CFP is a microcosm of the EU itself. The question is, as I tell the Congress for Democracy rally on 18th December, where should competence for Fisheries lie – in Brussels or at Westminster? I suggest that the assembled company ask their own MPs this very question or, alternatively, whether their MP believes in European integration rather than freedom and democracy.

As the year draws to a close Wm. Hague addresses the full '22 Committee and demonstrates some of the leadership qualities that have been so lacking in the Conservative Party these past 8 years. All except the 'malignant tendency' applaud his remarks and I am reminded of what he had told us when the '22 Executive met him on 25th November. On that occasion '22 Chairman, Archie Hamilton, had expressed concern about the Conservative Party's very low ratings in the opinion polls, in reply to which William had said that it is going to take time before the electorate accept that they've made the wrong choice and that, in the meantime, he will go on being consistent, spelling out what it is that he and his Party stand for and opposing the Government when they are wrong. This is a point of view with which I personally have great sympathy and only hope that he will stay true to his word.

The final curtain call for 1998 features Minister without Portfolio, Peter Mandelson (Hartlepool), who resigns at 1 pm on 23rd December as a consequence of having failed to declare a large loan from Paymaster General Geoffrey Robinson (Coventry North West) in connection with a mortgage application he had previously submitted in respect of a not inexpensive property. The sequel to this is the resignation of Geoffrey Robinson himself, less than four hours later. Thus ends the first full year in office of a Government that Tony Blair had said would be 'whiter than white'!

1999

1

" Traitors in our Midst "

Notwithstanding that we are now into a new year, some topics simply don't go away. On Tuesday 12th January, Shadow Chancellor of the Exchequer, Francis Maude (since 1997 representing Horsham, having lost his Warwickshire North seat in 1992), is the guest speaker at a '92 Group dinner. When it comes to questions I say that he is probably aware of the very excellent and courageous speech made by our new Fisheries spokesman, Patrick Nicholls, in the House on 15th December when he said that "we have to bring fisheries policy back under national control". Since this now appears to be Party policy, as endorsed by a letter from the Leader's office addressed to a fisherman in Fleetwood (retired trawler skipper Mark Hamer) which states that "we believe that the only solution to the problems facing the fishing industry is for our fishing grounds to be brought back under national control" could he give me an assurance that the Manifesto Committee, of which he is a member, will include this new policy in our manifesto for the forthcoming European Parliament elections in June. Furthermore, does he share my concern that this would be incompatible with the joint statement rumoured to be being agreed between our existing MEPs and the EPP?

On the first part of my question he answers by saying that if I've got a letter from the Leader's office saying that that is so, then that must be the new policy although he was personally not aware of it. It will therefore, he says, have to go into the manifesto. On the second part of my question he 'verbalises' until concluding that it would be wrong to agree anything which might lock us into a situation which would prejudice our own position.

The following day, at the meeting of the '22 Executive, I ask the Chairman whether he supposes there is any truth in the rumour that our MEPs are proposing to issue a joint statement with the EPP group. Michael Mates (Hampshire East) says that we don't want to open up old sores, new Member, John Bercow (Buckingham), takes my part, whilst John Butterfill (Bournemouth West) says that he can see no harm in a joint statement on subjects where there is agreement! Given the all too apparent ambivalence of shadow Cabinet ministers on this subject I have, earlier in the day, written to Francis Maude, Michael Howard and Michael Ancram stating my concern about the mixed messages that we are in danger of sending out ahead of the EP election and also about the prospect of Conservative MEPs issuing a joint statement with the EPP.

When on Thursday I join colleagues Chope, Forth, Howarth and Leigh at table in the tearoom they are discussing Francis Maude's reaction to the questions that I had put to him on Tuesday. Eric Forth says that Francis didn't know what to say! That evening there is an adjournment debate on the 'sustainability of fisheries' sponsored by Shaun Woodward (Witney). Although I am able to make several interventions I regret missing the opportunity of referring to my Right Honourable Friend, the Member for Suffolk Coastal, as a 'collectivist' but his contribution to the debate confirms that this is precisely what he is. Like others of his ilk, John Gummer has absolutely no shame about masquerading as a Conservative even though much of his ideology would not disgrace any one of the socialist Parties.

In a book published in April, entitled 'Mandelson, the Biography', author Donald Macintyre reveals how, prior to the General Election, the said John Gummer and fellow arch-Europhile Ken Clarke were in secret negotiation with Peter Mandelson (Hartlepool). The purpose of their collaboration with the enemy was to strike a deal whereby in exchange for an undertaking by Mandelson, in his then capacity as Labour Party election campaign manager, that he would do the same, the traitors would do their best to ensure that the question of the single currency did not become an election issue. Clarke and Gummer wanted to keep the option of joining the single currency open but feared that Labour might conceivably rule out that possibility for at least the duration of the next Parliament. This was a prospect that Clarke and Gummer were determined to head off because not only would it give Labour an electoral advantage but, more to the point as far as they were concerned, it would effectively scupper their plans, as rabid integrationists, to see membership of the single currency brought to fruition sooner rather than later.

When on 28th April I tackle Ken Clarke about the revelations and ask him if he will be suing Macintyre and/or his publishers he answers in his usual off-hand and dismissive way. 'No', he says, 'in grown up politics one is always talking to the other side and doing deals'!

Unwilling to let that be the end of the matter I add it to the list of items that I want to see our Chief Whip about. On 4th May, when I request a meeting with him, I am mildly surprised to be ushered into James Arbuthnot's office there and then. I start by telling the Chief about the paragraph on the single currency in the European Democratic Union's position paper which must presumably have been sanctioned or endorsed by Conservative MEPs and go on to say that if the furore of the past fortnight, which includes an appalling speech by Deputy Party Leader, Peter Lilley, was because the public don't trust the Conservative Party on Health and Education he'd better understand that I and millions like me don't trust the Party on Europe either. I tell him that nothing matters more to me than the sovereignty of the United Kingdom and that having a public platform on 30th May the question I have to answer in my own mind is whether I exhort the assembled company to vote the ticket in June or whether, like Enoch Powell in 1974, I urge them to do otherwise.

On the question of the traitors in our midst who had secretly treated with the enemy I am able to draw the Chief's attention to pages 329/333 of the Macintyre book. He wants to know if I have spoken to Clarke and Gummer in reply to which I tell him what Clarke had said in response to my asking him if he was going to sue.

Having put Chairman, Archie Hamilton, on notice that I intend to raise the matter of the Macintyre revelations at the '22 Committee on 5th May he advises me to postpone my remarks until next week's meeting because he is anticipating a poor attendance. On the strength of this I write to Clarke and Gummer putting them on notice that I intend to raise the matter of their perfidiousness at the '22 Committee meeting on 12th May and lose no time at the weekend lobbying colleagues to attend.

On the eve of the '22 meeting I learn that John Gummer has rung my office, at home in the constituency, to find out what my letter to him is all about . The short answer to this request is to put on the House of Commons letterboard for his attention a copy of the review of the Mandelson biography which appeared in the edition of the ' 'Independent' newspaper published on 23rd April.

In spite of all the build up, the meeting itself is somewhat of an anti-climax. The point I make is that notwithstanding what individual colleagues may choose to do on the single currency front the Party itself must not be inhibited, as it clearly was at the time of the last General Election, as evidenced by the revelations in the Mandelson biography. Gummer, having arrived at the Committee Room twenty-five minutes before the meeting was scheduled to start, is as white as a sheet and visibly frightened. His partner in crime, Ken Clarke, treats the whole proceedings with the contempt that he obviously thinks they deserve and is nowhere to be seen!

After I have said my piece Gummer responds in a most belligerent manner which colleagues later tell me was no more or less than a threat to me personally. Alan Clark, who might have been expected to take my side, then, together with Tom King (Bridgwater), changes the subject to talk about the local elections and it is left to Teddy Taylor to bring the meeting back to my subject. Teddy says that Wm. Hague's little mantra about 'being in Europe, but not ruled by Europe' is just plain silly and that what the Party needs is a crusade. As soon as Teddy has spoken Archie Hamilton promptly closes the meeting but it is of course just possible that there were no other colleagues trying to catch his eye.

Anticipating their reaction to something controversial, I had prefaced my remarks about the Macintyre revelations and the double dealing of our two colleagues by teasing the committee, saying that I could confidently predict that those of them who didn't start to earnestly study their bootlaces would almost certainly be gazing intently skywards. In this respect I was not disappointed!

Collaboration between so-called Conservatives and the European integrationists in other Parties is not confined to Westminster. At the beginning of January Daniel Hannan had expressed his concern about reports that Conservative MEPs would agree a common statement with the federalist EPP in advance of the European Parliament elections to be held in June.

At a breakfast meeting of the European Research Group (ERG) held on 19th January it is agreed that a formal letter of complaint should be sent to Party Leader, Wm. Hague, regarding any possible joint statement being issued by the EPP and the European Democratic Group (EDG) to which the British Conservative MEPs belong. Already it is beginning to look as though such an EPP/EDG joint statement is a done deal and that the EP election will be fought on a Left versus Right rather than a Right versus Wrong basis. Former Party Vice Chairman Michael Trend (Windsor) wants to talk to me about the letter which I have written to colleagues on this subject. After some preliminary skirmishing he admits that privately he agrees with me. I tell him that at the EP election we need to have a distinctly British Conservative message and that the electorate will not otherwise be motivated to vote for us. To reinforce the message I quote George Eustice who had telephoned me from Cornwall on 6th January. George had rung to say that he was strongly of the opinion that the National Farmers Union (NFU) must be influenced to abandon its support for Economic & Monetary Union (EMU). During the course of our conversation he had told me that he had only been politically active for two years and, when asked, went on to explain that he had been inspired by the late James Goldsmith whom he thought had a message that was fresh and worth fighting for – a real object lesson for the Conservative Party!

Another colleague to mention receipt of my letter is Liam Fox (Woodspring) who tells me that in his capacity as Shadow spokesman on Constitutional Affairs he is off to visit Scotland. In response to that snippet of information I say that I very much hope that he will get the Scottish Conservative Party to toe the line on our new fisheries policy. Liam assures me that he 'most certainly will'.

The following day I waylay the Leader's Parliamentary Private Secretary (PPS), David Lidington (Aylesbury), to say that matters ought to be brought to a head regarding our European policy in the light of the possibility that there will be a joint EPP/EDG statement. I instance how even Michael Heseltine (Henley) and Douglas Hogg (Sleaford & N. Hykeham) appear to be coming round to our opinion and stress the necessity for Wm. Hague to take a much tougher line otherwise it is highly likely that it will go badly for him. I go on to point out that an EPP/EDG agreement would be manna from heaven for the UK Independence Party (UKIP) and a huge disincentive for disillusioned Conservatives to return to the fold at the EP election in June. I also take the opportunity of telling David that people like myself are not best pleased with the decision, which I have heard about from Michael Spicer, to make ex Chief Whip, Alastair Goodlad (Eddisbury) a European Commissioner and the message that that will send to our potential supporters. At a lunch yesterday Goodlad had apparently told Jonathan Aitken, Robert Cranborne, Richard Shepherd and Michael Spicer that his name is the only one in the frame for the pending European Commissioner vacancy. In the event our worst fears are not realised and ultimately Goodlad will be sent off to be the British High Commissioner in Australia!

Still on the subject of the threatened EPP/EDG joint statement, Deputy Party Leader, Peter Lilley (Hitchen & Harpenden) thanks me for my letter of 13th January but leaves me with the strong impression that he knew nothing about the rumoured deal. I am at pains to explain that, in electoral terms, such a deal would be the kiss of death.

On 22nd January news reaches me that the reward for all my efforts to save the Conservative Party from itself is that I am to be deselected. Former LCCA Chairman, Michael Wood, says that West Midlands Area Treasurer, Simon Lee, has been told by new West Midlands Area agent, a man by the name of Ashman, that moves are afoot to prevent me from being the Conservative candidate for Ludlow at the next General Election. Because I am a consistent thorn in their side I can well understand the attraction to the Europhiles of having someone more malleable as the elected representative for the Ludlow constituency but in terms of my credentials as a real Conservative I yield to no man. As an illustration of how the modern Conservative Party is controlled and manipulated by a clique of politicians who never were and never will be Conservatives this is as good as it gets.

With the weekly Whip which arrives in the post at home on the weekend of 23/24th January there is a request for Conservative MPs to sign a 'Charter for Britain'. My reaction to this request is to put a letter on the letterboard for Oliver Letwin, in his capacity as opposition spokesman for Constitutional Affairs, as soon as I get to the House on Monday and to determine to speak to as many colleagues about it as possible that evening.

The business of the House is the Second Reading of the Sexual Offences (Amendment) Bill for which there is only a one-line Whip and consequently a 'thin House'. Angela Browning (Tiverton) is very much on my side about this flim flam of a Charter and says that she has absolutely no intention of signing it, but goes on to say how much she regrets having voted for the Maastricht Treaty – now you tell me!

Opposition Whip, Oliver Heald (Hertfordshire NE) is taken aback by the vehemence of my opposition to the 'Charter for Britain'. Others in the tearoom take my part and far from being launched as planned tomorrow it subsequently appears to have been pulled. Oliver says the Charter is Liam Fox's idea and a subsequent word with David Lidington confirms this.

On 26th January, on the strength of what I have been told last evening, I fire off a letter to Liam Fox, with copies to selected shadow Cabinet Ministers including Wm. Hague himself. Hopefully this will put paid to the ridiculous 'Charter for Britain' idea once and for all.

Meanwhile I have received a response to my letter of 13th January about the rumoured joint EPP/EDG statement from Shadow Foreign Minister, Michael Howard. It is totally unsatisfactory – he neither denies the possibility of a deal with the EPP nor does he rule it out for the future.

Later in the day, wearing my Council of Europe hat, I arrive in Strasbourg where I am able to continue lobbying against the EPP/EDG concordat. When I buttonhole John Townend on this subject he is reluctant to accept that Michael Howard is a fifth columnist to which I am bound to say that even if Michael's motives are beyond question his stance on this issue will have the same effect as if he was. John undertakes to raise the matter with senior colleagues and I ask for the question to be put on the agenda for the forthcoming '92 Group officers meeting with Wm. Hague.

Over breakfast in the Hotel Gutenberg (former Nazi HQ in Strasbourg) I take the opportunity of briefing David Wilshire (Spelthorne) on what is going on apropos Conservative MEPs and the EPP. David, having told me that he would seriously consider moving to the Isle of Man if Britain adopts the single currency, promises to add his pennyworth to my agitation when he gets home.

That evening, over supper at 'Les Armes de Strasbourg' in company with Lord Northesk, Alastair Goodlad opines that Wm. Hague is doing exactly the right thing. He expresses opposition to any deals with the EPP and hints that he is not really in favour of a single currency. What I am unable to discern is whether he believes in what he is saying or whether he is saying it purely for my consumption – he is, after all, a member of the 'Blue Chip' group whose questionable belief in national sovereignty is reminiscent of an earlier gang of traitors with Cambridge University affiliations.

The following day I tackle our delegation Leader, David Atkinson (Bournemouth East), about the joint statement of Conservative MEPs and the EPP. It is apparent that he has not read the copy correspondence that I sent him a fortnight ago and gets rather cross when I push him on the question of European integration versus freedom and democracy and whether competence should rest with Brussels or Westminster. He argues that without an association with the EPP we will have no influence to which I retort that without seats in the European Parliament we won't even feature and that linking up with the EPP does nothing to improve our chances of winning any seats (at the forthcoming EP election). After this lively exchange of views David is clearly relieved to break off the debate in order to catch his flight home!

On 9th February the Steering Committee of the '92 Group meets Party Leader, Wm. Hague. The meeting goes well and William appears to be receptive to our views as well as welcoming our advice.

I take the opportunity of thanking him for his help and support on the question of fisheries policy but he is shaken when I explain what Agriculture spokesman Tim Yeo (Suffolk South) has, as reported in the edition of 'Fishing News' published on 5th February, told the Scottish Fishermens Federation (SFF) . I also draw William's attention to the 'Fishing News' headline which is "Speak Up Mr Hague".

At the 10 o'clock Division Richard Shepherd tells me that he has seen a letter on the desk of Beryl Goldsmith from the Leader's office. In it Beryl's boss, Party Deputy Chairman, Michael Trend, is instructed not to respond to letters from the fishing industry posing the question as to whether competency for fisheries should rest with Brussels or Westminster.

The following day I have a meeting with shadow Foreign Secretary, Michael Howard, which proves to be a total waste of time. He says that there is no deal with the EPP but that he is talking to individual European centre-right Parties. I tell him that from my experience as a delegate to the Council of Europe I have concluded that there are no other political Parties in Europe that think as we British Conservatives think and that there is therefore no electoral advantage to be gained by being associated with them – quite the opposite! Knowing that we are in any way linked to them will simply be playing into the hands of the UK Independence Party.

On the question of fisheries he is equally hopeless saying that I, meaning me, "will not be displeased" with what finally emerges in the EP election manifesto.

That evening, at the meeting of the '22 Executive, Bowen Wells (Hertford & Stortford) complains about the way in which policy decisions are reached. His particular interest is Overseas Aid and he is annoyed that he has not been consulted about changes of policy in that area. That is my cue to flag up the differences between what shadow Fisheries Minister, Patrick Nicholls, is saying and what Tim Yeo, the shadow Minister of Agriculture is reported in 'Fishing News' as having told the SFF. I also draw attention to the memo from the Leader's office instructing a member of the Euro manifesto committee not to reply to George Forman, the Chairman of the Fishermens Association Limited (FAL), until a draft response has been agreed.

It later transpires that, in my absence, I have been elected Commodore of the House of Commons Yacht Club in its 50th anniversary year.

At a meeting in my office on 11th February I bring fisheries spokesman, Patrick Nicholls, up to speed on the developments of the past two days. He is particularly frank about Michael Howard – 'unctuous and oleaginous' – and Yeo – 'if he swallowed a nail it would come out a corkscrew'. I assure Patrick that he's got plenty of support on the backbenches and that we shan't let him down.

Next in my sights is shadow Defence Secretary, Iain Duncan-Smith, but his failure to keep our 19.00 appointment means that I shall have to speak to him by telephone before next week's meeting of the Shadow Cabinet. When I finally make contact with Iain on 16th February he says that he thinks that the Shadow Cabinet will meet that day and that the vexed question of Fisheries will be discussed. In the meantime, on 15th February, I have spoken to shadow Trade & Industry Secretary, John Redwood - who has assured me that he is already up to speed on fisheries - and fired off an article about fisheries to the 'Daily Telegraph' having also spoken to Charles Moore, the editor, on the telephone. Charles is kind enough to call me back to suggest that my article would be best turned into a letter.

On the strength of my conversation with Duncan-Smith I telephone the Leader's PPS, David Lidington, who confirms that the Shadow Cabinet will indeed be meeting later in the day and that the question of fisheries may very well be discussed. He says that he will definitely be seeing Wm. Hague before the Shadow Cabinet meeting and I tell him how important it is that the Leader comes down firmly on one side of the fisheries argument or the other; that I am not the only one who thinks that he should come down on the side of Patrick Nicholls and that, frankly, if he doesn't, then there's trouble on the line. I also take the opportunity of telling David that I don't know what Michael Howard's game is but could it be that he is calculating that if Hague does badly at the EP election in June he, Howard, could become Leader?

In the lobby I talk to Patrick Nicholls about the prospect of mobilising the '92 Committee if we don't get the right answer out of Shadow Cabinet. In the event Shadow cabinet does not reach a conclusion in spite of fighting talk from Duncan-Smith, Liam Fox, David Heathcoat-Amory and John Redwood. 'Two brains' Willetts (Shadow Education Secretary) argues the other way saying that it is 'better to stand and fight on bigger issues' to which Iain D-S apparently retorted that if we can't make up our minds on small issues what chance do we have when it comes to the big ones! Iain is clearly very angry about the way things went and is only too willing to give me a shot by shot and blow by blow account of the whole proceedings. He tells me, for example, that Michael Howard 'wasn't too bad'. When I ask Tim Yeo how things went he says that it's just a matter of finding 'the right form of words' to say that we are going to get tough but without actually threatening to leave the EU. At a meeting with Patrick and his wife, Bridget, in the Pugin Room we review the events of the day and agree to speak again in the morning.

My first action on Wednesday 17th February is to draft a strong letter to Wm. Hague which is acknowledged next day by a telephone call from David Lidington who says that William will see it when he returns to the House on Monday. In the meantime Patrick has 'phoned to say that things are looking better. He has been assured that Hague is prepared to make strong speeches and write articles in support of our position.

On Thursday 18th I cannot get beyond Charles Moore's secretary to explain what has gone on since we last spoke. Knowing that Owen Paterson is a close friend of Charles I enlist his support and between us Patrick, Owen and I agree the text of a letter to the 'Telegraph' and then set about obtaining other MP signatories. That evening Michael Spicer rings, possibly on a pretext, to say that he doesn't want to sign the letter unless 30 or 40 others do likewise. I sense that he might well go back to Michael Howard or others to warn them as to what is going on.

Things are hotting up!

At 08.30 on Friday 19th the chief Whip telephones me with a request that I speak to Michael Howard. I regret not being able to see the Chief's face when I tell him that he mustn't think that because I am personally mild mannered, self-effacing and polite that I am not also ruthlessly determined. For good measure I also tell him that I don't depend upon politics for a living and that I have two choices viz; to carry on as an MP or to stand down and force a by-election. As a parting shot I tell him that I didn't join the Conservative Party to support Leninist policies i.e. collectivist policies like the CAP and the CFP.

The upshot of this conversation is another 'phone call from an anxious Michael Spicer who seeks to dissuade me from going ahead with my letter to the 'Daily Telegraph'. This is followed by yet another 'phone call, this time from the Chairman of the '22 Committee, Archie Hamilton, also in reaction to my proposed letter to the 'Telegraph'. Archie assures me that he has not been put up to 'phoning me by the Chief Whip but the coincidence is just too great to ignore.

When I speak to Daniel Hannan at the 'Telegraph' offices his advice is to keep the letter in reserve just in case everything goes 'pear-shaped'. The 'Telegraph' will, for their part, publish a strong leader on the strength of the speech which Patrick Nicholls is scheduled to make to the Bruges Group on Monday.

On Saturday 20th February I answer my telephone expecting the caller to be a colleague wishing to pledge support for my letter, only to find myself speaking to the Shadow Foreign Secretary. He sounds rather peeved that he hasn't been able to get through to me sooner – I wonder why! On Sunday I turn to to draft a letter to supportive colleagues explaining why I have pulled our letter to the 'Telegraph'. On Monday this letter goes on the Members letterboard with copies to Wm. Hague, Michael Howard, James Arbuthnot, Iain Duncan-Smith, Liam Fox, David Heathcoat-Amory, John Redwood and, of course, Patrick Nicholls who will be addressing the Bruges Group later in the day.

In the event Patrick does an excellent job of explaining to a packed audience that for the UK to get its way on Fisheries we cannot simply negotiate in the conventional way but must show our determination by using the same tactics that Margaret Thatcher adopted when she re-negotiated Britain's contribution to the EU budget and secured the British rebate. He avoids the use of the word 'ultimatum' but this is surely what he means.

Another speaker at the Bruges Group event is journalist Christopher Booker who having made very disparaging remarks about Parliament in general and MPs in particular, goes on to say that 'there is one shining exception, who is here with us tonight – Christopher Gill'. That is all very flattering but the stark reality is that because I have no powers of patronage the number of colleagues that I can ever hope to win over to the cause is limited to those who are genuinely patriotic, or those relatively few whose ambition for office is not all-consuming, or those for whom the prospect of office is no longer a realistic expectation. There are of course many other facets of patronage which lie within the gift of Party leaders but my own patronage is limited to promising my colleagues that if they don't do the decent thing they won't even get a mention in my memoirs – always supposing I ever get round to writing them!

Earlier in the day John Ashworth of the 'Save Britain's Fish' campaign has told me that he has been in touch with deputy Party Chairman, Archie Norman, and Daniel Hannan has confirmed that there will be an article about Fisheries and a strong editorial in tomorrow's edition of the 'Daily Telegraph'. In the event this manifests itself as a report by lobby correspondent, Robert Shrimsley, and a second leader written by Daniel.

Tuesday 23rd February is a doubly significant day because not only are matters coming to a head within the Conservative Parliamentary Party regarding Fisheries but also because Prime Minister Tony Blair is coming to the House to make a statement about the 'Changeover Plan' for the introduction of the single currency – the Euro. Blair does well but Hague does better, until it is pointed out that his defence of 1000 years of history is – by his decision to rule out the single currency only for the duration of the next Parliament – 'only for the duration of this Parliament and the next'. Unsurprisingly those called to speak from the Conservative benches include Ken Clarke, Michael Heseltine, Ted Heath and Ian Taylor – Europhiles to a man!

In the lobby at the 10 o'clock vote I go into overdrive, telling shadow Cabinet Ministers that they simply have to get their policy on Fisheries right by tomorrow. I speak to Hague, Lilley, Maude, Ancram, Yeo, Mackay and Arbuthnot, having already tackled Liam Fox earlier in the day. Archie Norman, although not a member of the Shadow Cabinet, is well aware of what is going on and appears to be sympathetic to our cause. John Townend and Owen Paterson both tackle David Willetts and Owen also tells Michael Spicer that we really do mean business – with any luck this will ensure that our message reaches the ears of his friend, Michael Howard.

John Townend assures me that he has written to all shadow Cabinet Ministers in membership of the '92 Group telling them where their duty lies and, just for good measure, I tell Wm. Hague that whilst it isn't Trafalgar Day, nevertheless, 'England expects...........

Wednesday 24th February is the day of decision. What will the Shadow Cabinet decree as being the Conservative Party's future Fisheries policy?

That morning William Hague and Owen Paterson both make excellent speeches to a mass meeting of Road Hauliers in the Methodist Central Hall. Afterwards I tell Owen that the Hauliers will obviously march to his drum as indeed I believe that the Fishermen would march to mine. The trick is to get all the many and various sectional interest groups marching to the beat of Wm Hague's drum!

Later in the day I tackle Francis Maude about the outcome of the Shadow Cabinet meeting but he stonewalls and refers me to shadow Minister of Agriculture, Tim Yeo. Iain Duncan-Smith is more forthcoming but similarly refers me to Tim Yeo. Shadow Fisheries Minister Patrick Nicholls, John Townend and I then collectively tackle Yeo. The conversation gets rather heated so I drag John aside so that Patrick and Tim can fight it out amongst themselves but Yeo continues to argue in favour of conventional negotiations within the EU and definitely not ultimatums.

That evening Patrick joins the assembled company for a supper meeting of the European Reform Group (ERG) in Archie Hamilton's apartment in Tufton Street. Patrick seems reasonably satisfied that the statement which Yeo will issue in the morning will be satisfactory.

Having asked Wm Hague what our fisheries policy now is I subsequently challenge the Party's Chief Whip as to why it is that it is always left to a few people like myself to persuade our Party to be Conservative – the task is akin to shovelling steam up a ladder!

On the strength of Archie Hamilton telling me that the UK should be a European Singapore – a Free Trading, Low Tax, sovereign Currency, offshore Tax Haven – I jokingly say that instead of him moving, as intended, to Shropshire where he will be able to vote for me I'll move South so as to be able to vote for him! And speaking of Shropshire it is only the tutors who are disappointed with my views on the Single Currency when I address students at the Shrewsbury College of Arts and Technology at the weekend.

Back at the House on Monday 1st March I am flat-out putting envelopes on the Members letterboard containing a letter that I have written to colleagues, supported by various Press cuttings, seeking backbench support for Wm Hague's new fisheries policy and his reported more pro-active campaigning against the Single Currency. Due to the restriction on the number of letters that can be placed on the letterboard at any one time it is the following day before the exercise is complete but by that time my letter has gone to all Conservative backbenchers. Archie Norman, Conservative Party Chief Executive and Deputy Chairman, tells me that he thinks things will be entirely different after the European Parliament elections in June. I don't really know what he means by that but when on Thursday I suggest that the game-plan may be to delay putting all our goods in the proverbial shop window for fear that the window will be smashed on 10th June he responds by saying that he doesn't think that the planning is really that sophisticated!

On the following Monday, due to the 3-line Whip for business in the House having been reduced to 1-line, only nine colleagues attend a '92 Committee convened to discuss the Common Fisheries Policy (CFP) with shadow Fisheries Minister, Patrick Nicholls. My own contribution to the debate is an attempt to explain that EU policies such as the CFP are no more Conservative than a lot of other EU collectivist policies and that, given that 20 members of the Labour Cabinet are paid-up members of the Fabian Society, we really ought not be surprised at the direction in which things are moving.

This is a theme that I pursue when the CFP is mentioned at the early evening meeting of the Forward Look Committee. I am at pains to point out that both the CFP and the Common Agriculture Policy (CAP) are collectivist policies which have more in common with socialism, communism and the old USSR than they do with conservatism and that, more to the point, I didn't join the Conservative Party to promote the policies of Lenin!

The following day (9th March) the Chancellor of the Exchequer comes to the House to present his Budget proposals for the year ahead. In the Members tearoom afterwards I am able to congratulate Wm Hague on his brilliant response to the Budget statement and also take the opportunity of handing him a copy of my letter of support for his fisheries and Single Currency stance, now endorsed by no less than 49 colleagues – had it not been for the inclusion of the reference to the Single Currency the addition of Sir Peter Tapsell's signature would have brought the total up to 50.

At a private meeting with Wm Hague on 15th March he tells me how well his mention of our new Fisheries policy went down at the Party's Spring Conference in Reading at the weekend. In return I tell him how much easier it has been for me to collect the names of colleagues in support of him now that he has made the decision (on Fisheries). I emphasise that in the absence of a natural consensus on European issues it is down to him as the Party Leader to decide and for the rest of us to either follow or do the other thing! I go on to explain that what we are up against is a Cabinet which includes twenty paid-up Fabians pursuing a radical socialist agenda which includes the destruction of our constitution and the undermining of all our institutions - as evidenced by the increasing talk of institutional racism in the Police, the Education service, the Armed Forces etc. Yet again I make the point that EU collectivism has more in common with Communism than it does with Conservatism and go on to remind William that whenever I raise these matters in Party committees colleagues quickly change the subject! That being said I impress upon him that I am not interested in petty point scoring but only in winning, both the argument and the next election.

Unbelievably and totally illogically there have been calls from Labour MP supporters of the Single Currency for a preferential interest rate for the North East region of England. It is therefore my pleasure at a working breakfast attended by Eddie George, the Governor of the Bank of England, on 10th March to congratulate him on having slapped down this ridiculous notion when he recently told the North East that we cannot possibly have differential interest rates within the UK.

Ever since the BSE (Bovine Spongiform Encephalopathy) scare the sale of 'beef on the bone' has been prohibited and it is to this theme that I return when I have the first question to the Prime Minister at PMQs on March 3rd. Such is the vocal support from colleagues that I am barely able to hear myself speak when I ask Tony Blair if he will 'now revoke the ridiculous and discredited ban on beef on the bone, or is it the case that his EU puppet masters will not let him'? At the following week's briefing for PMQs, having extracted undertakings all round that the Party will get stuck in on the question of small abattoirs, I allow myself to be persuaded to follow the Party line and ask the PM about the level of tax on road fuel. In the event my question at number two on the Order Paper goes very well and subsequently in the tearoom Wm Hague remarks that I've got lucky in the draw for PMQs – 'luckier than you' I reply, 'you've got to do it again next week and every week thereafter'!

Following my question to the PM about beef on the bone I speak to Minister for Agriculture, Fisheries and Food (MAFF), Nick Brown, who assures me that he is willing to meet a deputation representing small abattoir owners to discuss Meat Inspection charges but that the meeting cannot go ahead tomorrow as planned because he has to go back to Brussels. In the light of this cancelled meeting I raise the question of small abattoirs again at the weekly 'Business of the House' session and later receive assurance from my 'pair', Jeff Rooker, the Minister of State at MAFF, that both he and Nick Brown are sympathetic to my concerns. Subsequently I tell Deputy Chief Opposition Whip, Patrick McLoughlin, that small abattoirs are a good political topic for us to run with but that there seems to be a reluctance on the part of our Frontbench to do so. Since the beginning of January I have nagged Tim Yeo, as well as Agriculture Whip, Caroline Spelman, and others to pick up this particular ball and run with it but all to no avail. Patrick Nicholls agrees that they are most likely inhibited from doing so by their Europhilia! My efforts on this subject appear to be making more impression upon the Government than upon our own side because in the House on 11th March I am able to congratulate the Minister on the Press Release issued by MAFF saying that he would reconsider the position of small and low-throughput abattoirs. Notwithstanding this welcome development I am on my feet again at Business Questions a week later calling for an emergency debate on the future of small abattoirs which is followed by an interview on College Green for Midlands Today TV. Either because I was too robust or because it didn't suit the left-wing editors, this interview was not I think screened. Possibly for the same reason the BBC Countryfile programme cancelled their appointment to feature the abattoir owned by the Bishop's Castle Meat Company, in my constituency, about the threat to its business posed by the proposed increase in Meat Inspection charges.

Aside from the mundane concerns about abattoirs and questions about the automatic reselection of sitting Conservative MPs there is the urgent topic of hostilities in the Balkans. On 24th March Shadow Foreign Secretary, Michael Howard, and Shadow Defence Secretary, John Maples, attend a full meeting of the '22 Committee where I find myself third in a string of colleagues who wish to express views on the prospect of bombing Serbia. I say that I wish our Leader had not been so quick to offer the Government our support, that there is no recognisable British interest at stake, that it is doubtful whether bombing alone will achieve the desired effect and that it is quite wrong to prejudice the integrity of NATO in this way. I conclude by telling colleagues that there are undoubtedly other countries who would like to see NATO discredited. My overall impression is that colleagues are less than happy with what the Government intend but shortly after our meeting ends the bombing begins!

Instituting offensive action would be contrary to both the constitution and the ethos of the North Atlantic Treaty Organisation which had been founded in 1949 as a purely defensive pact. This would be the first occasion, but by no means the last, on which this cardinal principle, established in Article 5 of the founding treaty, was to be broken.

The House is at its best on 25th March when the debate about Kosovo produces some first rate speeches on both sides of the argument but unease on the Conservative benches continues. In fact when I speak to the Chairman of the '22 Committee at the weekend to highlight my own concerns Archie Hamilton tells me that it is hard to find any colleague who actually supports the bombing.

On 29th March, five days after he has declared war on Serbia, Tony Blair comes to the House to make a statement about Kosovo and the EU summit meeting in Berlin which, ironically, is where he was when hostilities commenced. When, in his capacity as Leader of the Opposition, Wm Hague responds, I am personally disappointed that the first thing he says is that we support the action taken by the Government – in spite of all the forebodings previously expressed by so many of his own backbenchers. Not content to give up without a struggle I have written an article on the subject which the Birmingham Post publishes on 30th March and the following day make a point of telling the meeting of the '22 Committee that we should not be involving ourselves in the civil war in Kosovo and that our policy ought to be based upon the defensible principle of not attacking another sovereign nation in the circumstances in which that other country has neither attacked us, nor our allies nor even its own neighbours. There is good support in the committee for my stance to the extent that after the meeting Alan Clark (Kensington & Chelsea) congratulates me on what I had said and the manner in which I had said it.

At lunchtime on 30th the Institute of Management stage a meeting to discuss the Euro. Illustrative of the woolly thinking that surrounds the question of joining the Single Currency, guest speaker and euro enthusiast Lord Simon of Highbury, Minister for Trade & Competitiveness in Europe, refuses to come clean on the question as to how and by whom the rate at which we might enter the Euro would be set. Woolly thinking is not however confined to the Labour benches as at dinner that evening I hear Peter Brooke (City & Westminster) aver that socialism is dead – if only!

As Parliament heads towards the Easter recess my perseverance regarding the plight of small abattoirs is recognised and I am called early in the Easter Adjournment debate to make a final plea to Government to make concessions regarding the astronomical increase in Meat Inspection charges scheduled to apply as from the following day. I acknowledge that Government ministers are on the horns of a dilemma. "On the one hand they are under enormous pressure from the European Union to implement fully the Meat Inspection Directive but on the other hand they know that if they do so scores of small abattoirs will close and there will be knock-on effects for other small businesses". The prospect is that small abattoirs will, like their counterparts in the fishing industry, be consigned to the scrap-heap because the political objective of 'ever closer union' and EU-wide 'harmonisation' of standards comes first.

1999

2

" Time to fire off another broadside "

After the recess, on 21st April, there is an Opposition day debate on the British Livestock Industry during the course of which Agriculture Minister, Nick Brown, announces an investigation into the dynamics of the slaughtering sector and the deferral for 12 months of Specified Risk Material (SRM) inspection charges. Shadow Agriculture Minister, Tim Yeo, says that we must spin this announcement as being the result of today's debate – never mind my three months hard work without the least help, support or encouragement from the Frontbench!

Earlier in the month I have been briefly to Greece with the Agriculture Committee of the Council of Europe. My host at dinner one evening is employed as architect to the local authority in Larissa, a Greek town which in the fullness of time will achieve a degree of notoriety as the place where British tourists are arrested for allegedly taking unauthorised photographs at the nearby military airfield. The so-called 'Greek plane spotters' will lose several weeks of their lives banged up in a Greek prison because in Greece, as in other European countries, such protections as we enjoy against State coercion simply do not exist. They have no equivalent of our law of habeas corpus, trial by jury, the presumption of innocence etc. etc. and the onus is upon the defendant to prove their innocence, rather than, as in the UK, upon the prosecution to prove guilt. In other words the defendant has to prove the negative which is, as anyone who has had to do this will know, an extremely difficult thing to do. Almost daily throughout the BSE scare, Labour, in opposition, would come to the House and taunt the Conservative Government by challenging them to prove that beef was safe to eat. They couldn't provide the evidence to prove that it wasn't safe but what they could do was to invite the Government to prove the negative which, as they well knew, effectively meant slaughtering every beast in the land and examining its entrails to establish that there were no signs of the disease and that, therefore, the carcase meat was safe!

Corpus juris – i.e. the system of criminal justice that the 'plane spotters' will fall foul of in Greece and which the EU aims to impose upon Britain – is top of my agenda when I meet Opposition Chief Whip, James Arbuthnot (NE Hampshire), on April 20th. I tell him that I am not best pleased about being expected to work to secure the re-election of Conservative MEPs who repeatedly vote against my interests. The Chief is grateful to me for providing him with the information as to how our MEPs voted on corpus juris in the European Parliament last week and leads me to believe that he will be taking appropriate action. I explain that people are monitoring our every move in relation to the EU because they do not trust us on this subject, as neither do I for that matter. I warn him that the information that I have received and passed on to him will doubtless have gone to many others who will have no compunction about publicising the dastardly actions of our MEPs. The following day, at the regular Wednesday meeting of the '22 Committee, I go round the track again concerning the MEPs and the EP vote on corpus juris. I get a good level of support and a promise of action but shadow Foreign Secretary, Michael Howard, says that voting for corpus juris was as a result of 'a cock-up' – just like last year's vote on the Single Currency says I! No, says Michael, that wasn't a cock-up!

A couple of days later, as I am leaving the House, I run straight into Edward McMillan-Scott, Leader of the Conservatives in the European Parliament. When I castigate him for voting for corpus juris and also for failing even to get all his colleagues into the same voting lobby he excuses himself by saying that there were 'hundreds of votes' that day and that their adviser had told them that there was nothing of any special importance on the Order Paper for that particular day!

As a consequence of stopping to remonstrate with McMillan-Scott I miss my train to Wolverhampton and find myself in the company of The Lord Hurd of Westwell on one going to Birmingham. Douglas tells me that he has never been a 'pro-Euro man', but a 'wait and see man'. From the lips of a former Foreign Secretary who signed the Treaty on European Union (Maastricht) which categorically states that 'the currency of the Union shall be the Euro' this is most illuminating, although to be fair to my former colleague it is alleged that only when he got home after signing the treaty did he say that he then needed to read what he had signed, or words to that effect.

The following week I am breakfasting at the Hotel Gutenberg in Strasbourg when Lord Lucas of Crudwell, a former Government Whip in the Lords and a fellow member of the UK delegation to the Council of Europe, says how pleased he is to meet me and how much he is in agreement with me and Save Britain's Fish (SBF) regarding the CFP. He agrees that the problem is that a big lie was told in 1972 and that, instead of admitting it, successive Ministers have sought to perpetuate it. The big lie, of course, was that told by another Balliol man, a man by the name of Ted Heath!

Back in the House later that day for the meeting of the '22 Committee it's time to fire off another broadside. For what it's worth I tell my colleagues that, regardless of the quality of the advice we might give our Frontbench colleagues, without the right people in post we'll do no good. I repeat what I had said to the '22 in the last Parliament and call for all the old relics of the previous administration to be cleared away. I point out that a disastrous speech recently made by Peter Lilley was a re-run of the totally unhelpful antics of the top brass when we last had District Council elections and that really, if after all this time he didn't know better, then he should go. A somewhat subdued '22 welcomes the Leader, Wm Hague, to our meeting but for the benefit of the 'journos' gathered in the committee corridor outside Room 14 there is the usual ritual desk banging both before and after his address.

The issue of the Euro keeps recurring. At an Aluminium Federation lunch at the end of April my constituent Derek Peden, Managing Director of Lawson Marden Star's aluminium processing factory in Bridgnorth, is adamant that the Single Currency is essential for business survival. Similarly when I ask Walter Schwimmer, a candidate for the position of Secretary General of the Council of Europe whom I happen to sit next to at a lunch at the Austrian Embassy, if he supports the Single Currency it is no surprise when he says 'Yes'. I then ask him if he has ever had any doubts about it. 'None' he replies but when I then go on to ask him if he can tell me the difference between old style USSR collectivism and current EU collectivism he is completely floored.

Other straws in the wind are when on May 11th Giles Radice (Durham North) says "you've won the argument in your Party". This is a quite fascinating comment coming as it does from no less a person than the Chairman of the European Movement and unofficial arch-Druid of the integrationists. Sadly winning the argument is not the same as winning the battle which will continue for many more years yet to come. A couple of days later Michael Clark (Rayleigh) tells me that he had told his Whip more than two years ago that until the Party's policy on Europe was sorted out he would please himself whether he voted or not. Of no less interest, particularly in the light of his subsequent political odyssey, is a remark at dinner in the Members Dining Room (MDR) by John Bercow (Buckingham). He tells me that the Deputy Chairman (Political) of my Constituency Association is not one of us!

With less than a month to go before the European Parliament elections I meet with shadow Foreign Secretary, Michael Howard, to discuss the letter which I had sent him last week about Kosovo and the common election statement recently issued by the European Democratic Unionists (EDU). The reason for Michael's tetchy response to my opinions is subsequently provided by Bill Cash (Stone) who, in a later meeting with MH, concludes that MH has virtually written the statement himself.

The EDU is the group to which British MEPs belong in the European Parliament. My attendances at Council of Europe meetings have taught me that there is no direct equivalence to the British Conservative Party on the continent so this arrangement is essentially a marriage of convenience.

During my interview with MH he quite revealingly tells me that he definitely does not want us to get out of the European Union to which I retort that there is no point arguing about that when, on 10th June, the electorate will deliver its own verdict, it being my belief that the UK Independence Party manifesto, a copy of which I had previously handed to the Chief's secretary, Shana, for her to pass on to her boss, will resonate with millions of voters, as indeed it resonates with me.

On 19th May the executive of the '92 Committee meet Wm Hague, having previously discussed amongst ourselves the importance of keeping William in the saddle and the likely political scenario after the EP elections. The meeting goes well. Eric Forth (Bromley & Chislehurst) is, with good reason, very blunt about the calibre of the people William has around him; Michael Colvin (Romsey) is unnecessarily fulsome in his praise for our EP election manifesto published yesterday; Michael Clark gives the Peter Lilley fiasco another airing and John Townend does his own thing on matters not entirely related to the issues we had identified at our pre-meeting! For my own part I tell William that what we need is a crusade and that Europe is the issue we should be crusading on. William responds by agreeing that we do indeed need a crusade but on other issues too.

The following Monday evening I find myself dining in the MDR with the Leader's Parliamentary Private Secretary, David Lidington (Aylesbury). I take the opportunity of saying that I hope William realises that as far as he's concerned it's going to be, as I'm told they say in Yorkshire, 'muck or nettles' time after the EP election and that unless he comes out of his corner fighting the 'left ' will have him! David leads me to believe that this is already understood but seems rather more interested in hearing my views on the vexed question of reform of the House of Lords (see Appendix B).

On 25th May the business of the House includes a debate on 'European Union'and the Europhiles in our party such as Andrew Tyrie (Chichester), Bowen Wells (Hertford & Stortford), Andrew Lansley (S. Cambridgeshire), Nicholas Soames (Mid-Sussex), Stephen Dorrell (Charnwood), Anne McIntosh (Vale of York), Michael Jack (Fylde), Francis Maude (Horsham) and Ian Taylor (Esher & Walton) are queuing up to speak. To be fair to Stephen Dorrell, he has some discernible conservative aspirations but, like so many of my other colleagues, cannot see that they are simply not achievable within the totalitarian EU. The breaking news that same day is that former Conservative Government Chief Whip, Alistair Goodlad (Eddisbury), is to be the next UK High Commissioner in Australia. Is this Britain's answer to the fictitious Australian ambassador, 'Sir Les Paterson', as portrayed on screen by Dame Edna Everidge? The following day's newspapers report that he has been displaced as successor to Leon Brittan as our next EU Commissioner by none other than Chris Patten, another Europhile of the first order. At the Dispatch Box, in a previous incarnation as Minister of State at the Foreign & Commonwealth Office, Goodlad had been the butt of one of Denis Skinner's more amusing jibes. At the best of times Goodlad's delivery was ponderous and almost embarrassingly hesitant. In company with others in the House on that occasion the 'Beast of Bolsover' was becoming rather bored with it all. 'Come on Duracell, charge yourself up a bit'!

Two days before the EP Election my constituent and former Conservative MP for Aldershot, Julian Critchley, tells the listeners to the 'Today' programme that he will vote 'pro-Europe Conservative'. In an uncertain world one can always rely upon the pro-EU biased BBC to give prominence on its programmes to the likes of EU fanatics Critchley, fellow Old Salopian Michael Heseltine and Ken Clarke - as if they are representative of opinion within the Conservative Party. In this way, according to their own selective interpretation of their Charter, the BBC discharge their responsibility to be fair and impartial!

Later in the day, at a meeting between the Officers of the '92 Committee and the Chief Whip, I venture to say that as Dr Adrian Rodgers, Conservative candidate in Exeter at the last General Election, was chucked out of the Party for alleged unacceptable pronouncements I presume that Critchley will be too. I go on to repeat my plea that in the forthcoming 're-shuffle' the Party must rid itself of the last remnants of the failed previous administration. He is definitely not best pleased when I follow this by saying that there must be no back-sliding, irrespective of the outcome of Thursday's EP Election. He says that 'we have a policy' and that 'we shall stick to that policy'. On a less confrontational note he is interested to be shown broadcast schedules indicating that the Conservative Party Political Broadcast will be going out only in England whereas tomorrow's PPB on behalf of the Labour Party will go out in all parts of the UK except Northern Ireland.

On the eve of poll, when asked on the 'Today' programme whether Critchley will be thrown out of the Party for having championed another Party, Francis Maude can't or won't answer the question. When I tackle the Chairman of the '22 Committee about this issue Archie says that Maude should have known that the rules say that anyone who votes against the Party is automatically disqualified. He goes on to suggest that the Chairman of the local Constituency Conservative Association (CCA) should deal with this problem. When I say that Maude's procrastination on the 'Today' programme will cost us votes and that I have already provided the Ludlow CCA Chairman with proof positive that Critchley should have been chucked out of the Party a long time ago - but that he remains, making a laughing-stock of us all - Archie says that he will get the Party Chairman to have a word with LCCA Chairman, Justin Caldwell. I am not holding my breath as to the outcome because the man in question is an unmitigated Europhile and the rules seem to be interpreted differently for people of that ilk!

On 11th June, the day after the Election, I learn that the turn-out in my Ludlow constituency has been 30% but to comply with EU requirements it will be Sunday before the votes can actually be counted. In the event the local count reveals an amazing 42.9% for the Conservatives, 17.7% for Labour and 13.6% for the rabidly europhile Liberal Democrats. The unanswered question as far as I am concerned is whether, because of my well known hostility to European political union, I am in effect acting as some sort of decoy duck for the Conservative Party. Because I stand as a Conservative and genuinely am a conservative the electorate might be being fooled into believing that my views are consistent with Party policy. Clearly they are not, but that doesn't deter the Party, either at this election or other elections, from asking me to endorse their candidates – presumably because the Party recognises that my beliefs are more in line with voters thinking than the official Party policy itself! At this particular election I have even been 'slipped' from voting one Thursday evening so as to allow me to get home in time to glad-hand Conservative candidate, Philip Bushill-Matthews, around the West Midlands Agriculture Show at Shrewsbury the following day.

With the election behind us the fear is that Conservative MEPS will want to affiliate with the federalist European Peoples Party (EPP). As long ago as 24th October 1993, former Conservative Party Chairman Norman Tebbit had told the BBC's TV programme 'On the Record' that "the European People's Party is a federalist party, it believes in a central European state in which Great Britain and various other parts of the (European) Community would be provinces."

With that thought very much in mind, at the Forward Look Committee meeting on 14th June, I seek an assurance from Wm Hague that we will not be linking up with the EPP. The Leader's response is somewhat ambivalent. He says that the matter needs careful consideration and that he will have to consult the MEPs. At the same meeting, Robert Key (Salisbury) asks what we are going to do about UKIP which last week won three seats in the EP. This is a fair question but I am not convinced that Robert has made the connection between the singular unattractiveness of our own totally indefensible European policy and the popular appeal of a Party like UKIP which is committed to the restoration of the sovereignty of the Westminster Parliament.

In the lobbies later in the day I tackle William again about the EPP question and am encouraged to hear him say that he realises that the decision has to be his and that he will make that decision. This vexed question of whether or not our MEPs should join the EPP group is going to predominate much else for the next several weeks. Later still the names of the members of the new Shadow Cabinet are announced and I immediately go into overdrive telling them what they must do vis-a-vis the EPP.

At dinner the following evening I am mildly surprised when shadow International Development Minister, Gary Streeter (Devon SW), does not reject my proposition regarding the EPP. A day later I tell Archie Hamilton that whilst I do not believe in making threats I do have a bottom line on this issue. Knowing of my interest in this matter Shadow Trade & Industry Secretary, Angela Browning (Tiverton & Honiton), tells me that the matter was discussed, but only briefly, at this week's Shadow Cabinet meeting and that the Leader will discuss the matter with our MEPs before making his final decision.

My next step is to put my case in writing to the Leader with copious copies to all and sundry including my old friend newly elected MEP Daniel Hannan, Party Chairman Michael Ancram, his new PPS Robert Syms (Poole), '22 Committee Chairman Archie Hamilton, Wm Hague's new PPS John Whittingdale (Maldon &Chelmsford E.), Angela Browning and, by Fax, to newly elected MEP Philip Bushill-Matthews, who may or may not be on side. When fellow Maastricht rebel and Sshadow Defence Secretary Iain Duncan-Smith tells me that he is seeing Hague later and will tell him that he must finish the job that he's started and that he'll never have a better time than the present I tell Iain, he being a former Army officer, that I am 'four-square' behind him.

Early the next morning (18th June) the 'Today' programme announces that Conservative MEPs are meeting today at Conservative Central Office

(CCO) and that one of the topics to be discussed will be their future relationship with the EPP. At home on Sunday I receive a 'phone call from Daniel Hannan who says that he thinks Wm Hague ought to be grateful to me for bringing the EPP issue to his attention. Daniel is very much of the opinion that unless I had done so then it would simply have gone through last Friday's meeting of MEPs as just an ordinary piece of business.

Back in the House on Monday 21st I put a letter in the internal message service urging approximately 45 colleagues to make sure that they attend tomorrow's meeting of the '22 Committee which will also be attended by our MEPs. Before that though I have yet another meeting with the Leader. As usual our meeting goes well and inter alia I tell William that it is my sincere belief that he could be a latter-day Winston Churchill – Prime Minister of the United Kingdom and 'beacon of hope' in Europe where only the British, by dint of our different political system, have the ability to break the totalitarian mould. British MPs are reliant upon the local electorate for the position they hold. Not so on the continent where MPs, elected on the 'list system', must, if they wish to retain their seats, unfailingly tip their caps to the Party bosses.

As an additional reason for not joining the EPP I cite the fact that it is not as if we are trying to form a government, added to which, if Tony Blair thinks that it would be a mistake for us to leave the EPP, then that is probably a sound enough reason for doing just that! That aside though, with so many more Conservative MPs to please than MEPs it should be fairly obvious which side of the EPP argument the Leader of the Party should come down on. I urge him to dig in on this defining issue and start setting the political agenda. I am also able to tell William how at an old boys reunion at Shrewsbury School I had recently met his former constituency Chairman, David Tiptaft, who confirmed my opinion that William is tougher and more determined than most people give him credit for. I go on to say that I am telling people that, in my opinion, he has courage, that quality which is such an essential prerequisite of true leadership. My parting shot at this meeting is to tell William that I want to help him to succeed and that in my life to date there is nobody who is worse off as a result of knowing me.

Later that day (22nd June) MEP Leader, Edward McMillan-Scott, and other MEPs are present at a well attended meeting of the '22 Committee which lasts for an almost unprecedented one and three quarter hours. There are nine speakers in favour of EPP affiliation - all bar one of them being former ministers – sixteen against and Douglas Hogg (Sleaford & N. Hykeham) manfully searching for a middle way! None of the pro-EPP speakers gets applause but for those against the applause is generally thunderous, the most going to Roger Helmer, the newly elected MEP for the East Midlands. Young Daniel Hannan MEP bravely explains how, at the beginning of his political career, he finds it hard to be put in the position of having to choose between, on the one hand his Party and on the other hand, loyalty to those who elected him and that, in the final analysis, he will do the latter. Desmond Swayne (New Forest W.) says that when he has to explain a deal with the EPP to his constituents they will say to him "right Party, wrong bloody planet"!

The following day the ineffable Critchley takes to the airwaves again to give listeners the benefit of his opinion which is that Wm. Hague 'is only a little boy' and that people (wets) like former Cabinet Minister Ian Gilmour are the real greats in the Tory Party! That they are both on the way out gives new meaning to the old cry of 'good riddance to bad rubbish'. Politically speaking Critchley is 'dead' but the old rascal simply 'won't lie down', as evidenced by an article published under his name in today's 'Independent' newspaper. By sheer coincidence Critchley is one of the topics of conversation when my former Constituency Chairman, Councillor Michael Wood, telephones me that morning. He relays the news that when current Ludlow CCA Chairman, Justin Caldwell, recently interviewed him Critchley wanted to know 'who this chemist chap from Bishop's Castle is who keeps ringing me up to ask how we can get rid of our MP'. How the chemist from BC is thwarted in his attempts to become the next Chairman of the LCCA is a story for another day!

Back in the Palace of Westminster Michael Spicer (Worcestershire W.) is not untypically generous when he says that I should be proud of what I have achieved in getting the question of the EPP properly aired, but I'm far from finished yet.

Before the Chief Whip goes off to the Shadow Cabinet meeting on 23rd June I am at pains to impress upon him that the decision about the EPP is a critical one and that he must recognise that the future of the Party lies with the 'young Turks' who want to dissociate, as opposed to the 'old guard' – yesterday's men – who want continued affiliation. I go on to say that this is all about perception and keeping faith with the people who voted for us. In the event, I gather that the subject was not discussed at this particular meeting and the next morning the 'Today' programme is running with the story that a decision about Conservative links with the EPP was not likely to be made yet a while.

On 24th I fire off yet another missive to the Leader about the wretched EPP, vowing that this really will have to be the last in the present series.

That weekend, at a Shropshire Conservative Forum organised by my trusty secretary, the incomparable Vicki Stevens, I am asked by our elected councillors why the Party allows the likes of Nicholas Soames (Sussex Mid) to appear on BBC 'Question Time'. I guess that because he tends to create an unfortunate impression as far as the Conservative Party is concerned that is precisely the reason why the BBC chooses to screen him. On 1st July the said Soames tries to tell me what a wonderful deal we've got with the EPP. This is 24 hours after the Party issues a Press Release which makes it apparent that we have not got the clean break that so many of us wanted. All that I can do is to try to humour the buffoon – his grandfather, Sir Winston Churchill, must be spinning in his grave at the way in which we are so fecklessly turning our backs on the freedom that his generation and he in particular, fought so hard to protect.

Very much tongue in cheek I ask newly appointed shadow Foreign Secretary, John Maples, whether I can tell the world that we've made a clean break with the EPP. His response is that what we can say is that we've made a clean break with the past! I then ask him if he has met M. Pasqua to which he retorts that Pasqua doesn't speak English but that he has met his emissary. The significance of my asking Maples if there has been any contact with M. Pasqua is firstly because this is a question that I had previously asked Wm. Hague at our meeting on 22nd June and secondly because when I met Paul-Marie Couteaux MEP yesterday he told me how keen his group of 13 Pasqua Gaullists (RPF) were to form a group with British Conservative MEPs as an alternative to the federalist EPP.

In the re-shuffle Archie Norman (Tunbridge Wells) has been appointed number two in the shadow FCO team and when I congratulate him upon becoming our 'Mr Europe' he says that he would very much like to talk to me about the EU because 'you know so very much more about it than I do'. Whilst on the subject of the EU, Patrick Nicholls is still 'fizzing' about his fellow Sshadow Agriculture Minister, Michael Jack, for continuing to undermine our new fisheries policy. All the indications are that Jack has gone 'native'.

A week after congratulating Archie Norman I have a long chat with him about his life and times at CCO where for the past two years he has been Chief Executive and Deputy Chairman of the Party. He agrees that immediately following the General Election we should have seized the initiative and divorced ourselves from the EPP. At CCO Archie will undoubtedly have encountered my constituent Robin Hodgson, chairman of the National Conservative Convention. Knowing him as well as I do it is my opinion that Robin's agenda is somewhat different to that of our Leader, but on this point Archie is reluctant to agree.

On 6th July I am up with the lark to go to the Royal Show at Stoneleigh where I am lucky enough to encounter most of my quarries. A few minutes alone with Ben Gill, President of the NFU (National Farmers Union), is enough to convince me that he is irreconcilably europhile, notwithstanding his utterances on yesterday's 'Today' programme. On air he had bemoaned the fact that reform of the Common Agriculture Policy (CAP) is not happening fast enough and that the burden of legislation is intolerable. Like so many others who refuse to face the facts, Ben clearly doesn't understand that without the unanimous agreement of each and every one of the other EU member States there simply cannot be any meaningful reform of the CAP. That being said, surely he must realise that the prospect of getting the French to agree to the sort of reform of the CAP that Britain wants is just as remote as the possibility of getting the Spanish to agree to reform of the Common Fisheries Policy. In both these areas the prospect of achieving unanimity for reform is no more or less than pie in the sky. As far as his complaint about the burden of legislation is concerned, tough luck! Most of it is coming from Brussels where it is initiated, within the European Commission, by unelected and unaccountable eurocrats. By way of contrast I have been elected by the voters in a predominantly agricultural constituency and am ultimately answerable to those same voters but the reality is that there is virtually nothing that I or other MPs can do to resolve Ben's problems – by dint of the EU treaties, with which he apparently agrees, the matter is entirely out of our control. It makes a mockery of democracy, but that's the way it is!

Back in the House that evening I recount my conversation with Ben Gill to Wm. Hague (who has also been to the show) and am pleased that he appears sympathetic to my opinion which is that the real problem is the system into which we have allowed ourselves to become so totally enmeshed.

That same day I have a fascinating late night chat in Members Lobby with Jeff Rooker, Minister of State at MAFF. Together we hatch plans for me to ask a question about abattoirs at tomorrow's Prime Ministers Question Time where I have drawn Question No.6 on the Order Paper. Jeff tells me that he, plus both the departmental Parliamentary Secretaries (Elliot Morley in the Commons and Bernard Donoughue in the Lords) AND the Prime Minister are all on side on the issue but that the problem is the MAFF Minister himself , Nick Brown. Jeff then goes on to tell me that in all of Nick Brown's 12 months in office as Agriculture Minister never once have all four of them met as a group without either civil servants or hangers-on. He further confides that the plight of small abattoirs is the only problem keeping him awake at night!

In the morning I get on to Wm. Hague's new PPS, John Whittingdale, to tell him that there has been a change of plan since I spoke at the Forward Look Committee on Monday and said - much to their amusement - that I would like to ask a question about the Single Currency. John is happy with this and so my next move is to get on to the PM's PPS, Bruce Grocott (Telford), at No. 10, to brief him on my question about small abattoirs. As far as I am concerned it is highly unusual to be 'consorting with the enemy' but the reality is that only the Government can deliver the goods in terms of rescuing the small abattoirs on whose behalf I have been battling all year and frankly, in the circumstances where a consensus of opinion apparently now exists, I would be looking a gift horse in the mouth if I didn't take advantage of it. An important ally in this battle has been Jeff Rooker, my Parliamentary 'pair'. Politically we are as chalk and cheese but, because we both say what we mean and mean what we say, there is the sort of mutual respect between us which it is almost impossible to achieve with the 'mugwumpers'.

In the event my question to the PM goes well with plaudits afterwards from several of my colleagues. Later Jeff Rooker and his PPS, Richard Burden (Birmingham, Northfield) say that it went very well, but when I say that I had hoped for better in the PM's answer Jeff says that a fortnight ago all that I would have got was something to the effect that 'due to EU rules there is nothing that the Government can do' instead of which I got "we are

reviewing the charges to ensure that they are fair and sustainable............
I am sure that the hon. Gentleman's comments will be taken into account".

The abattoirs issue temporarily parked whilst Government conducts its review, attention now reverts to the old chestnut of our relationship with the EPP. Rumours abound that the EPP have rejected the terms of a deal with our MEPs but Whitto, alias John Whittingdale, tells me that his boss, Wm. Hague, has gone to Marbella to talk to Silvio Berlusconi and others with a view to signing an agreement. John assures me that it will be something that I can live with and volunteers to make arrangements for me to meet William again before the Summer recess. Although scheduled for 27th July this meeting is subsequently cancelled, very much at the last minute, and it will be the end of October before William and I enjoy another of our tete-a-tetes.

Upon returning from Eddisbury in Cheshire, where I have spent the day electioneering in the by-election caused by Alistair Goodlad's imminent move to Australia, there is a message to 'phone Daniel Hannan. He tells me that the British Conservative MEPs will be re-joining the EPP so as to be able to vote on the deal to implement the terms which the Westminster MPs were told we had secured last week. This all sounds rather rum to my mind and I conclude by telling Daniel that I need to sleep on it! Having done just that, the following morning I ring the Pairing Whip, my old friend James Cran (Beverley & Holderness), to say that unless and until I have a piece of paper in my hand setting out in satisfactory terms the relationship between our MEPs and the EPP, signed by someone in authority in the Party, I shall only be voting in the House when it suits me. James suggests that I speak to Whitto and when I do John assures me that our MEPs affiliation to the EPP is purely technical until the new deal is agreed. Furthermore, he says that if we don't get the terms that we have negotiated then we'll be out altogether. He goes on to say that this could be done next week or failing that, in September. My response is to tell John, that regardless of how long it takes, my decision stands.

On Saturday 10th July Michael Spicer rings and I take the opportunity of telling him what I have said to James Cran and Whitto. He tells me that the Congress for Democracy which he organises each year went well yesterday and that Patrick Nicholls, our Sshadow Fisheries Minister, was one of the star turns. Michael also confirms newspaper reports that Wm.

Hague was not prepared to attend the Congress if UK Independence Party Leader, Michael Holmes, was also going to be present.

That evening there is a Conservative Party dinner in Shropshire where the guest speaker is shadow Health Secretary, Liam Fox (Woodspring). In the audience are well known local Europhiles including Christopher Prout, former Conservative MEP Leader and now Lord Kingsland, my tiresome constituent Rupert Blum and Petronella Matson, to mention but a few. They are less than pleased when Liam tells the assembled company that the Party is opposed to a Common Defence policy, a Common Foreign & Security policy etc. which is, of course, music to the ears of most.

Back in the House on Monday there is a little bit of sport to be had! Last Wednesday, walking home at night, I fell in step with Douglas Hogg who put it to me that when the Government introduce their anti-hunting Bill we should disrupt the business of the House to demonstrate that we were not going to take this matter lying down. With no less than seven hunts in my constituency this suggestion has an immediate appeal and so it was that we combined to keep the Government out of their beds long after the traditional 10 o'clock vote. After several Divisions, triggered by the simple device of shouting 'Object' when measures that would normally have gone through on the nod were called out by the Speaker, I was asked by one of the Government Whips, Bob Ainsworth (Coventry North E.), 'what's this all about', to which I replied, 'in a word, hunting'. Ainsworth's response was priceless. Without having the least knowledge or understanding of the function of hunting with hounds he simply blurted out "I'm all in favour of continuing the class war". With little more than this sort of naked prejudice upon which to base their arguments Members will spend endless hours in debate before the Hunting with Hounds Bill finally reaches the statute book. The battle lines are now clearly drawn, but not all the antis are necessarily on the benches occupied by the Government.

On 13th July I spy Ann Widdecombe (Maidstone & The Weald) sitting alone in the Aye lobby during a Division and decide that this is my opportunity to speak to her about hunting. She is adamant that she is not going to be silent on this issue and that thousands of Conservatives are opposed to hunting with hounds. At the end of our private but prickly conversation she has the nerve to bounce up from the bench where we have been sitting to tell Deputy Chief Whip, Patrick McLoughlin (Derbyshire

West), that I have asked her to shut up for the sake of Party unity. I catch the tail end of this outburst and have to ask her to repeat herself before telling her that that is not what I had said at all. What in fact I had said to her was that for the sake of her many colleagues, such as myself, who had several hunts in their constituencies it would be appreciated if she would pipe-down on this emotive and controversial issue – not for the sake of Party unity but for the sake of not making matters worse for her colleagues.

There is good news on Wednesday 14th July when the Minister of Agriculture, Nick Brown, makes a statement in the House about beef exports, in these terms. "I am very pleased to inform the House that, this morning, the European Commission adopted a decision that has the effect of lifting the beef ban for the whole of the United Kingdom", as if we needed any reminding as to who calls the shots as far as the whole of the agriculture industry is concerned.

At the '22 Executive meeting later that day I point out that three Conservative MEPs are running for Vice Presidencies of the EPP. Archie Hamilton responds by saying that Eric Forth (Bromley & Chislehurst) has put him on notice that he intends to pursue this matter at the full '22 meeting which follows. I am not myself able to attend this meeting but Eric assures me that he did raise the matter and also that he was part of a 'peasants revolt' against new rules governing the reselection of sitting MPs.

The fact that Conservative MEPs are seeking election to office within the EPP goes a long way towards explaining why they are so keen to belong to this group in the first place. The group effectively has the power of patronage which appeals to many of our brethren who would otherwise be denied office and/or opportunities to travel the world at taxpayers expense. In the face of this seductive patronage the ideology of the group appears to be of secondary importance - a place on the 'gravy train' is so much more appealing!

Still on the subject of the EPP, Daniel Hannan rings on 19th July to say that he thinks that he now has sufficient undertakings that the terms of our association with the group will be as was promulgated on 30th June. When I tackle Shadow Foreign Secretary, John Maples (Stratford-on-Avon), later in the day he says that Daniel is satisfied and that that is, in effect, the acid test. My response is to tell him that the original deal was barely acceptable and that there must therefore be no back-sliding.

With fellow Shropshire MP Owen Paterson on the Countryside Alliance protest march against banning hunting with hounds.

On my feet at the Council of Europe in Strasbourg.

Speaking at a 'Save Britain's Fish' campaign meeting at the 1999 Conservative Party conference in Blackpool.

Lord Tebbit, former Conservative Cabinet Minister and Party Chairman.

With Speaker Betty Boothroyd waiting to welcome HRH The Princess Royal.

William Hague, Conservative Party leader throughout the period of these memoirs.

With the Princess Royal in Speakers House to celebrate the 50th Anniversary of the House of Commons Yacht Club.

Aside for a moment from the nitty gritty of politics I had that morning telephoned one of my constituents who was scheduled to be presented with a prize at Lancaster House early that same afternoon. Having previously volunteered to be at Lancaster House to support him I wanted to be sure that he was going to be there before I caught an earlier than usual train to London. In the event I was there in good time but of my constituent there was no sign. Searching for him amongst the horde of other attendees every time I re-entered the main reception area I was struck by the warmth of the smile that I got from the young lady on duty at the entrance who reminded me of someone that I had once met. As I passed her yet again, in my vain attempt to locate my constituent, I couldn't help saying " has anyone ever told you that you bear a striking resemblance to Ffion Hague" to which the said young lady replied "I am Ffion Hague"!

A conversation with Archie Hamilton about properties in Shropshire that might suit he and Ann concludes with him extending an invitation to my wife and I to join them for lunch at Harrington, a large house on the Apley estate belonging to LCCA President, Lord (James) Hamilton, his elder brother. Amongst the other guests will be Denis and Margaret Thatcher. Come the day, at the end of August, Margaret confides in us by saying that we should get out of the EU. She also says something else that I find hard to disagree with, namely that Wm. Hague needs to be more assertive. Very sadly her conversation becomes rather repetitive but it is nonetheless a great privilege to have met her on these terms.

On 22nd July I have the anticipated meeting with Shadow FCO Minister, Archie Norman, who has special responsibility for Europe. Our discussion is, unlike some of my meetings with Party spokesmen, a genuine dialogue, during the course of which we discuss the intellectual honesty of different stances on the vexed question of our relationship with the EU. The outcome is inconclusive but I get the impression that he is somewhat swayed by my arguments.

Amongst other things I make the point that politically we potentially have the best tune and that we must not be afraid to whistle it. He is less enthusiastic about ending the tug-of-war within the Parliamentary Party, within constituency Associations, within the group of Conservative MEPs and amongst Prospective Parliamentary candidates (PPCs) by adopting a more robust position on the Euro etc. He describes me as being an 'absolutist' to which I reply that 'I haven't got where I am today without being positive and determined '!

On the question of PPCs I have recently told Roger Freeman (formerly the Member for Kettering and now elevated to the House of Lords), who advises the Candidates Committee, that putting forward 'integrationist' candidates is not helpful and will simply perpetuate divisions within the Party and prolong our time in Opposition. Concerned by reports that former colleagues who lost their seats in May are not getting a fair deal in terms of being selected as PPCs, John Townend raises the matter at the weekly meeting of the '22 Committee but there is no discussion about it because of the imminent arrival of the Leader to address us before we break for the Summer recess. Wm. Hague gives a good account of himself – he is fluent, coherent and most importantly, cheering.

The news as we leave London for the long recess on 23rd July is that the Conservatives have held on to the Eddisbury seat with a slightly increased majority in the by-election caused by Alistair Goodlad's pending move to Australia.

1999

3

" Tony Blair, the Revolutionary "

Highlights of the Summer recess as far as I am concerned are addressing a crowd of literally thousands in Gibraltar on their National Day; obtaining 69 signatories from 24 countries and 4 political groupings for the resolution I table in the Council of Europe on the subject of Asylum seekers; getting articles published on the repatriation of Agriculture policy and a standing ovation from the audience at a 'Save Britain's Fish Campaign' fringe meeting at the Party Conference in Blackpool where retired trawler skipper Tom Hay is kind enough to say that without me they could never have achieved what they have achieved – a radical change in Conservative Party policy.

By dint of my being one of the British representatives on the Council of Europe I am also expected to attend meetings of the Western European Union (WEU). The Western European Union is a military defensive organisation supported by a group of exclusively Western European nations which, unlike NATO, does not include the USA and Canada.

At a group meeting of WEU European Democrats and Christian Democrats on October 18th the outgoing President, Jose Luis Lopez Henares, comes down heavily on my side of the argument after my colleague Michael Colvin (Romsey) had contradicted my assertion that the EU is an essentially Political entity and had stated his own view that it is principally Economic. Henares pointed out that, from the very beginning – the Treaty of Rome, 1951 – the intentions had been, indisputably, Political. The significance of this exchange is that it perfectly illustrates the dichotomy that exists between the continental understanding of European Union and the British interpretation of it, which is quite different. Our continental 'partners' in this joyless endeavour are quite open and frank about the aims and objects of 'ever closer union' – it is a political construct and they make no bones about it. British politicians, on the other hand, pretend that it's all about trade and jobs and economics. Why? Because they know that if they came clean and told the great British public what it is really all about then British acquiescence would quickly turn into outright opposition. Only by deceit is it possible to sell this totalitarian project to British voters and that is precisely what we have been getting ever since Ted Heath told Parliament, way back in 1970, that "there will not be a blueprint for a federal Europe". On BBC 'Question Time' two decades later Heath was asked "......the single currency, a United States of Europe; was that in your mind when you took Britain in?" "Of course, yes." He replied!

At that same WEU meeting I had the satisfaction of being able to fix Jacques Santer with a steely stare whilst I sought to demolish the case for the EU taking over defence responsibilities from the WEU. A former Prime Minister of Luxembourg, Santer has the dubious distinction of having been President of the European Commission until he and the rest of the Commission were sacked earlier in the year for failing to tackle the excessive levels of fraud endemic within the EU.

Whilst separate from and independent of the EU the WEU is coveted by the EU. Speaking in Oxford on 2nd November 1995, then European Affairs spokesman for the German CDU Party, Wolfgang Schauble, had said "It should be our goal to integrate the Western European Union into the European Union and thereby create a European army."

During a lull in proceedings on the second day of the WEU meeting I take the opportunity of telling the leader of the British Conservative delegation, David Atkinson (Bournemouth East), that I should like him to find a replacement for me on both the Council of Europe and the WEU. No one in either organisation appears to hold views that are remotely like those of British Conservatives and regardless of Party affiliations, they are all intent on going, like lemmings, over the cliff towards European integration. That is quite apart from the fact that I have better things to do with my life than spend endless hours in airports getting to and from Strasbourg and occasionally, Luxembourg.

Addressing the Annual Dinner of the Streetley branch of Richard Shepherd's Aldridge & Brownhills CCA on 22nd October my theme is Tony Blair, the Revolutionary – overturning all our democratic institutions, disorienting the populace by undermining all the fixed points in our society and establishing alternatives to our traditional form of government with his Community Forums, Regional Assemblies, devolution and in the context of Europe, promoting the EU as the alternative to NATO and the WEU for Defence and the Council of Europe as the arbiter of Human Rights respectively, all at the expense of national Parliaments as representative of the sovereign voices of the people.

When I meet Wm. Hague the following Tuesday I run through the theme of my Aldridge Brownhills speech to which he listens with great interest and is kind enough to say that I 'always say something to make him think'! I tell him that I am not intending to pressurise him on the subject of agriculture in the same way that I have pushed him on fisheries because of the proximity of the next election and he agrees that his EU 'shopping list' is already long enough. As I am leaving his office William says that he hopes that I have noticed how much of my advice he has already taken. In answer to that very generous comment I respond by saying that I've got no complaints on that score but that what I have had to tell him is, after all, only common sense! When I bump into William's PPS later that evening I make the point that a counter revolution based upon common sense policies would, in my opinion, be an effective antidote to the revolution being prosecuted by Blair.

The next day I attend the Conservative backbench Defence Committee intent upon making a contribution based upon the theme of my speech at Aldridge Brownhills. In the event the only other attendees are Robert Key (Salisbury) and Richard Ottaway (Croydon South) – it later transpires that Iain Duncan-Smith and the other officers of the committee were, at the same time, sitting in a completely different committee room!

At the '22 Executive meeting on Wednesday 27th the Chairman voices his concern about the Party's failure to vote last night against the abolition of hereditary Peers. This is fair comment but symptomatic of the fundamental problem that is dogging the contemporary Conservative Party i.e. the fear of standing up for traditional conservative values, without which we can, of course, kiss goodbye to any prospect of winning the next General Election. In a nation that is intrinsically conservative it makes no sense to be tacking to the left – if the voters want socialism there is no shortage of political parties offering them just that. Throughout the land they can vote Labour or Liberal Democrat or, in Scotland, SNP and in Wales, Plaid Cymru. The Conservative Party is the only party that could, if it was so minded, offer a real alternative to this drab and dreary prospect but for as long as it continues to ape the socialists and ignore its USPs (Unique Selling Points) it will fail to realise its full potential. Why can't the Party hierarchy recognise that clinging to the concept of Economic and Monetary Union, the concept of 'ever closer (political) union' within the benighted EU and a host of other misconceived notions, is the way to political oblivion? The answer to that question may not be so hard to discern. We have in our midst a number of senior colleagues who are not conservatives at all. They probably never ever were conservatives in the first place but attached themselves to the Conservative Party simply because it offered 'wannabee MPs' their best chance of being elected or, as seems to me more likely, for the enhanced opportunity that it would give them to promote the collectivist agenda. Are these people the latter-day equivalent of Burgess, Philby, Maclean and Blunt, infiltrating arguably the world's most successful political party so as to destroy it from within?

Whilst Archie quite rightly raises the question of our stance on reform of the House of Lords I for my part say how disappointed I am that we did not oppose the Food Standards Agency Bill and warn colleagues that others will inevitably raise questions at the next full '22 meeting about our failure to oppose the Financial Services and Markets Bill.

That evening, in my capacity as Commodore of the House of Commons Yacht Club, I find myself sitting next to the Speaker, Betty Boothroyd, at a celebratory dinner in Speaker's House to mark the 50th anniversary of our club. On Betty's other side sits Her Royal Highness, the Princess Royal, who has graciously agreed to be our Guest of Honour. During the course of dinner Betty tells me that she doesn't recognise some ex MPs present but that as far as I am concerned "you've made your mark on this place and no mistake"! Her observation is rather underlined by Agriculture Minister, Nick Brown, who the following day accuses me, in a jocular fashion, of being a 'trouble maker'. When I ask him why he thinks that, he says because 'you ask awkward questions'! In reply I tell him that in my book that is precisely what backbenchers are supposed to do – to hold the Executive (the Government) to account.

18 members of the Shadow Cabinet would doubtless endorse Nick Brown's assessment of me when on 2nd November I write inviting each one of them to respond to the challenge issued by Sunday Telegraph journalist, Christopher Booker. Christopher's challenge is for them to come up with positive benefits of belonging to the EU. With this letter I also enclose another one explaining that in the event of us joining the single currency that would not be at a rate plucked out of the air simply to suit ourselves but at a rate determined by the EU itself.

At the '22 meeting on Wednesday 3rd November, Andrew Lansley (Shadow Minister for the Cabinet Office) addresses us on the subject of Party policy. This is only spoiled by Douglas Hogg's insistence that saying that we will take fisheries back under national control is not deliverable. After the meeting I explain to Hogg and Lansley that it is only the commitment to take fisheries back under our own national control that gives some of us any hope for the future and that otherwise it is a) a waste of time attending Parliament and b) that our future as a nation is going to be precisely as determined by the EU Treaties.

Earlier in the day we have learnt that Michael Portillo has won the nomination for the vacancy at Kensington & Chelsea caused by the demise of one of Parliament's more colourful characters, Alan Clark. Also in the running had been the former Member for Shrewsbury & Atcham, Derek Conway. As a professed eurosceptic, one of only eleven Tory MPs to have voted against the Single European Act in 1986, it is disappointing to hear that at one of the K & C selection meetings Derek had laid the blame for the Conservative defeat at the last General Election at the door of the Maastricht rebels and the 'Whipless Eight'. With friends like that who needs enemies!

As guest of the Shepherd family, whose family business purveys groceries to the Royal household, I am invited to attend the Warrant Holders banquet where guest speaker, Robert Worcester of MORI poll fame, talks about the inevitability of the single currency. There is little doubt that the single currency is still the received wisdom but for the life of me I cannot understand how so many otherwise successful and presumably intelligent people continue to be so blinkered and utterly deluded by this totalitarian project.

One of my least admiring activists in the Ludlow CCA has long been one Katherine Lumsden. On 5th November, when invited to address the West Midlands Conservative Women's half-yearly meeting, I am able to have a little bit of fun at her expense. Whilst congratulating Anthea McIntyre on securing the nomination as candidate for Shrewsbury & Atcham I am able to point out that she's a jump ahead of me in as much as I have yet to submit myself to re-selection and that I have to confess that there are still a handful of people in the LCCA who will never forgive me for having stood up for our country's freedom and independence. The ladies appear to be genuinely interested in what I have to say on the Aldridge theme and are not at all shocked when I cite Soviet Russia as the historical precedent for what is now happening to us. Also that weekend, at my instigation, Graham Brady, the new Member for Altrincham & Sale West, is the guest speaker at an LCCA lunch but such is the level of harmony between myself and the officers of the Association that I am neither asked to introduce my Parliamentary colleague nor to thank him for giving up his Sunday to visit us!

Back in the House on Monday 8th November Shadow Transport Secretary, Bernard Jenkin (Essex North) tells me that my letter about the benefits of the EU has caused a lot of grief amongst his colleagues in Shadow Cabinet. He is honest enough to admit that he himself can think of no benefits accruing to the UK as a result of EU membership.

The passage of the Food Standards Agency Bill onto the Statute book is an appalling indictment of our ineffectiveness as Her Majesty's Loyal Opposition. It has had an unopposed Second Reading, a truncated Committee stage, a guillotined Report and Third Reading and now time-tabled final stages without an opportunity to debate the guillotine motion. In bemoaning these facts to the Chief Whip I also make the not insignificant point that because the Bill is an 'enabling' Bill it will doubtless in future spawn a plethora of regulations over which Parliament itself will have little or no say.

Reverting to my recent meeting with the Leader I probe John Whittingdale, Hague's PPS, to see whether William has hoisted in what I had told him. Whitto says that it is quite likely that William will read the 'Perestroika Deception', a book that I left with him published by my friend, Christopher Story, whose insights into what is happening in the field of international politics is, to say the least, both revealing and instructive.

The following day I suggest to William that he gets the former 'Whipless' taken off what I suspect is a black-list so that we can be used to speak in support of his 'back of the lorry' campaign against the single currency. He says that he is not aware of any black-list and that he will speak to the Party Chairman about my suggestion.

On November 10th I receive a curt note from my Whip, Eleanor Laing (Epping Forest) asking for an explanation as to why, without telling her, I had defied a 3-line Whip to vote against an amendment to the House of Lords Bill – the Bill to reduce the number of hereditary Peers to 92. My short answer to her query is to tell her that I made the mistake of listening to the debate and that in any case my constituents don't like me voting with Labour!

My appointment with the Chief Whip at 11.10 on 11th November is postponed until 11.30 when I have his undivided attention for nearly half an hour. I go round the track with him on my Aldridge theme at the end of which he says that every time I go to see him I really do give him something to think about and that he has to admit that he has no rebuttal to what I am saying. He reminds me that he is not responsible for policy to which I retort that this issue will become his responsibility if people like myself conclude that the Party is delivering us into the hands of international socialism, in which eventuality he will find it difficult, if not impossible, to get us through the lobbies. I make a point of telling him that I have written to 18 Shadow Cabinet Ministers inviting them to tell me what the benefits of EU membership are but that, so far, the response has been very poor!

That evening I spend an hour at the Bar of the House of Lords at its last sitting before the ban on hereditaries comes into effect. There is to be no period of grace before the terms of the Bill come into force. Such is the prejudice of our new masters that the axe will fall just as soon as it receives the Royal Assent – a sad and depressing end to an era.

The Aldridge theme is one that I am only too pleased to rehearse, not only with colleagues but also with audiences and individuals beyond the Westminster village. In responding to a question at a meeting of the Oswestry Men's branch of the North Shropshire CCA I find an unexpected level of support for my theme as indeed I do when I speak at a meeting of the Ludlow Rotary Club. There the headmaster of Bedstone College,

Michael Symonds, is bang on side and expresses the opinion that there are more people than I realise thinking the same way.

On 17th November the new session of Parliament opens and I am in immediate trouble with the Whips because I am unaware that the Party has issued an embargo on intervening on the PM during the course of the opening speeches of the debate on the Queen's Speech. I have a run-in with Richard Ottaway (Croydon South) who says "that was a bloody silly thing to do" and only after the moment has passed do I realise that I have missed the opportunity to point out that, in terms of the team effort, photographs of his old boss, Michael Heseltine, on a platform with Tony Blair and Ken Clarke, promoting the Euro, was hardly helpful either. Assistant Whip, Jacqui Lait, who was sitting next to me on the green benches could have pulled me down but didn't and my own Whip, Eleanor Laing, is miffed because, on account of me, she is in trouble with the Chief Whip!

There is a letter from Shadow Transport Secretary, Bernard Jenkin, in this morning's post saying that Shadow Cabinet have agreed that Shadow Foreign Secretary, John Maples, be deputed to respond to the letter which I had written to them all on 2nd November.

Following on from yesterday's fiasco I am cross when Deputy Chief Whip, Patrick McLoughlin, orders our side not to stand at Business Questions because Deputy PM, John Prescott, is not yet in his place to open the second day of debate on the Queen's Speech which follows. The title for the debate is 'Environment, Transport and the Countryside'. McLoughlin comes over to tell me that it would have been a news story if the Minister responsible for Transport had been late on parade. He also says that whilst he doubts it would be the sort of book I would choose to read, Ted Heath's book says that the best form of opposition to Bevan (or it might have been Bevin) in the Chamber was absolute silence because, shades of yesterday, without interventions he was lost. On the strength of this I retrieve my 'open letter' to the Chief Whip and substitute a revised version!

After speaking in the debate, during the course of which the Agriculture Minister responds to all my comments and concerns about British agriculture, I tell his shadow, Tim Yeo, that this is the third time that he, Tim, has used the Minister's answer to the intervention that I made on 1st July and that if he intends to use it again I had better let him have details of the events either side of that date. I also tell him that some form of attribution would not be entirely inappropriate although, ironically, I am more likely to receive recognition from the Labour Minister, who confirms his anxiety to address the issues I raise, than to get any credit from our own Agriculture team whoich does not share my views on the iniquities of the CAP.

On 23rd November the '22 Executive hold a meeting with the Leader at which William appears to be very phlegmatic about the latest Jeffrey Archer embarrassment. News has broken that Archer had persuaded a friend to provide a false alibi in his libel case 12 years ago. William says that he just has to press on regardless but after two and a half years into the job he is already quite used to that!

Bernard Jenkin is refusing to tell me whether the decision to depute John Maples to reply to my letter of 2nd November in which I asked for a statement of the benefits of EU membership, was taken formally or informally. Maples himself is reluctant to meet me before he has, as he claims, finished setting out his stall during the course of the next two weeks which includes a debate on the EU scheduled for next Wednesday. Angela Browning (Tiverton) is at pains to tell me that she is not the only Shadow Minister who disagrees with what Maples has said to me in his letter of reply, on behalf of all Shadow Ministers, which I have yet to receive.

At a meeting with Archie Norman on 24th November regarding the Aldridge agenda which he says he accepts, there is nothing to indicate that he would consider disengagement from the EU, in spite of all the evidence that it is so totally alien to traditional British Conservatism. He does not accept that the alternative to 'In' is 'Out' which he says is totally negative and that what is necessary is to come up with a positive alternative.

That same day I get voted off the '22 Executive. John Townend, who lost his place on the Executive last year, says that it is more than a coincidence that he and I, respectively Chairman and Secretary of the '92 Committee, have both suffered the same fate. The finger of suspicion points to the Whips office. If that is the case it should perhaps not surprise me as I have done much to incur their displeasure and it is, of course, true to say that I will not have made too many friends within the Shadow Cabinet as a result of having asked them all to tell me what are the positive benefits of our membership of the EU.

Life is full of coincidences and it is, as they say 'a small world'. Aside from my ongoing endeavours to persuade the Conservative Party that

European Union is not for us I am, inter alia, a member of the All Party OP Group which is battling to try and get satisfaction for those farmers and farm workers whose health has been impaired by contact with organophosphate prophylactics whilst compulsorily dipping sheep and treating cattle for the eradication of warble flies. In this connection the group goes to meet the new Agriculture Minister in the Lords, Baroness Hayman, who, as I was able to confirm, had been 'the little girl next door' when we were both children and living on Penn Road, Wolverhampton.

On 29th November, those of us who are still here, hold a dinner to mark the fifth anniversary of being thrown out of the Parliamentary Party for defying a 3-line whip to vote for a motion to send more money to the sink in Brussels. The enjoyment of the evening is rather spoilt by our guest, Patrick Nicholls, who insists upon making a speech justifying his own actions – or, from our perspective, inactions - the upshot of which is that Richard Shepherd walks out in disgust. Patrick's behaviour will be somewhat redeemed by the quality of the speech that he makes later in the week in a debate on the European Union. Over a late nightcap at the St Ermine's Hotel I talk to Christopher Booker about my Aldridge agenda and am pleased that he doesn't dismiss it as a conspiracy theory.

Next day there is good news and bad. The good news is that the Agriculture Minister announces the lifting of the ban on the sale of 'beef on the bone'. I am also pleased when John Redwood accepts my Aldridge proposition and presents me with an autographed copy of his latest book, 'The Death of Britain', hot from the press. The bad news is that the discussion at a meeting of the backbench European Affairs Committee in advance of tomorrow's EU debate leaves me smouldering – I conclude that, were he alive today, Lenin would be really proud of some of my colleagues! My faith in human nature is only restored when at dinner that evening Bowen Wells appears to be coming round to my point of view on the European question and Peter Viggers (Gosport) tells me that his constituents just want out.

Learning that our Leader is going to be making an important speech in Poland in January I importune Whitto and say that I would like to talk to William before he sets off.

On Friday evening, at a Midlands Area Freedom Association dinner attended by my old colleague Teresa Gorman, she doesn't let on that she is about to chuck her hat in the ring to be Mayor of London. The news breaks on Monday 6th December but by Tuesday her candidature will have been rejected out of hand. The same fate awaits another member of the 'Group of Eight', John Wilkinson, who has also applied to be considered for this newly created position. That we are all marked men (or woman) is rather borne out by my being informed at the Freedom Association dinner by a man from Llandrindod Wells that Jonathan Evans had once told him that I would be de-selected in Ludlow and how that would make a nice safe seat for JE! Jonathan Evans is the 'wannabe' MP for whom, at the time of the 1992 General Election, I travelled a long way to speak in his support at a hustings in Radnor. I had agreed to do this having first received his assurance that he shared my views on the vexed question of European Union. Once elected, it soon became clear that this was far from the truth but once again it had been demonstrated how the Conservative Party and its acolytes are prepared to use eurosceptics to enhance their electoral prospects because they know as well as we do that euroscepticism has far more popular appeal than the Party's true agenda.

In pursuit of an old theme, at a meeting of the European Research Group on 7th December, I berate my colleagues for supporting the collectivist policies of the EU. I ask them if there is nothing that will convince them that we have to get out. I instance how the opinion polls show 40/45% of the population wanting to leave and point out that the public have come to that conclusion under their own steam without any political guidance in that direction whatsoever. I go on to tell them that, as politicians who depend upon votes, being afraid to upset the cognoscenti is not the point and that when I was thrown out of the Party it was the people who sustained me – not my colleagues in Parliament who wouldn't even speak to me, nor CCO who went into overdrive to get me deselected. As per usual – no response!

On 8th December I brief our new Fisheries spokesman, Malcolm Moss (Cambridgeshire North East), in advance of next Monday's debate. He accepts that if he backs away from the new Party line, as expressed in Wm. Hague's letter to Peterhead Harbour Commissioners Chairman, George Wiseman, dated 9th March, then people like myself, John Townend and Patrick Nicholls will be down on him like a ton of bricks. In the event the start of the annual Fisheries debate is somewhat delayed whilst the PM makes a statement to the House about the outcome of the Helsinki European Council and becomes almost farcical when Fisheries Minister, Elliot Morley, in opening the debate, takes up 54 minutes of the 140 minutes available. I make sure that my Whip understands that I am only able to support our Opposition amendment to the main motion because Malcolm Moss has categorically stated that "we shall insist on repatriation of national control". Conspicuous by their absence amongst the 131 Conservatives and Ulster Unionist Party Members who vote for "negotiating a reform of the CFP that will devolve power to national, regional and local levels" are former MAFF Ministers John Gummer and David Curry and a number of other unreconstructed europhiles such as Ken Clarke and Michael Heseltine.

At the regular weekly meeting of the '22 Committee former Lord Chancellor, Lord Mackay of Clashfern, is not much taken with my idea of abolishing the House of Lords and creating a Federal Parliament in its place to be responsible, on a UK-wide basis, for Defence, Foreign Affairs, the Law of the Land and federal Taxation, thus allowing the Commons to become an English Parliament to replicate the, albeit unicameral, Scottish Parliament. This proposition gets the enthusiastic support of Peter Luff (Mid Worcestershire) and, after the meeting, Michael Jack (Fylde). They both being such ardent Europhiles I wonder what sort of EU federalist trap I might be falling into!

My meeting with Shadow Foreign Secretary John Maples on 9th December goes better than anticipated. I take him through the Aldridge agenda and he says that maybe he should be using these ideas in future speeches. I tell him that whilst that might be difficult the important thing is that he accepts this as the background against which to view future relations with the EU. Maples says that the policy which we now have was arrived at after consultation with Hague and Howard. This contrasts with Bill Cash's assertion that Maples had consulted Geoffrey Martin, the EU representative in London and Iain Taylor MP, the pro-EU fanatic representing Esher.

On Friday 10th December there are some excellent speeches at the Congress for Democracy organised by Michael Spicer in Church House, Westminster. US Republican Senator, Gordon Smith, describes the EU as being a socialist project which, whilst undoubtedly true, is a bit of a slap in the face for the Labour MP, Austin Mitchell, who is chairing the meeting and Labour peer Lord Shore and Independent Labour peer Lord Stoddart who are in the audience.

First thing on Saturday I telephone my area Whip, Eleanor Laing, to say that I am not pleased to hear about the softening of the Party line re Section 28 of the Education Act (which prohibits the promotion of homosexuality in school teaching) and that I will have to honour the pledge given to my constituents to oppose its repeal. Eleanor says that she too thought that that aspect of Party policy was clear and thanks me for letting her know. Given that Shaun Woodward (Witney) has just been sacked from the Front Bench for saying that he could not support the Party line on this very issue it seems unfortunate, to say the least, that the Party might now be contemplating a U-turn. This disappointing news prompts me to call John Townend to say that yes, it would be a good idea for the Officers of the '92 Group to seek a meeting with Wm. Hague, particularly in the light of the speech that John Maples made to the Centre for Policy Studies last Monday.

After chivvying Whitto and Hague's diary secretary we get our meeting and on 14th December Messrs Colvin, Forth, Gill, Townend and Roe, bearing the apologies of Clark and Hunter, troop into the Leader's office. In spite of time spent in an ante-room discussing tactics John Townend puts me on the spot, in front of Hague, by asking me to open the batting. I defer by suggesting that others should speak first. In the event I have the last word, pointing out that 45% of respondents to a MORI poll in October wanted out of the EU and that that is without being given any lead from any political Party whatsoever and that, more importantly, what elects us to Parliament is not the votes of the bosses of multinational companies but the votes of the proverbial 'man in the street'. William says that he doesn't want to risk splitting the Party! Where have I heard that before?

Back in the House on Monday I meet up with Angela Browning to discuss the Aldridge agenda. She is very much on side and gives me the impression that she wishes somehow to atone for her failure to oppose European Union in the last Parliament. On the same tack, i.e. the Aldridge agenda, I meet Andrew Mackay (Bracknell). He is sympathetic and recommends me to read an article by Stephen Glover in the current edition of the 'Spectator'.

My next target is Andrew Lansley who may or may not be hoisting in what I am telling him about the Aldridge agenda. He ripostes by giving me the text of his 'Nicholas Ridley Memorial' lecture which I will read and subsequently respond to. In exchange I give him copies of a quote by Soviet defector Anatoliy Golytsin and an article by Mark Seddon published in the 28th August edition of the 'Spectator'. The fact that he is interested to hang on to these items I take to be a sign that he might possibly be buying into my proposition.

The following day I am up at 03.55 to draft letters to Maples and Lansley in confirmation of what we have previously discussed. I also write to my Whip confirming that my vote for our Fisheries amendment was strictly conditional upon the assurances given.

A chat with Richard Shepherd reveals that he too is very fed-up – not least because of the way in which people of our ilk are being deliberately sidelined. He instances how both John Wilkinson and Teresa Gorman never got as far as the final selection for London Mayor. For my part I tell him that I went home last night thoroughly depressed after the meeting with Hague.

At 17.50 on Saturday 18th December I learn that Shaun Woodward has defected to Labour. This gives a whole new meaning to the lecture that I had once been subjected to by his father-in-law, Tim Sainsbury (formerly the MP for Hove), about the importance of loyalty to the Party! Woodward's defection gives me a good peg to hang my hat on when I address the Wrekin CCA's Christmas Supper Party at Albrighton Hall that evening. I give them part of the Aldridge agenda and by sheer coincidence their Chairman, Peter Forgham, corroborates what I say because he is currently reading a biography of Lenin! Their President, Vesey Holt, congratulates me on a good speech and says how glad he was that I said what I said about Blair because his wife Liz, a veritable pillar of the Conservative movement, "has quite a soft spot for him"!

As the Christmas recess beckons I am very disappointed that Transport Secretary John Prescott refuses to let me intervene on him during the Second Reading debate of the Transport Bill. His excuse that "I have made it clear that the hon. Gentleman has never made a sensible intervention. I have no intention of conceding to him" is followed by uproar, but as far as I'm concerned this is a simple case of the bully being frit because of fears that I shall ask him something that he will struggle to answer.

Before we leave for our respective constituencies there is a joint meeting of the Foreign Affairs and the European Affairs committees in John Maples' room. When Oliver Heald says that we must look at EU enlargement from the standpoint of those countries which have been under the yoke of

Communism I fairly explode, telling the assembled company that the EU is collectivist, just like soviet Russia, and that the question they should all be asking themselves is why we, as Conservatives, are going along with it all. I perhaps overstep the mark by saying that whilst I could never defect to a socialist Party the Whips need to start thinking about how they are going to keep me in the (collectivist) Conservative Party.

We will continue the dialogue in the new Millennium!

2000

1

" Even Gorbachev agrees with me "

The best news as the New Year gets underway is that the long expected 'millenium bug' doesn't materialise. The less welcome news is that Ken Clarke, Geoffrey Howe and John Major have chosen this moment to denounce, what they term to be, the Conservative Party's 'lurch to the right'. For a former Leader of the Party to be party to such a gross act of disloyalty, whilst not unknown, is nevertheless unacceptable and provokes the Chairman of the '22 to pen the rejoinder which appears in the 'Daily Telegraph' on 6th January. I am so pleased that such a senior and influential figure in the Party has put these serial 'wreckers' back in their box that I call Archie Hamilton to congratulate him on his article and to thank him for speaking up for the rank and file, as indeed the Chairman of the '22 should do.

It's business as usual when the House reconvenes after the Christmas recess. At a meeting of the backbench European Affairs Committee held in John Maples' office I try to get him to address the fundamental question posed in my letter of 16th December, but without success.

Whilst I am sitting on the green benches, minding my own business, Shadow Foreign Affairs spokesman, Cheryl Gillan (Chesham & Amersham), asks me whether I would leave the Party over the issue of European Union. She says that it would be silly for us to go too far at this stage in the electoral cycle and that it would be better to keep our powder dry until nearer the next General Election. Needless to say that is an opinion that I do not share, not least because there is a real fear that Blair may, in the meantime, shoot our fox by himself ruling out joining the single currency for the duration of the next Parliament. He might even call an election this coming autumn so as to avoid getting wrong footed by the impending Nice Treaty in the way that his predecessor, John Major, got snarled up by the Maastricht Treaty. This possibility is, I believe, causing the Party's top brass to face up to the real need to widen our attack. At the Maples meeting Julian Lewis (New Forest East) had made positive suggestions as to how this could be done – by staking out our rejection of a European Army, the Single Currency, the CFP and uncontrolled immigration.

Charles Wardle (Bexhill & Battle),Parliamentary Under-Secretary of State at the Home Office in the last administration, tells me that he has more or less concluded that we have to get out. One swallow doesn't make a summer but I sense that Charles is not alone in thinking that there is a better future for us outside of the totalitarian EU.

Discretion being the better part of valour I decide that I am not the right person to stand up at the '22 to suggest that colleagues having differences of opinion with the Party might choose to express them in this forum rather than in the media but nevertheless regret not having taken the opportunity to congratulate Archie Hamilton on his 'Telegraph' article in the hope of sparking off some discussion in an otherwise silent meeting. I doubly regret failing to do this because the meeting is well attended in anticipation of an address by Liam Fox on the subject of the Party's new thinking on the subject of Health.

Later in the day Deputy Chief Whip, Patrick McLoughlin, invites me into his office to ask me to go onto a Select Committee – the vacancy that he has to fill is on Richard Shepherd's Select Committee on Public Administration. When I discuss the matter with Richard he makes the comment that at the beginning of this Parliament, when the chairmanship of the Select Committee on Agriculture was in their gift, the Whips didn't send for you then!

On 18th January a useful breakfast meeting of the ERG decides to try to persuade Wm. Hague that the Party's best tactic, in the circumstances in which it is wedded to its policy of 'flexibility', is to declare that it will ring-fence defence, immigration, health, education etc. as being the non-negotiable, exclusive responsibility of the Westminster Parliament. Walking back to the House with Daniel Hannan he volunteers to write up our proposal as a discussion paper and, true to his word, sends me his homework by FAX the following Monday (24th January).

At his own request I have arranged to meet Yorkshire entrepreneur Paul Sykes on Wednesday 19th January at his hotel in St James Place. As I arrive, Michael Portillo is just leaving. I talk Paul through most of the Aldridge agenda in response to which he says that I am direct, clear thinking and can see ahead, but clearly in the wrong job! He says that he just cannot get the European issue out of his head. I know the feeling and tell him that I too am a driven man. He seems genuinely grateful for the chat but, once again, there is no outcome although, years later, he will tell me that he always carries a copy of one of my speeches in his pocket to show to people that he meets.

Meeting with Shadow Home Secretary, Ann Widdecombe later in the day to go through the Aldridge agenda, I am pleased when she questions me on three points. She then invites her Central Office researcher to question me. I am reasonably confident that I have answered his question about New Labour's 'means' and 'ends' satisfactorily by saying that the 'ends' are the same as they always have been i.e. state control, but that the 'means' are different in the sense that they now manifest themselves in terms of intrusive 'regulation' rather than outright 'nationalisation'. Whilst talking to Ann I warn her that I have put in for a debate on Asylum Seekers. Later in the day I am able to tell her that my application has been successful and that I have been allocated a slot next Wednesday.

At the '22 meeting I row in behind Michael Howard and Bill Cash who both say that we should be opposing the Second Reading of the Disqualifications Bill. The Bill will permit members of the Irish Republic legislature to be members of the House of Commons, the Scottish Parliament, the Welsh Assembly and the Northern Ireland Assembly. Owen Paterson (Shropshire North) and Stephen O'Brien (Eddisbury) speak up in our support but in the event our opinions are ignored and next Monday our Shadow Home Secretary will tell the House that "we shall therefore give the Bill a fair passage to its next stages". On Saturday morning I telephone my Whip to ask why we are only on a 1-line whip for the Second Reading of this Bill and whether the 3-line Whip imposed for Tuesday's business is for us to vote For or Against the Third Reading. She doesn't know the answer to the latter question but undertakes to get Andrew Mackay to ring me. He never does.

On Sunday I resolve to be in the House tomorrow, come what may, to vote against Second Reading. I am extremely annoyed that the Party has not imposed a 3-line Whip to oppose this measure and in the lobbies I find myself in the company of 12 other Conservatives and, not surprisingly, half a dozen Ulster Unionists.

Over dinner that evening, former Europe Minister David Davis (Haltemprice & Howden) appears to relish discussing the European issue and concludes by taking me to the library to see an article by Alan Judd in the 30th December edition of the 'Daily Telegraph' which, he says, is based upon a speech that David had made in America.

The next morning I am up with the lark to complete preparations for my Adjournment debate on European asylum seekers. In the event my debate is overshadowed by the Home Office release of the latest statistics at 11.00 which is right in the middle of my allotted time (10.00 – 11.30). I am extremely disappointed at the poor attendance and lack of Press coverage, notwithstanding the fact that the timing of the debate could not have been better, nor the subject matter more topical. I feel that the Party really could have rallied round but it is as though they have imposed a boycott. The Home Office team could hardly have been unaware of the debate as I had given Shadow spokesman for Home Affairs, David Lidington, all the dope in October when I had raised the matter at the '22 and only last week had informed Ann Widdecombe that I had secured an allocation of time in Westminster Hall. That afternoon I take off to the Imperial War Museum to get away from it all, having first told my Whip that I could not support the Party's amendment to the Disqualifications Bill and that I would in any case be voting against the Bill at Third Reading. What at the time I thought to be a rather rash statement of my intentions subsequently proves not to be the case because when we finally reach Third Reading after an all-night sitting, which results in Wednesday's business being lost, we are whipped to vote against!

Shadow Agriculture Minister Tim Yeo is is my next victim. Our meeting on 26th January goes better than expected and whilst his question is tangential to the theme of the Aldridge agenda he at least listens and appears to be interested in what I have to say. After leaving Tim I am hard pressed to make it to CCO in time for my meeting with the Leader when, once again, I am given a good hearing. I tell William that I do not want him to compromise his position by what he says in Cracow at the weekend and to bear in mind that the Central and Eastern European countries (CEE) see the EU as a home from home after the supposed 'collapse' of the Eastern bloc and that, furthermore, many of their political leaders are the very same people who held sway under communism. I say that I believe that the EDG seminar provides him with the opportunity to make a 'wind of change' speech if he is so minded and flatter him by telling him, once again, that he could become a latter-day Winston Churchill. I urge him to plant his standard firmly in the ground in Cracow and challenge all those European countries who believe in genuine free trade to reject the totalitarian customs union that is the EU and join us in a re-vitalised European Free Trade Area (EFTA).

In the event, William's speech to the Centre for Policy Studies (CPS) that same evening, figuratively speaking, pokes a stick in my eye and is further proof that, in spite of all the rhetoric to the contrary, the Conservative Party will not reverse course on the European issue. The only question now is what do those of us who see the European trap closing - and who believe that the only way is OUT - do, to head off the impending tragedy.

On the way to the House the next morning I bump into my old friend James Cran (Beverley & Holderness), the Pairing Whip. I offer to buy him a cup of coffee – being a canny Scot he never carries money – and tell him that I was just on my way to see my own Whip, Eleanor Laing, to tell her that I am totally browned-off as a result of events this week. Firstly, the Party's refusal to oppose at Second Reading the principle behind the Disqualifications Bill. Secondly, the Party's apparent lack of interest in the problem of Asylum Seekers and thirdly, the Leader's poke in the eye for all that I had said to him yesterday morning. As the Member with the second best voting record when, I ask, is my support for the Party going to be reciprocated. James agrees that if we don't win the next General Election the European issue will be a foregone conclusion but, even if we do, it is unlikely that the Conservative Party will live up to its rhetoric.

James assures me that whilst I am perceived to be hard-working and persistent I am not regarded as a trouble-maker. My next encounter is with Eleanor whose opinion might be somewhat different! She agrees to meet me next Monday but, notwithstanding that she is anxious to get off to an appointment, she has to endure much of what I have just told James.

Later in the day I find myself sitting opposite John Major in the Members Tea Room. He doesn't much relish having to speak to me but is nevertheless civil. Also in the Tea Room is Eric Forth who opines that as we have a consensual Shadow Leader of the House in Sir George Young (Hampshire North West) and a consensual Opposition Chief Whip in James Arbuthnot, there's only one thing for it – we shall have to run our own Whip!

A meeting with representatives of the German CDU and CSU Parties under the auspices of the CPS and chaired by John Maples gives me the opportunity to ask whether, in the light of the fact that one of the Germans has stated that 'there will be no negotiation' regarding EU new entrants – 'they will have to accept the acquis communautaire', he fundamentally disagrees with the British Conservative Party's policy of 'flexibility'. After a pause for thought he says 'Ja'. Later I tell Maples, who clearly wishes he hadn't called me to ask the second question, that he's stuffed - the paymaster won't play ball! His response is to say that Britain is a big contributor too. He then says it's no good going on about it to him – the policy has been agreed by Wm. Hague, Michael Howard and himself and that's it!

Returning from a Meat Training Council annual luncheon at Butchers Hall on 1st February where, incidentally, the Master, Graham Jackaman and another member of the Company's Court, Brian Wheatley, both say that we have to get out of the EU, (The significance of these two entirely unsolicited and separate remarks is that they go way beyond the reticence that has previously prevailed on this subject) I pick up a 'phone call from Vivian Bendall, formerly the Member for Ilford North, who tells me that there has been a re-shuffle and that John Redwood has been sacked from his position as Shadow Trade and Industry Secretary. This development ensures a record turnout at a '92 Group dinner that evening when Wm. Hague is given a hard time by John Bercow (Buckingham), David Wilshire (Spelthorne) and Julian Lewis to mention but a few. William refuses to give reasons for Redwood's sacking other than to say that he had to make room in the Shadow Cabinet, the beneficiaries of which are Michael Portillo and Archie Norman. John Maples is the other casualty so maybe that is the quid pro quo – one anti-EU out on his ear, together with a rabid europhile to balance the equation. Our Whips have been helpful in ensuring that there are no votes after 19.30 so there are no time constraints on what may yet prove to be a watershed day in the narrative of the Conservative Party in this Parliament. Having assured Whitto that since Sir George Gardiner, the former Member for Reigate, ceased to be chairman, our group didn't leak, I am embarrassed when subsequent press reports of our dinner prove to be uncannily accurate.

On Wednesday 2nd February my appointment with Liam Fox is cancelled but my half hour with Shadow Social Security Secretary, David Willetts, is worthwhile. He says that he doesn't agree with everything that I say but nonetheless appears to accept the gist of my argument (on the theme of my Aldridge agenda) and sends me away with a copy of his booklet 'Blair's Gurus' and a recommendation to read 'Capitalism v Capitalism' by a Frenchman called Albert.

A meeting that I had arranged with my area Whip, Eleanor Laing, has to be postponed because I wish to attend a debate in the Chamber on 'Immigration and Asylum Seekers'. When we do eventually meet it is my intention to tell her that the sacking of Redwood, the non-opposition to the Disqualifications Bill, the lack of support for my Asylum Seekers debate and Wm.Hague's stick in my eye over Europe are making it difficult for me to be so wholeheartedly in support of the management as my previous voting record might indicate. When I collar her the next day she agrees that the interference of the Party Chairman, Michael Ancram, in the affairs of the Ludlow constituency, without any reference whatsoever to the Member, is not on. What the Party is trying to achieve in terms of re-organisation is not the subject of this book – suffice it to say that more than a little of it seems to be designed to ensure that there can never be a recurrence of the circumstances which allowed someone like myself to become an MP without ever having been on the Party list and who was not, in the final analysis, prepared to kow-tow to the Party hierarchy. In our brief encounter I am only able to cover part of my agenda but she takes the point that there has to be a degree of give and take in these matters.

On Friday 4th I journey to Much Marcle in Herefordshire to meet representatives of the 'Commercial Farmers Group'. The experience is disappointing and somewhat depressing. My point to them is that unless they are prepared to think 'outside the box' (of the CAP) there is really nothing that I can do to help them. Henry Fell won't even address his mind to that possibility, Robin Malin says there's no point – we're in and we've got to make the best of it – Eric Drummond says nothing and only Anthony Colburn is brave enough to suggest that maybe we should be thinking in terms of getting out. I am at a slight disadvantage as a result of not having yet had the opportunity to read this morning's 'Daily Telegraph' in which the group is featured.

As a still loyal member of the Conservative Party my wife and I pay good money to attend the Party's Winter Ball. This is held on Monday 7th February and our table has been organised by Malcom Moss. I am not sure that he is being serious when he tells me that in the forthcoming debate on the Fishing Industry I should talk about 'renegotiation'. Is he telling me this to wind me up or has there been a change of policy and a reneging on the commitment to bring Fisheries back under national control?

I get my final bite of the cherry with Eleanor Laing on Tuesday 8th. She is now doing a survey of Members views and attitudes which suits me fine. Afterwards I entertain my wife, Patricia, to tea in the Pugin Room where she suggests that I am being too frank in baring my soul to Eleanor. It would be an exaggeration to say that I am past caring but on the other hand I am in no mood to equivocate. As far as I am concerned, back home in Shropshire, I am an archetypal Conservative but within the Parliamentary Party I can't help feeling quite untypical. The Party, I tell her, needs to use language that the proverbial 'man in the street' can understand – our problem is too many professional politicians and too little common sense!

Being called to speak third in the debate on the Fishing Industry initiated by Tim Loughton (East Worthing & Shoreham) in Westminster Hall on 9th February I make a 'no holds barred' speech in the vain hope that this will precipitate some reaction within the Party but sadly I am almost inevitably going to be disappointed.

In the afternoon I bob up and down throughout yet another Prime Minister's Question Time but by now the Speaker is well aware that I only stand when I've got an awkward question to ask. The chances of 'catching her eye' are therefore not good. Later in the week I will be furious at not being called at Agriculture Questions when it proves necessary for me to stand at Business Questions, which follows, to make my point there.

Speaking up at the '22 about constitutional matters meets with greater success. As a consequence of what I have to say on that subject I subsequently receive a 'phone call from Lord (Philip) Norton who invites me to join him in the House of Lords smoking room for a very long chat about the difficulties of strengthening Parliament. Unlike other previous so-called consultations his Lordship is genuinely interested to listen to my views and I am left feeling that if my view does not prevail it will not be because it hasn't been fully considered.

A casual conversation with John Bercow confirms that he has been carpeted by the Chief on account of his criticism of the Leader at last week's '92 Dinner – something that Shadow Ministers really shouldn't do!

A rumour is circulating that the new Shadow Foreign Secretary, Francis Maude, is going to change our policy on Europe. This is the man who, together with Douglas Hurd, signed the Maastricht Treaty on behalf of HMG, a point of fact that Foreign Secretary, Robin Cooke, will allude to when, on 15th February, he launches a White Paper in advance of the forthcoming Inter Governmental Conference (IGC). A joint meeting of the Foreign Affairs and European backbench committees, also on 15th, proves a lively forum, particularly when I drop my own little pebble into the pond. In answer to my question as to whether it is the new Shadow Foreign Secretary's understanding that it is Party policy to take back control of fisheries out to 200 miles, or the median line where applicable, Francis Maude bluntly says NO! John Townend then goes ballistic and the shock waves are soon extending far beyond the confines of Francis Maude's office.

On 10th February I take time out to compliment John Redwood on the article that he has written for this morning's 'Daily Telegraph' and also on the responsible way in which he is conducting himself in the aftermath of last week's sacking. This is in stark contrast to the behaviour of the other defenestrated Shadow Cabinet Minister, John Maples, who will have an open letter to Wm. Hague in the 'Times' newspaper on 15th February criticising the Leader for 'surrounding himself with too many right wingers'! John Townend asks JR if he is going to lead the Get Out of Europe campaign to which he replies by saying that the country is not yet ready for that and that we must concentrate on winning the argument over the single currency which, in turn, will then lead to the unravelling of the rest of the EU project. Realistically this is probably the way it is going to have to be but leaving the

EU would negate the need to win the battle of the Euro and doubtless save the nation an awful lot of headaches and cost, not just in treasure but in political capital too. Later in the week, at dinner in the Members Dining Room, JR will tell me that whereas prior to the last election Ken Clarke was in league with Mandelson it is now Michael Portillo! He reckons that the new common purpose is to topple Hague.

Continuing my round of one to one meetings with individual members of the Shadow Cabinet I find Party Chairman, Michael Ancram, surprisingly receptive when I explain my Aldridge agenda. He does, however, suggest that the real genesis of what I am describing is Hegel rather than Marx or Engels. Our meeting is generally satisfactory because neither of us chooses to refer to the controversy surrounding his proposals for Party re-organisation in so far as they affect my own home county of Shropshire.

The following day, 16th February, I arrive at the office of the Shadow Culture Secretary, only to discover that he, Peter Ainsworth, has cried off. This is not entirely bad news because I am able to spend the time in Westminster Hall participating in a debate on the EU draft Charter of Fundamental Rights. I am glad of the opportunity to make the point that this is yet another instance of the EU seeking to duplicate what is already being done by other bodies, in this case the Council of Europe and the long-established European Charter of Human Rights, administered by the European Court of Human Rights.

At my meeting with the Shadow Foreign Secretary later in the day it is a very much more emollient Francis Maude than I had encountered yesterday. He accepts that both the CAP and the CFP are collectivist policies and that it therefore follows that they have more in common with communism than conservatism. He tells me that he would like to talk to me again about these two subjects as he has at some stage to decide what our future strategy should be.

At a well attended meeting of the '22, Lord Wakeham, chairman of the Royal Commission on Reform of the House of Lords, having listened to a whole raft of Members' views says that he has heard nothing to make him want to change any of his proposals. In the circumstances I am glad that I hadn't wasted any breath propounding my own ideas. Wakeham is positively rude to Geoffrey Clifton-Brown (Cotswold) when Geoffrey points out the desirability of keeping an open mind.

On 17th I get a positive response from Shadow Health Secretary, Liam Fox, when I meet him to talk about the Aldridge agenda. He is quite clear that he wants low taxes, minimum state interference and for politicians only to be involved in creating the environment in which individuals can go about their legitimate business. When I say that I am concerned about the future of our country and the future of our Party he retorts by saying that once upon a time these two things were synonymous – I cannot but agree!

Following my meeting with Liam Fox I next go round the track with Shadow Fisheries Minister, Malcolm Moss, as a prelude to explaining the relevance of fisheries to the Aldridge agenda whilst at the same time putting him in the picture regarding what has transpired in the recent meetings with Francis Maude.

My next appointment is with Shadow Education Secretary, Theresa May, who buys into the Aldridge agenda to the extent that she says that under New Labour the education and bringing up of children is being collectivised. She is less convinced that collectivisation is operating across the board but assures me that she will think about the big picture in the light of my presentation.

On 21st February I have a surprisingly good meeting with Shadow International Development Secretary, Gary Streeter (Devon South West) who, in spite of his past membership of the Social Democrat Party (SDP), does not demur when I explain the Aldridge agenda. He is anxious to know how many EU get-outers there are but I don't know the answer to that question. All that I can do is to point to the increasing number of people of that persuasion as revealed in recent opinion polls.

At an ERG breakfast meeting on 22nd February I listen to a lot of waffle before telling the assembled company, which includes Shadow Foreign Secretary, Francis Maude, and Shadow Chief Secretary to the Treasury, David Heathcoat-Amory, that I have spent seven years of my life trying to persuade Conservatives that it is neither in the Party's interest nor the country's interest to pursue European Union. The time has come, I say, when I shall stop trying to persuade them and that they, on the contrary, must now try to persuade me, and millions like me, why we should continue to vote Conservative. Furthermore I say that to talk about 'reform', 'renegotiation', 'flexibility' etc. is simply unrealistic, not least because the UK Independence Party will be saying 'Better Off Out'. I conclude by saying that nothing short of a commitment to outright repatriation of control over Agriculture and Fisheries will now do.

Making a presentation of my Aldridge agenda to Shadow Chancellor of the Exchequer, Michael Portillo, later in the day, I am taken by surprise when he asks me if I am thinking of leaving the Party. This is an opportunity which I regret missing for me to spell out, in terms, exactly how I am feeling. Michael appears to be under considerable pressure which ties in with something that David Heathcoat-Amory had said to me as we walked back to the House after breakfast this morning – are they at loggerheads I wonder.

On 7th March I spend half an hour with William Hague during which time I take him through an agenda that will form part of my address to the AGM of the Ludlow CCA on Friday. On the perennial question of Europe I am left not knowing whether he is being craven or calculating. In the light of our previous meetings I cannot believe that he is ignorant of these matters but just like all his Shadow Cabinet colleagues he makes no attempt to refute my argument that EU policies are essentially collectivist i.e.communist.

Much more encouraging is the message that I receive from retired trawler skipper Tom Hay who tells me that Mr Stephen, the fisherman that I had quoted in my last speech on fisheries, had insisted that my letter to him be read out to the recent Fishermens Association meeting and that another fisherman, seeing me on TV speaking in the House as he lay in hospital recovering from a heart bypass operation, had rung to say that it made him feel like a man with a new heart!

My postponed meeting with Shadow Culture Secretary, Peter Ainsworth, takes place on 14th March. It goes well. Peter says that one of the classic areas exploited by international socialism is the Arts. He tells me that the first time he was eligible to vote was at the Referendum in 1975 when he voted 'NO'. Later in the day Martin Holmes, co-Chairman of the Bruges Group, will tell an audience how he too, as a young student, also voted 'NO' in that referendum.

At lunch at the Austrian Embassy that day, Professor Gerhardt Bruckmann, a Peoples Party member of the Austrian Parliament, tells me privately that he was afraid to answer Patrick Nicholls' question. Patrick had asked him whether he resented EU interference in Austria's internal affairs. What is it about the EU that even grown men are afraid to speak their mind? This incident perfectly illustrates one of the most fundamentally important differences between British politicians, who are ultimately answerable to their electors, and continental politicians, who are generally dependent upon the political party bosses for their place on the party list (of election candidates) and, therefore, for their livelihood and careers as Parliamentarians. This fact goes a long way towards explaining why so many continentals look to us to point out that the king has no clothes because we can, on a matter of principle and if so minded, risk incurring the wrath of our respective Parties and fall back upon the mercy of the people who voted us in. Oh that William Hague would only recognise this fact of European political life and lead us to a better future instead of following the herd in the direction of the supposed nirvana.

At a Marine Stewardship Council reception on 15th March I am greeted by the Chairman himself, one John Gummer, who then spends time talking exclusively to myself for what seems like a very long time – wonders never cease! I then spend an equally long time talking to the 'Daily Telegraph' Agriculture correspondent, David Brown, who promises to wear the £ lapel badge that I am pleased to give him! Clearly JG has forgotten what he said in the Fisheries debate because when he addresses the assembled company he instances Iceland as a discrete fishery as though 'discrete fisheries' might be preferable to 'common fisheries'!

Once again I fail to catch the Speaker's eye at Agriculture Questions on 16th March but as I am leaving the Chamber the Speaker beckons me over to apologise for not reaching me – I was next on her list Betty says, whereupon I explain that I have several times had to resort to asking my Agriculture question at Business Questions!

At a meeting that same day regarding the draft EU Charter of Fundamental Rights, Keith Vaz, Minister for Europe, says that the proposed new Charter will simply restate existing rights and responsibilities; Win Griffiths (Bridgend), the House of Commons representative on the drafting committee, says that the draft Charter is very closely based upon the European Convention (ECHR) and Lord Goldsmith, the PM's personal representative on the committee, says that they are, as far as possible, sticking to existing rights! All this begs the question as to why it is thought necessary to be doing anything – but, of course, the answer is so as to create the EU supra-state.

As previously stated it is not the purpose of this narrative to record all the shenanigans regarding Party re-organisation – suffice it to say that over a cup of tea in the Members Tea Room former Party Chief Executive, Archie Norman, has previously told me that in spite of all the changes the same old faces have emerged at the head of the voluntary side of the Party and that, more to the point, nobody is thrusting to take their place – principally because the ladder that aspirants had previously climbed has now been removed! At constituency level things have come to such a pass that on 22nd March I tell my friend James Cran, the Pairing Whip, that I can no longer be relied upon to respond to the Party Whip as I shall have to devote more of my time to constituency matters – something which, even in the darkest days of the Maastricht rebellion and, subsequently, during the time when I was deprived of the Party Whip, I had never had to do. A letter from Party Chairman, Michael Ancram, is the last straw and I tell James that the ultimatum that Ancram has just issued, in effect saying that regardless of the objections of Party members, as expressed in a properly conducted ballot, his proposals for the Shropshire constituencies 'that grouping would take place in any event and urgently' is totally unacceptable.

Walking to the House on 27th March, for some inexplicable reason, instead of going via Lord North Street as is my wont, I go via Gayfere Street where I bump into frontbench spokesman for Trade and Industry, Alan Duncan (Rutland & Melton) coming out of his house. When I ask him about a newspaper report in Friday's 'Telegraph' he says that he and Mikhail Gorbachev are old friends; that Gorby's here on a private visit; that he thought it would give Francis Maude a publicity boost if the two of them met and that 'my line about the EU being a European soviet' was one that he, Gorbachev, agreed with!

At an ERG breakfast on 28th at which Michael Portillo is invited to address us, I ask the first question. Michael's reply is not memorable other than that he says that he will make Wm. Hague aware of my concern. My fear is that whilst we will never say 'never' to the Euro, the Leader has, only last month, said that 'we will never leave the EU'. That evening I make a special effort to travel to Birmingham to hear the Leader address a 'Save the Pound' rally of Party members so that I can judge how his policy on the single currency issue is going down with Party activists. To say, as William does, that he rules out joining the Euro for the duration of the next

Parliament is totally illogical – either one is for it, in which case one should commit to joining it as soon as possible, or one is against it, now and for all time. It is, when all said and done, a fundamental matter of principle as to whether we retain control of our own financial destiny or whether we cede that control to the unelected and unaccountable in Brussels. I sense that the feeling of the meeting is that William's speech is good in so far as it goes but undoubtedly I am not the only one to be disappointed that he doesn't go further.

2000

2

" He thinks the whole idea is crazy "

Within the Parliamentary Party there is cheer for us so-called Eurosceptics when Julian Lewis beats Nicholas Soames in an election for the position of Vice Chairman of the backbench European & Foreign Affairs Committee and Owen Paterson is elected unopposed to the Executive of the '22. Less welcome is the letter that Edward McMillan Scott and Timothy Kirkhope, Chairman and Chief Whip respectively of the UK delegation within the Group of EPP and European Democrats in the European Parliament, have written to Chairman of the Group, Dr Professor Hans-Gert Poettering. In this letter, a copy of which has been handed to me by 'Group of Eight' PR man, Mike Penning, McMillan Scott and Kirkhope assert that the majority of British Conservative MEPs elected to the EP do not consider that they have been elected on a eurosceptic manifesto! This letter reaches a wider audience when in the 'Sunday Telegraph' on April 2nd there is reference to it in Christopher Booker's column. When a meeting of the Freedom Association Council is held on Wednesday 5th it is apparent that several of those present have read Booker's piece in the Sunday paper and whilst I am happy to tell them that we appear to have won the battle of the Euro within the Conservative Party they should not assume that that is the end of the matter and that they would be well advised to start campaigning to get out of the EU altogether. I instance how Wm. Hague has sent word to the Rushcliffe constituency urging the members there not to de-select Ken Clarke whilst CCO, with Hague's knowledge, is doing its level best to de-stabilise the CCA's in Shropshire.

On Thursday 6th April I receive a letter from my area Whip saying "Thank you for your letter regarding the vote which you missed on 30th March. It has been noted that you have missed several more votes - which is unlike you! I wondered whether there was a problem and would welcome the opportunity to have a quick word". Too right there's a problem and so the following Tuesday afternoon I go to the Whips' Office in search of Eleanor Laing to have it out with her. Unfortunately she is not there but, finding James Cran alone I take the opportunity of bringing him up to date with what's going on regarding CCO and the Shropshire CCAs. James says that he will speak to Eleanor on my behalf and seeks my permission to use the information that I have given him at a Whips meeting tomorrow. He says that he has previously spoken to Michael Ancram following our brief discussion on 22nd March. I tell James that Ancram had best get his tanks off my lawn, or else! Later that evening I try to talk to Eleanor but it is obvious that she has dined too well to pay the slightest attention to what I am trying to tell her and so I have to content myself with telling her that I shall in future only be voting when it suits me.

In the meantime I have taken Richard Shepherd as my guest to the April Court and Livery Luncheon at Butchers Hall where I take him into my confidence regarding the sinister developments in Shropshire. Richard instantly recognises the danger to other Associations and urges me to raise the matter at the '22. I tell Richard that I am just biding my time. Just as we are about to leave Butchers Hall I espy my fellow Liveryman and Conservative Party Board Member, Raymond Mombiot. We are soon into an acrimonious exchange during the course of which he says, inter alia, that it's time I made up my mind as to whose side I am on because I am perceived to be 'not on ours'! I retaliate by telling him that if he prefers to believe what others are telling him and to ignore my voting record that's his problem. Furthermore, having worked for the Party, man and boy, for 50 years, I cannot believe what is now happening – it is unprincipled and truly despicable. As a result of what Mombiot says during this heated exchange I now realise that the real motive for the proposed amalgamation of constituency Associations in Shropshire is to settle old scores. The fact that

Mombiot is, or was, President of Michael Heseltine's constituency Association is a fair indication of where his sympathies lie – not on the side of the independent nation state, that's for sure! Thankfully I am not entirely without friends as the Master Elect, John Jackaman, who has overheard the altercation with Mombiot, tells me that he agrees with me!

When, on 12th April, I warn Archie Hamilton that I intend to raise the matter of the proposed constituency amalgamations in Shropshire at the '22 he infers that the LCCA is no longer in the frame. I have to tell Archie that that's news to me but then again we'll probably be the last to know! James Cran assures me that he has had a word with the Party Chairman and been told that Ancram has written to me, in response to which I feel constrained to say that, given Ancram's track record, I'll believe that when I see it.

At the '22 meeting, colleagues are scarcely able to credit what I am telling them and only Bill Cash, whom I had briefed beforehand, speaks up in my support. In conclusion Chairman Archie says that he will report the feelings of the meeting to the Board! Precious little good that will do for it is precisely the Board itself that is the architect of this whole sorry business.

After the meeting several colleagues are wanting to discuss the matter further. Michael Spicer suggests writing to the '22 Executive; Bill Cash suggests getting others to co-sign the letter and Richard Shepherd is adamant that the matter must be pursued to a conclusion.

The following day Laurence Robertson (Tewkesbury) pours his heart out to me in Members Lobby regarding the total ineffectiveness of our Frontbench and the total lack of any discernible policy, not least on Europe. John Randall (Uxbridge) joins in and in spite of being a Whip can't wait to tell me that he cannot credit the way in which Party policy is made and is appalled that so many colleagues see the whole thing as a game. I tell John that in New Zealand, according to my dinner guest last evening, the Party caucus simply would not allow this to happen.

At the St Stephen's entrance to the Palace of Westminster I am accosted by Tony Baldry (Banbury) who wants me to tell him more about the Shropshire grouping project. Like so many others he thinks that the whole idea is crazy.

Whilst working in the library on Friday 14th pending the vote on Ann Winterton's anti-euthanasia Bill, Charles Wardle (Bexhill & Battle) approaches me to ask whether I am angry with him for agreeing to take a job with Mohammed Fayed. These are personal decisions I tell him, to which he replies that he may be stubborn but what he is not is dishonest or corrupt. Having been subjected to a torrent of propaganda from both sides of the Tiny Rowland v Fayed battle concerning their business rivalry I think that it would have probably been rash of any MP to get involved with either one of them.

On Sunday 16th I am obliged to spend all day putting together backing papers to accompany a letter to all members of the '22 Executive concerning the CCA in the adjoining constituency of the Wrekin. That afternoon their Chairman, Peter Forgham, comes to my home to hand me a schedule of the events that have occurred since 'supported status' was imposed upon the Wrekin CCA in March last year. Back in the House on Monday I have to explain to Gillian Shephard (Norfolk South West) that her letter suggesting twinning the Ludlow Association with the Wrekin Association comes at an odd time when CCO are hell-bent on sacking the Wrekin officers two weeks before the local elections.

John Redwood suggests I should talk to Ancram who has told him that everything has been amicably resolved! The letter I receive from Ancram today is dated 12th April – the same day as the last '22 meeting – and says that the ballot of Ludlow members (on amalgamation of Shropshire constituencies) is postponed until after the next General Election! As well as suggesting to '22 Executive committee member Gerald Howarth (Aldershot) that a reasonable question to ask '22 Chairman, Archie Hamilton – our representative on the Party Board - would be what part he has played in the decision to sack the Wrekin officers I also ask Whitto if his boss knows about these sackings. Whitto is slightly evasive and seems relieved when I volunteer to send him all the relevant paperwork.

A disproportionate amount of Tuesday 18th is taken up collating the papers to go to the 18 members of the '22 Executive and a dozen others, on the Wrekin question. In the House, Ray Whitney (Wycombe), seeing Bill Cash and I together, says that he is always suspicious when we two are seen working together and so I appeal him to try and look at this particular issue impartially. Bill says that he thinks that the Wrekin officers have a case in law (about being arbitrarily sacked) but on 19th April Peter Forgham tells me that he has no interest in pursuing that course of action. More importantly he gives me an assurance that he will not cave in to the ultimatum to sign a CCO declaration by noon that day. It is certainly a talking point amongst colleagues and hopefully the air will be cleared at the meeting of the '22 Committee later in the day. In the meantime David Wilshire (Spelthorne) has raised the interesting question as to who would elect new Association officers – if it is to be the Association members then surely they will want to elect the same ones they voted for only last month.

During the course of the day I tackle Archie Hamilton about his role in the Wrekin affair but all that he will say is that 'it's a Board decision'! My apprehension about this evening's meeting of the '22 increases when Bill Cash, Eric Forth and Julian Lewis all tell me that they are not going to be there. My apprehension increases further still when I encounter, standing outside Committee Room 14 waiting for the Executive meeting to conclude, a whole phalanx of 'wets'. As things turn out my worst fears are not realised. Before the meeting gets underway it is apparent from what Gerald Howarth is able to tell me that we have won. Only one colleague, Desmond Swayne, speaks in my support and tells the meeting that when he was working as a schoolmaster in Shropshire he knew Peter Forgham when Peter was previously Constituency Chairman and that 'a more conformist, less rebellious man you've yet to meet'. Archie Hamilton then reports that the Executive have considered the matter and that he will be reporting their views to the Chief Whip and the Party Chairman. After the meeting Laurence Robertson gives me the lowdown on the Executive meeting and says that everybody was on my side barring only the Chairman!

Easter intervenes before the next meeting of the '22 at which I ask the Chairman if he will make a situation report on the Wrekin affair. All that Archie will say is that he will raise the matter at the next meeting of the Party Board but Gerald Howarth tells me privately that Archie has informed the '22 Executive that there will be no more enforced groupings of constituency Associations. This confirms what James Cran had told me yesterday when he said 'you WON'! Richard Shepherd thinks that I should have sent details of the Wrekin fiasco to all colleagues - it really seems to have got home to at least some of my colleagues that the new Party rules are seriously bad news.

On 2nd May I have Question 4 on the Order Paper for Prime Minister's Question Time. My question: "Doubtless, the Chancellor of the Exchequer will have told the Prime Minister that more than half the Bank of England's gold and currency reserves are now held in euros. Will the Prime Minister take this opportunity of telling the House by how much the value of the nation's reserves have slumped since the decision was taken to sell off the nation's gold? On gold is he aware that Germany has increased its holdings of gold threefold, from £10 billion 12 months ago to more than £30 billion today?" The PM's answer, described in a message from a member of the public as 'the worst answer I have heard yet', is: "I cannot work out the precise point that the hon. Gentleman is making, but I am sure that it is against Europe; of that we can be sure. The Bank of England has a diverse range of assets, as do other countries. Some countries have sold gold; some countries have not. I am entirely content with the way in which the Bank of England has handled the matter. I suggest to Conservative Members that they get a new obsession, as that one is wearing rather thin." Perhaps he should have a word with his Minister for European Affairs, Keith Vaz, who, that very same day, tells me that 'the more he has to deal with Europe the more eurosceptic he is becoming'!

May 4th is Polling Day for local authorities and also in the Romsey constituency where there is a need to elect a new MP to replace Michael Colvin who has sadly been killed, together with his wife Nicola, in a fire at their home. I am personally feeling slightly fraudulent at not being involved in any electioneering simply because I am finding it so hard to whip up any enthusiasm in the wake of Peter Forgham's sacking. Potential Conservative voters in Romsey are apparently feeling equally disillusioned because the seat goes to the Liberal Democrats who overturn a Conservative majority of 8585 in an election in which the Labour Party actually lose their deposit.

Walking home at night on Monday 8th May, Michael Spicer tells me how, in conversation with himself and Archie Hamilton, John Major had told them that the thing that really matters to him is the Constitution! He apparently went on to complain about being hauled up in front of the 'Standards & Privileges Committee' regarding his earnings as an outside speaker and as a writer. He admits to having made a few mistakes as PM but, as the one responsible for establishing the wretched committee in the first place, it looks like this is a case of the biter bit.

In the morning the constitutional lawyer Martin Howe addresses a breakfast meeting of the ERG. He tells me that European law overrides Magna Carta, the Declaration of Rights 1688 and the Bill of Rights 1689.

Eric Forth surprises me by seeming to go along with the idea that we have to be careful about what we say on the European issue for fear of splitting the Party. This, to my mind, seems like a sure-fire way of not only ensuring that we lose the next General Election but also of perpetuating the differences of opinion in the Party for ever more.

It's either feast or famine in this job – after breakfasting with the ERG my next engagement is to entertain Roger Helmer MEP to lunch in the Strangers Dining Room. Roger and his MEP colleagues are going to see Francis Maude this afternoon and I urge him not to give Francis any quarter. Although he appears to be instinctively a Party loyalist, Roger is nevertheless determined to go on putting forward his own views and seems interested when I say how certain events have caused me to think that the Party is not so eurosceptic as we might have thought and that it will therefore take longer than we would like to reach our eventual goal.

Next day I stand John Redwood a lunch at Rules where he tells me that the Party is still as divided as ever with both Portillo and Maude briefing against the Leader. He stresses that the difference between them and us is that we do what we do out of conviction whereas they are driven by personal ambition. He agrees that if the Nice Inter Governmental Conference (IGC) goes ahead the game will be up – the eurosceptic sandcastle on the flooding beach will be washed away by the incoming EU tide. He shows no sign of bitterness or ill-will towards Wm. Hague for sacking him. On the contrary, John seems to be determined to give Hague his total loyalty which, were it not for the events of the past few months regarding the grouping of Shropshire constituencies, I would have no trouble doing myself.

Later that day Mike Penning tells me that Shadow Trade & Industry Secretary, Angela Browning, is spitting feathers about CCO telling my secretary, Vicki Stevens, that they didn't want me at the launch of Angela's pro-business/anti-bureaucracy campaign – a fact subsequently confirmed to me by Angela herself. One can only imagine how appallingly awful it would have been if the launch had been attended by one of the very, very few MPs to have actually run a business, especially a successful one!

In one other respect I am also one of a dying breed in the House of Commons. Whereas in the not too distant past quite the best attended of all Conservative backbench committees would have been the Agriculture Committee there are now only a handful of MPs with practical farming experience. In advance of the debate on the CAP on 11th May I determine to put both the Government and the Opposition frontbenches on the spot but, needless to say, so committed are they to European Union, that they cannot possibly bring themselves to agree with what I have to say. Subsequently, when I ask John Randall, the Whip on duty during the debate, if there had been any reaction to my contribution he simply says that my remarks have been noted, which is tantamount to saying that, as far as our own frontbench team is concerned, 'our mind is made up, don't confuse us with the facts'! John then tells me that what the Party really fears is that I will jump ship – although he doesn't say it, I presume that he means to the UK Independence Party. I tell him that they need have no fear of me crossing the floor – nor is there because one thing that I am not, is a socialist.

A line is finally drawn under the saga of Association amalgamations when, on 15th May, Michael Wood telephones to say that he's heard that Chris Poole, Secretary to the Party Board, has advised the Board to drop plans for Association groupings because of the "fiasco in Shropshire"!

A couple of days later James Cran asks me if we can meet at 16.20, but won't say why. When we do meet it is to discuss the rumours that I am about to jump ship. I assure James that I am not but, upon reflection, I feel bound to tell him later in the evening that whilst that is the current position I can give him no guarantees regarding the future. James says that I am entitled to feel very angry about these rumours but I tell him that I'm really unconcerned and won't be doing anything to discourage them – not least because privately I'm inclined to think that they may even have been deliberately started by the Whips themselves! Whilst talking to James I take the opportunity of taking him all round the track in the hope that he will make sure that the 'top brass' are made aware of the causes of my continuing dissatisfaction with the Party's stance on Europe. I tell James that the rumours may of course emanate from those who a) failed in their efforts to get me deselected, b) failed to annihilate me when they chucked me out of the Parliamentary Party and c) failed yet again when, most recently, they tried to effectively destroy my constituency Association. For the avoidance of doubt, the very next day, I make it a priority to confirm the salient points of our conversation in a letter to James.

Fast forward to June when on 5th I make my way to the BBC studios at Millbank expecting to record an interview for tomorrow's 'Farming Today' programme. When I get there it is quite apparent that the producer has absolutely no intention whatsoever of having me on the programme and I am told that they have been trying to reach me all day to cancel me. There are no messages at my office, nor my home, although I do subsequently find one timed 14.52 when I get back to the House. The BBC know full well that I have initiated a debate on the plight of rural abattoirs but they neither trail the debate on 6th June nor report it on the 7th. On the 6th the 'Farming Today' programme concentrates on GM crops and on the 7th it features the usual crop of minority interests! My debate is not entirely ignored by the Press but it is more than apparent that as far as the Beeb is concerned my views are generally unacceptable, opposed as they are to their own agenda in which the European Union and all its works is a perceived good that can do no wrong.

The backbench Foreign & European Affairs Committee meets on 7th June, on the eve of Francis Maude delivering a speech in Berlin on the 50th anniversary of the Schumann Plan. When I ask whether or not he will use the word 'repatriate' in respect of Agriculture and Fisheries he says 'No'. When I remonstrate with him about the futility of using language that the electorate will not understand he is equally undeterred. Going on to explain that voters don't trust the Conservative Party on the European question; that they are getting fed-up with the issue dragging on and that other Parties will have a much more intelligible message, e.g. 'Better Off Out', makes not the slightest difference to Maude's intransigence. At this late stage it seems that nothing will make any difference and it is obvious that this meeting is no more than 'going through the motions', as evidenced by Maude's early departure from the meeting, ostensibly to attend Shadow Cabinet.

The following Monday I drop Paul Sykes a line to say that, in the light of Maude's Berlin speech, we need to talk urgently. Doubtless influenced by the Berlin speech Paul will, within the next few days, announce his backing for his fellow Yorkshireman, Wm. Hague. Later in the day a rather chastened Andrew Lansley, Shadow Minister for Cabinet Office & Policy Renewal, leaves my office after I have let him have it regarding our European Policy. I resist the temptation to tell him what I hope to say in Thursday's debate on the European Union but put him on the spot by asking how the Party is going to deliver on its publicised aspirations regarding the Common Fisheries policy; lifting the burden of bureaucracy etc. etc.

I intend that my contribution to the debate on the European Union will be a 'no holds barred' commentary on Francis Maude's Berlin speech and I spend a considerable amount of time preparing to say things that he won't much like. It is therefore perhaps providential that when Thursday comes, notwithstanding that I am in the Chamber for the whole duration of the debate, I am not successful in 'catching the Speaker's eye'.

On 20th June I am in Peterhead, one of the biggest, if not the biggest fishing port in the UK. There the Chairman of the 'Save Britain's Fish' campaign, Tom Hay, has laid it all on for me – a report of my visit in the 'Aberdeen Press & Journal'; all the local fisheries movers and shakers on parade, together with a Press photographer, at the Fish Market at 07.30; a meeting with the Chairman of the Peterhead Harbour Commissioners, George Forman, in their offices; followed by a Press Conference in the Seamen's Mission attended by a goodly number of Fishing skippers. I later learn that one Jimmy McGregor, Conservative Fisheries spokesman in the Scottish Parliament, had, in high dudgeon, tried to contact Malcolm Moss about my impending visit and what I might have to say in Peterhead!

At a meeting of the British Weights and Measures Association – motto, 'Feet and Inches are Miles Better' – on 22nd June, Lord (Peter) Shore throws caution to the winds and speaks with passion about, in essence, getting out of the EU, which course of action will, I believe, only be accomplished with the help of pressure from the UK Independence Party whose Leader is also in attendance. As far as I can recall this is my first encounter with the charismatic Nigel Farage MEP whose presence on the political scene will undoubtedly become more and more prominent as time goes by.

Not untypical of the reaction that mention of European Union provokes is that of Ludlow CCA Chairman, Justin Caldwell. When on 23rd June at his Linley Hall home I try to engage him in discussion of the big issue he is not much interested. He thinks that whilst we remain in opposition our policy on Europe is purely academic. In response to this entirely unsatisfactory reaction I leave Justin with a copy of Maude's Berlin speech but don't feel that our dialogue has progressed sufficiently far for me to give him a copy of the speech that I would have made in the debate last week had I been called.

In another constituency, far away in Yorkshire, the Chairman of the Ryedale CCA is 'Save Britain's Fish' champion, John Ashworth. John telephones me on 27th to say that he has just been told by Party Board member John Taylor that if he sends any more letters to his opposite numbers in other CCAs he will be thrown out of the Party! John makes the point that he is not objecting to the Party's policies but simply to its refusal to tell the truth. In reply to this Taylor says 'are you accusing members of the Shadow Cabinet of telling lies?' to which John says 'Yes'. Knowing that moves are afoot to ditch the Party's 'Torch of Freedom' emblem I can only speculate as to whether the first casualty of this change will be Freedom of Speech!

That afternoon a meeting has been arranged in Room J by Bill Cash. This is in response to a request from European Commissioner Frits Bolkestein who has expressed a wish to meet eurosceptic Conservative MPs. Amongst those attending is the Member for Woking, Humfrey Malins, who says that quite apart from being an MP he is also a judge and he would like the commissioner to say something about 'corpus juris'. 'Ah' says Bolkestein 'what you have to understand is that throughout the European Union the people are saying that the law must be brought back under democratic control'! Upon hearing this, former Home Secretary Michael Howard, positively explodes, telling the Commissioner that in Britain the law is made here, in this very building, by the Members democratically elected to Parliament by universal suffrage and that if the people don't like the laws that are being made in their name then they boot those MPs out at the next General Election and vote another lot in. To this, Bolkestein's response is to the effect that 'maybe in England it is different but I can assure you that in the rest of Europe the people are saying that the law must be brought back under democratic control'.

Incensed by what I have just heard I am only too happy to agree to being interviewed for the 'Today' programme by BBC reporter Robin Crystal who waylays me as I am leaving the Palace on my way to my next appointment. How Crystal knew that I had been at the meeting with Bolkestein I shall never know but when he asks me what the Commissioner has said I answer by saying that 'he has said enough to convince me that we have to get out of the EU'. 'Oh' says Crystal 'why do you say that'? 'Because', says I, 'it is obvious that this particular Commissioner and perhaps the whole Commission are living in an ivory tower if they are so ignorant of the way in which the British democratic system works'. 'Is that the only reason'? says

Crystal. 'Far from it ' says I. 'Well what other reasons do you have for saying that we should leave the EU'? says Crystal. 'Well there's the Common Fisheries policy, the Common Agriculture Policy, all the mindless regulation, not to mention the cost. How many more reasons do you want'?

As far as I am aware this is the first time that any Member of Parliament has unequivocally and publicly stated that we should get out of the EU. So concerned am I that this is a potential bombshell that on Julian Lewis' advice I 'phone CCO to warn them that this is what I have done. One half of me is willing the BBC to use my interview, the other half worrying that it will queer the pitch for my scheduled meeting with Francis Maude the following day. At the ERG dinner that evening, but in another context, Wm. Hague says that if individual colleagues want to express different views then that's up to them. Has he already heard what I've been up to?

In the event I need hardly have worried because on the 'Today' programme the following morning, of my interview there is not a mention! The sequel to this particular anecdote occurs when, on the 28th September, the same Robin Crystal telephones me to see if I would be willing to do an interview with him on the subject of what I intend to say at the Conservative Party Conference where I am scheduled to address a fringe meeting organised by the Freedom Association. Immediately smelling a rat, that the BBC would use any such interview as a pre-conference spoiling exercise, I tell him that if he wants to know what I am going to say in Bournemouth then he'd best come to the Hilton Stakis Hotel at 12.45 next Tuesday and hear it for himself.

Come the 3rd October and there, to my great surprise, sitting on the front row of the Freedom Association meeting at the Hilton Hotel, is the said Robin Crystal! When he sees where I am going to sit on the podium he deliberately jumps up and places a microphone right in front of me. The chairman of the meeting, Norris McWhirter, thinking that the microphone is being provided courtesy of the hotel, moves it so that it is in front of him for when he comes to open the meeting. At that, Robin Crystal jumps up again and deliberately replaces the microphone back in front of me. The time comes for me to give the audience the benefit of my views on the EU at the end of which I recount the story of the events of 27th June, as already narrated, but with the added embellishment that such is the bias of the pro-Brussels Broadcasting Corporation that they did not use my interview on that occasion for fear that a call to get out of Europe would strike a popular chord with the British people. All of this, as they say in the business, goes into the can – again – and so next morning I am awake early to listen to how the 'Today' programme reports my second recorded call to quit the EU. What I hear is not a mention of my clarion call to quit the EU but an interview with the Europhile German Ambassador to the Court of St James, Herr Ploetz!

But that is not the end of this tarrydiddle. Months later the 'Today' programme will once again seek my views on European Union and I will oblige by giving them my views in no uncertain manner. The reaction from the interviewer is 'my, Mr Gill, that was powerful'! There are no prizes for guessing what that means. Yet again, I have wasted my time giving the BBC an interview that they will never use. Such is their political bias that there are no depths to which they will not sink in order to ensure that their listeners and viewers are deliberately denied the knowledge that not every Parliamentarian believes that we should remain in the benighted EU.

My meeting with Francis Maude, scheduled for 18.40 on 28th June, does not take place because he is detained in Shadow Cabinet. I am not best pleased by this turn of events and the following morning instruct my secretary, Vicki, to get me an appointment to see either Maude or the Chief Whip before the day is out. At the ensuing meeting with the Chief that afternoon his main interest is in whether or not I am intending to defect to the UK Independence Party. In response I tell James that should the Conservative Party straitjacket prove too uncomfortable then my likeliest course of action would be to become an Independent. I tell him that the main problem is that the Party is not being honest with the electorate and, more to the point, simply isn't trusted. To illustrate the point I show James a recent opinion poll showing Wm. Hague's trust rating on European Union at a minus. Furthermore there is nothing in Maude's Berlin speech to convince me that the Party will not renege, just as John Major has done in a recent newspaper article. James says that he anticipates that there will be a few who will not be able to sign up to the Party's election manifesto including, he says, myself and Ken Clarke! I stress that I am anxious to make my own position clear before the manifesto ballot of Party members in September. I also explain that it is totally dishonest to hold out the prospect of taking back control of fisheries waters by negotiation when, as we all know, this would simply be thwarted by a Spanish veto. Maude's speech is, I say, defective in that it fails to spell out exactly how we could possibly get powers back from the EU.

My meeting with Maude is re-scheduled for 6th July but in the meantime he chairs a meeting of the backbench Foreign & European Affairs Committee addressed by Sir Oliver Wright. Sir Oliver is a former ambassador to Bonn and Washington and in spite of his being a self-confessed Europhile I find myself in total agreement with all that he has to say, including his opinion that there isn't room for three in the marriage between France and Germany. (I shall have cause to remember this observation when, later in the month, at an International Butchery Skills dinner, the French President of the International Butchers Confederation accidentally sweeps my spectacles off the dinner table and the German Secretary General accidentally puts his foot on them!) After the meeting ends I look out for Francis Maude with a view to preparing the ground for our meeting next Thursday but I suspect he has made a quick getaway in order to celebrate his 47th birthday. What an irony that Francis Maude was born on Independence Day!

Come the 6th July and my meeting with Maude is disappointing in the extreme. He refuses to give me a copper-bottomed guarantee that Fisheries will be returned to national control, neither will he say how we will achieve the aspirations set out in his Berlin Speech. I tell him that I don't trust the Party on the European issue and explain that given my own personal experiences and the Party's track record there really is no reason to do so. Maude is a hard man to pin down as he wastes so much time giving long waffly responses to every point I make. I am obliged to remind him that only last Tuesday Sir Oliver Wright had told us to make up our minds as to where we wanted to be and then to spell it out with clarity. On balance I fear that there is a determination not to do anything to unsettle the existing treaties and no real commitment to recover lost powers. When I say that he is expecting me to take a lot on trust, he agrees! The question is, will I?

After my meeting with Maude I have a long chat with James Cran who expresses the opinion that I will just have to go on doing more of the same i.e. remonstrating with our senior colleagues. Personally I feel that I have done quite enough of this already and so the question as far as I am concerned is do I now start saying 'get out of the EU' from within the Party or as an Independent.

Prior to going to Buckingham Palace on 10th July, to attend a reception given by the Queen for Members of Parliament, I spend a moment considering which necktie I should wear that is most likely to attract the attention of the Duke of Edinburgh. My choice of the Peterhead Harbour Commissioners distinctive and colourful tie works perfectly. On the receiving line the Duke asks me about it and in reply I tell him that the tie was given to me by the PHC in appreciation of all the work that I have been doing in Parliament in support of the 'Save Britain's Fish' campaign. Later I speak to one of HM's Ladies-in-Waiting asking how I should go about obtaining a private audience with the Royals to pursue the matter. In reply she says that my best chance is to waylay the Duke here and now which is precisely what I do. "Sir", I say, "you asked me about my tie" and then launch into my spiel about the iniquities of the CFP to which he says that the man to talk to about the CFP is John Gummer! "No Sir", says I, "John Gummer and I are like oil and water on this issue" to which the Duke retorts 'he's doing more about it than you are'. When I respond by saying that the fishermen are throwing back dead into the sea more fish than they land the Duke turns 180 degrees on his heels and stalks off, muttering under his breath how appalling the CAP and the CFP are! I am hard pressed to recall such a demonstration of bad manners to equal this, other than perhaps Ken Clarke at Eastbourne, but clearly the Duke didn't want to hear what I had to say. The really troubling aspect of this encounter is that it demonstrates that the Royals, if the Duke is anything to go by, are getting their information from extremely partisan quarters. The even greater concern is to know how to correct that unfortunate and potentially dangerous situation.

Next day I chat to our Fisheries spokesman, Malcolm Moss, about the state of play vis-a-vis the EU and Fisheries. During the course of our conversation Malcolm says that the 'top brass' know that they are in difficulty on this issue – little wonder given the impossible task of having to defend the indefensible!

That same day former Shadow Foreign Secretary John Maples introduces a 10 Minute Rule Bill for the holding of a referendum on the Single Currency. Dennis Skinner, the 'Beast of Bolsover', heckles him unmercifully with taunts about hypocrisy and saying, pointing in my direction, 'there's people behind you who've stuck to their guns – not like you'! Desmond

Swayne is more charitable and says, with reference to Maples, there's more joy in heaven over one sinner that repenteth etc.

The following day the Speaker, Betty Boothroyd, announces her retirement with effect from the end of the Summer recess. Known candidates to replace her are Menzies Campbell (Fife North East), Patrick Cormack (Staffordshire South), Gwyneth Dunwoody (Crewe & Nantwich), Nicholas Winterton (Macclesfield) and two of the current Deputy Speakers, Alan Haselhurst (Saffron Walden) and Michael Lord (Suffolk Central & Ipswich North). Dennis Skinner, still in high dudgeon about the sheer hypocrisy of John Maples and 'what the likes of him did to you and others', says that he could more easily vote for George Young (Hampshire NW) to become Speaker than 'Ming' Campbell. He is at pains to point out that, because, in his opinion, the procedure for the election of Speaker means that not all of the candidates get a proper look-in, some care needs to be taken to get the right candidates up to the mark.

Examples of how the Conservative Party is continuing to get itself into a tangle over Europe are provided by, first of all, Laurence Robertson (Tewkesbury) telling a meeting of the Freedom Association at Stanway Hall that we must not talk about getting out of the EU for fear of handing Labour a stick to beat us with and also that UKkippers must be made to realise that their only hope is with the Conservatives. This is the day after the Chief Whip has said that he would rather that Richard Shepherd and I didn't go to Hereford to accept a 'Keep the Pound' petition. When I ask why, James says that it is because our PPC, Virginia Taylor, doesn't want us there. Odd, that, because I was under the impression that Richard and I were doing this to help Virginia Taylor!

A few days later all will become clear because it then transpires that the real reason for Richard and I being warned off is because the Chairman of the local 'Keep the Pound' campaign in Hereford, one Captain Easton, has apparently announced that he is to be a UKIP candidate at the next General Election!

At an ERG breakfast on 18th July some very forthright views are expressed and there appears to be a general concensus that the Party's position on Europe needs to be spelt out with much greater clarity/honesty. My proffered opinion is that nothing less than that will be successful in terms of lessening the threat from UKIP. Malcolm Pearson brings to the meeting a hand-written letter from Francis Maude in which he says that he cannot find any evidence that the acquis communautaire cannot be unpicked! The real question is whether he is saying this out of ignorance (implausible!) or simply because that is the last thing he wants to happen, thus confirming my impression that he will do absolutely nothing that risks unsettling the existing treaties.

On 25th July Michael Portillo addresses an end of session '92 Group dinner but fails to impress. Questioned by Owen Paterson as to what plan B is if the other EU nations do not agree to our demands, he waffles. Notwithstanding Portillo's less than satisfactory response Owen subsequently says that it was a better answer than he got from either Hague or Maude! Later I speculate as to whether Portillo is distracted by the prospect of the vote on Section 28 which is scheduled for later that evening. Either way MP is not the MP we used to know but, as former Member Jim Pawsey says, he is probably having to be super careful so as not to encourage press speculation about bidding for the Party leadership. At the dinner I hand Wm. Hague and Anne Widdecombe copies of my letter of 18th July addressed to home Office Minister, Charles Clarke, regarding Corpus Juris. (Corpus Juris is the mooted EU criminal justice system which differs from the British system in several important aspects, the most significant of which is that there is nothing in it that equates to or replicates our own law of Habeas Corpus.) I suggest that they might use the questions posed in that letter to put the Government on the spot but since the prospect of having an entirely alien criminal justice system imposed upon us by the EU goes to the very heart of the European question I doubt very much that they will ever do so.

On 26th July Wm. Hague delivers a very adequate 'end of term' speech to the '22 Committee during the course of which he says, inter alia, that he is glad that we've put our European differences aside and are all now working together as an effective opposition! Such optimism hardly seems justified when I speak to Andrew Lansley on the 27th July. Talking about Europe and the Party's pre-manifesto document I tell him that it has to be honest and credible if we are to win the next election. From his response it is obvious that he is personally very committed to the Treaties and will not countenance any thought of leaving the EU.

2000

3

" The BBC refuses to run my 'get out of the EU' call "

As we break for the long Summer recess there is good news and bad. The good news is that Richard Shepherd is letting his name go forward for Speaker and that two other sound Conservatives in the shape of Graham Brady and Owen Paterson have been promoted to the Whips Office. The rather less inspired appointment is that of former Epping Forest MP Steve Norris as Party Vice Chairman. That this is almost bound to cause trouble is subsequently evidenced by Norris publicly laying into fellow Conservative, Gerald Howarth, on the 'Today' programme at the time of the Party Conference in October.

In Bournemouth for that Conference I am amazed to see so many delegates wearing the £ sign on their lapels, notwithstanding that this symbol is becoming increasingly to be associated with the United Kingdom Independence Party. What a turnaround there has been these past few years – no longer are people shy about demonstrating their opposition to the Single Currency, quite the opposite! That this is the case is more than adequately demonstrated in the Ludlow constituency where, on 22nd September, the LCCA meets to discuss the pre-Manifesto document 'Believing in Britain' and spontaneously passes a resolution by approximately 50 votes to 8 saying never to the Euro.

A sad encounter in Bournemouth is with Bob Spink, the former Member for Castle Point. Bob tells me that in spite of being a 'eurosceptic' he obeyed the Whips' order to toe the Party line at the last election and as a consequence had a Referendum Party candidate put up against him who took 2700 votes. This intervention caused Bob to lose his seat to Labour by a margin of 1116, having previously enjoyed a majority of 16,830. Poor sap, if he'd stuck to his principles he'd have held his seat but now he's lost both!

On 23rd October it's 'back to school' to elect a new Speaker. Out of a field of thirteen, Parliament elects quite the least suitable candidate in the shape of Michael Martin, the Labour Member for Glasgow Springburn, henceforth known as 'Gorbals Mick'. Thanks to the Labour Party chucking overboard all the old conventions surrounding the election of a new Speaker there is no question of them voting for the best person for the job nor any regard for the customary practice of letting the office alternate between the two main political parties. Using their massive majority the Labour Members vote along partisan lines and Parliament is saddled with a Speaker who will undoubtedly struggle to uphold the dignity and reputation of that most senior political position in the land. Patrick Cormack will subsequently tell me that Labour Members made a lot of money as a result of placing bets on the outcome of the election of Speaker.

During the course of our first day back I first of all suggest to our new Shadow Chief Secretary to the Treasury, Oliver Letwin, that in order to seize the initiative from Labour on the question of taxation we should state what we regard to be reasonable levels of tax across the board and tell the electorate that we would then cut our cloth according to those means. In other words we would, in Government, act like the people we represent and tailor expenditure to match income rather than tot up all the expenditure bids from every government department and then send the taxpayer the resultant bill. For someone of Oliver's great intellect this idea probably suffers from the fatal defect of being too simple by half!

Next in my sights is Wm.Hague. I ask him whether, in the circumstances in which Tony Blair has shot our fox on the Euro by saying that if a referendum on the Single Currency were to be held now he would vote 'NO' and in the light of the fact that France and Germany are determined to form a hard-core (an avant garde), this does not give us cause and opportunity to revise our own policies. William's answer is 'NO' but that we would not stand in the way of 'enhanced cooperation'.

When I accost the Chief Whip to tell him what I think about the appointment of Steve Norris as Party Vice Chairman he says that he has received similar comments from other colleagues. One can only imagine what those other comments might have been!

Towards the end of a busy day Teresa Gorman seeks my advice as to whether or not she should accept Norris McWhirter's invitation to succeed him as chairman of the Freedom Association. As far as I am concerned this is a bit of a bombshell because I had been thinking that this might be a billet for me if I decide not to contest the next General Election. My answer to Teresa is therefore to the effect that if she does decide to accept Norris's invitation she can be sure of one thing and that is that she will have a rival!

My final conversation of the day is with Humfrey Malins whom I try to encourage to take a greater interest in Corpus Juris, it being my belief and understanding that the prospect of having this imposed upon us represents a far greater threat to our nation's wellbeing than any other of the EU's impositions, past, present or future.

The following day Shadow Defence Secretary Ian Duncan-Smith assures me that we are totally opposed to the 'European Single Sky' project. He refers me to Shadow Transport Secretary Bernard Jenkin who says that he will definitely attend European Standing Committee 'A' to oppose it in person whenever it comes up.

At the regular weekly meeting of the '22 Committee I draw colleagues attention to the fact that within the past six months the £ Sterling has depreciated against the US Dollar by more than 13% and would need to be devalued by a further 20% if we were to join the Euro. I go on to express the opinion that the Euro is not a collapsing currency but one that has already collapsed and that it behoves the Party's top brass to revise our policy on the Euro so as to avoid being made to look faintly ridiculous, as indeed we were again at PMQs this afternoon. What ensues is not argument or dissent but complete silence!

Journeying back to London from Chatham by rail on Friday 27th October a German passenger spots my £ sign lapel badge and tells me that we are quite right to want to keep our own currency – he would too, but nobody asked him! The 'political elite' are clearly in no doubt as to what the proverbial 'man in the street' thinks about the Euro but sure as hell they are not going to give him the opportunity to express his common sense views for fear of de-railing the whole ghastly project.

On Saturday John Redwood's PA, Nikki Page, tells me that her boss, with the blessing of Wm. Hague, is addressing marchers against the Single Currency and the Nice Treaty. I can't help wondering why the organisers of this demonstration, the Democracy Movement, are giving top billing to such Johnny come latelies. Nikki also tells me that the problem people in Shadow Cabinet are Maude and Portillo but how much of this is, I wonder, part of the JR comeback fight.

The said Francis Maude gets a rough ride at the hands of the 'eurosceptics' when, on 31st, he attends the backbench Foreign & European Affairs Committee. The 'europhiles', such as George Young, sniff the air and slink away rather than stand and fight their corner. As for myself, it's a question of no holds barred. I tell colleagues that the last straw in my case was the meeting with Commissioner Bolkestein on 27th June. I ask when the Party is going to come to its senses and realise that Conservative principles and aspirations can simply never be realised whilst we remain a member of the EU. I further instance how the effective devaluation of the £ Sterling against the US $ would be 33% if, hypothetically, we were to join the Single Currency today. In his response Francis Maude concedes that the CAP and the CFP are collectivist so perhaps I should be grateful for small mercies. I try to have the last word by pointing out that the 30m voters aren't much interested in semantics - they just want to know whether we are FOR or AGAINST this racket!

Later in the day I learn from Owen Paterson that Michael Portillo was given an equally rough ride at a 'No Turning Back' Group dinner last Thursday. In the Members Tea Room Peter Luff tells me that he was 'on the same staircase at Cambridge' as Owen and that his views have never changed. When he goes on to tell me that another of his university contemporaries was Francis Maude and that he, by contrast, had moved from being extremely pink to being right-wing, Peter observes that I look sceptical – in my opinion, with good cause!

On 4th November, the eighth anniversary of the Maastricht Treaty paving debate, after attending the AGM of the Shropshire Association of Town and Parish Councils in the Shirehall, I journey to my constituency Chairman's home near Bishops Castle to tell Justin Caldwell that I shall not be seeking re-election. I subsequently regret not driving away when after three long rings on the Linley Hall front doorbell there is no response. I then make the mistake of going in search of Justin who I eventually find in the stables with his horses. Later events will demonstrate that his elusiveness is almost certainly a studied insult to myself. When we eventually get down to business in his snug I tell him that, quite apart from my age, the real obstacle to me standing again is the Party's European policy which I regard as being completely bogus. I also tell Justin that I am tired of banging my head against a brick wall on agriculture matters on account of having absolutely no say or influence over these matters which are essentially decided in Brussels by those that we neither elect nor can hold to account. Justin tries to argue that it's all the fault of our own civil service for gold-plating the regulations but I see little point in prolonging the discussion with someone who is so obviously blinkered. The atmosphere is cool, not to say frosty, and the only concern that Justin expresses is that I might change my mind! He is also anxious to hear whether I know anybody in the constituency who would be interested in succeeding me and goes on to say that he can think of a few from outside who would – I'll bet he can!

The sequel to my meeting with Justin is a telephone call at 08.30 the following Tuesday morning from my old friend and former LCCA chairman, Michael Wood, who tells me what transpired yesterday morning when Justin Caldwell met Party activists Vanessa Lee and James Gibson. Justin says that as my replacement they need a Centre/Centre Left candidate, describing me as an extreme Right-winger. He says that he puts all correspondence from me straight into the WPB, saying that it is right-wing garbage! He has apparently taken it upon himself to convene a meeting comprising himself, Celia Motley, John Wheeler, Paul Kidson, Katherine Lumsden and Vanessa to decide how to go about selecting my replacement. He has also told James and Vanessa that he had lunch on Sunday with two UKippers who allegedly said that they had known for a long time that I was definitely not standing again – impossibly they must have known this even before I did myself!

The choice of invitees to tomorrow's LCCA meeting of what Justin says is a meeting of the Policy & Campaigning Committee is interesting – some who are members of the committee have not been invited and some who are not, have! At the actual meeting the view is expressed that what Ludlow needs is a local person with a mind of their own and one without Ministerial ambition! Can you believe it!

In the meantime, out of courtesy, and at the very earliest opportunity, which is Monday 6th November, I ask Wm. Hague's PPS, John Whittingdale whether it is usual for colleagues not seeking re-election to inform the Party Leader. Without a moment's hesitation Whitto says that he will arrange a meeting which, to his credit, takes place the very next day. At that meeting I tell William that my decision to retire is not solely because of age but also because I would find it difficult, if not impossible, to defend the Party's policy on Europe at the hustings. I tell him that his slogan of being 'In Europe but not run by Europe' is a contradiction in terms and intellectually incoherent. I go on to say that he's the boss and that it will be no good looking back in years to come and saying 'if only' – he's got to assert himself now, not seek unattainable consensus. I leave him with excerpts from last week's 'Fishing News' which describe Conservative Party policy as 'vague and impossible to achieve'. He asks me whose European policy I want – his or Blair's. In response to that I say that we aren't going to get his unless he takes a stronger line and, frankly, unless he does take a stronger line he'll be in the same position as John Major with a rump of 'europhiles' holding him to ransom. He assures me that he does take notice of what I tell him and I conclude by recounting the sequel to the Bolkestein story. I then invite him to consider why else the BBC refuses to run my 'get out of the EU' call unless it is because they recognise that it would be extremely popular. I remind William how for 28 consecutive months, in 1937 and 1938 and even after war had been declared in 1939, the BBC, which then of course had the monopoly of broadcasting, kept Winston Churchill consistently off the airwaves. I tell him that whilst I'm no Winston Churchill he, as I've told him before, has the potential to be one – it's up to him! My parting shot is to say to William that if I thought he was going to lead a crusade for our country's freedom and independence I would be prepared to do another four or five years porridge but as he is clearly is not, then I'm off. As this fails to provoke any sort of reaction I can only conclude that the bottom line is that William is quite reconciled to my leaving, even at the risk of the Party losing the Ludlow seat.

Back in the house it's business as usual. My question to FCO Minister Keith Vaz asking him if he will veto Article 280A of the Nice Treaty which seeks to establish an European Public Prosecutor is answered evasively but, as with all straight questions regarding the EU, there are seldom straight answers! Strangely enough, Michael Mates, not by any means a paid-up 'eurosceptic', has told me that we should oppose the Treaty of Nice in its entirety although, that being said, he is much less sound in his views on the European Security & Defence Initiative.

On 8th November there is a very satisfactory meeting of minds at a Freedom Association meeting which may translate into my being invited to take over the chairmanship from Norris McWhirter, with Teresa Gorman as my deputy. The following day Mike Fisher telephones to say that the Association Management Committee are thrilled at the prospect of my becoming Chairman, with Teresa as deputy. (A meeting with Teresa at her home in Lord North Street establishes that there are no differences between us regarding aims and objects but, as my perceptive secretary has previously remarked, 'Teresa will take any job as long as it is the top one'!) When I ask him if I can go public with this news he says best to wait until the appointment has been ratified by TFA Council. Barely five days later I wake up to hear the 'Today' programme announce that the Conservative Party is abandoning the 'Torch of Freedom' as its emblem. The news that the Tories are jettisoning Freedom confirms me in my opinion that now is an opportune time to be taking a very much more active role in the Freedom Association.

Later in the day I waylay Party Chairman Michael Ancram in the voting Lobby to tackle him about dumping the 'Torch of Freedom'. He says that it's not true and that the 'Daily Telegraph' has got it all wrong. He then says that he's sorry that I'm leaving but I guess that the truth is probably quite the opposite. Others to express regret at my decision are John Bercow, Patrick Cormack, Andrew Lansley, Julian Lewis, Patrick Nicholls, Archie Norman, Marion Roe and Teddy Taylor. Next day Michael Howard expresses similar sentiments saying that notwithstanding the differences of opinion that we have had in the past he is genuinely sorry to hear that I am leaving. In response to that I tell Michael that my decision is not entirely due to age but principally the difficulty of standing behind our current contradictory and intellectually incoherent European policy. He says that he doesn't agree that the policy is contradictory and incoherent but as a certain celebrity once said – 'he would say that, wouldn't he'!

In the Tea Room I venture the opinion that there are too many lawyers, too much law and not enough justice to which Humfrey Malins says "you are a man of good sense whom I would rather have than 12 lawyers"! Richard Shepherd opines that to be called a man of good sense is the highest accolade one could wish for. Joining in the conversation Peter Luff says that he is surprised at himself for having regrets at my decision to leave Parliament but that he has a sneaking regard for my independence, consistency and thoughtfulness, even though we have often disagreed.

At the backbench Foreign & European Affairs Committee former Foreign Office Minister Lord Chalfont says that he might be going too far in suggesting that there is a political motive behind the creation of the European Rapid Reaction Force. I say that for my money, far from going too far, he doesn't go far enough and that the sooner the Conservative Party recognises that affairs are being driven by a political ideology which is entirely alien to British conservatism the easier it will be for all concerned to understand what is really going on.

At the weekly Forward Look Committee meeting on Monday 20th November I insist upon having my say on the European issue. I point out that the recent spat between Foreign Secretary Robin Cook and Chancellor Gordon Brown is much more than a personal feud – what it is really indicative of is the ferocious battle between a pro-European Union FCO and a Treasury that is fighting a rearguard action against tax harmonisation. I ask whether our Foreign Affairs team have yet decided whether or not they regard the Nice Treaty as 'integrationist', only to get a lot of waffle about the single currency from Richard Spring (West Suffolk), who is deputising for his boss, Francis Maude. I had already pointed out that the effects of Article 7 (Member States voting rights), Article 191(suspension of political parties) and Article 93 (tax harmonisation) would be totally unacceptable but once again it proves impossible to provoke a proper debate about these matters.

At a backbench meeting with Francis Maude the following day I say that I cannot understand why the Party finds the subject of Europe so difficult – the EU is driven by a political ideology which is totally alien to British conservatism and has more in common with communism than conservatism. I express the opinion that if the various EU policies had been initiated in the Westminster Parliament by a Labour Government then we would almost certainly have opposed each and every one of them. Nicholas Soames (Mid

Sussex) asks whether I am saying that we should get out of the EU to which I respond by saying that that is the inevitable conclusion that I have come to. I then tell Maude that he has to use language that the 30m voters can understand and support. Maude says, quite correctly, that any of the changes we might pledge to make could only be made at the next Inter-Governmental Conference – so much for national sovereignty, but that appears not to be a matter of concern to our EU besotted leaders. I leave the meeting more confused about the Party's direction than when I went in!

Andrew Hunter (Basingstoke) expresses his regret that I am leaving but goes on to say that whilst he had considered doing likewise, at the age of 57 he can't afford to quit. Archie Hamilton has heard a rumour and wants to know whether it is true, that my son Charles is going to follow me into the House, a rumour that I have no intention of quashing.

At a meeting of the Midland Industrialists Council on 23rd November I tell Wm. Hague's Chief of Staff, Seb Coe, that Francis Maude really must go and that if John Redwood were to be put in his place that would be worth a million votes to us at the next General Election. In order to speak in the debate on European Affairs that afternoon I apologise to MIC Chairman Michael Brinton for having to leave the meeting early and in an aside to Wm. Hague who is sitting next to him say that 'I've told Seb what needs to be done'.

In a 15 minute speech in the House that afternoon I end by saying: "My loyalty has been strained to the limit. In all conscience I cannot go to the hustings as candidate for a party that maintains that one can be in Europe but not run by Europe. I have therefore announced that I shall not seek re-election. That is my decision; I hope that my right honourable and honourable Friends are happy with theirs. It is still not too late for my right honourable Friend the Member for Richmond to say that there will be no single currency whilste he remains leader of the Conservative party and that, under his premiership, control over agriculture and fisheries would be repatriated. That message would resonate with the people of this country; it is the very least that he must do to ensure that socialism is defeated at the next general election".

After the debate the rabidly europhile David Curry (Skipton & Ripon) makes the damning observation that nobody on our side actually agrees with the Party's EU policy - 'you don't, I don't, who does'?

The next day there is a brief mention of my speech in the 'Times' but nothing in the Torygraph. Nearer to home the 'Birmingham Post' describes it as a 'blistering' attack on Hague – in point of fact if it was a blistering attack on anybody it was a blistering attack on Maude!

At the Bury & District Industrial Society where I am the guest speaker on 24th November their Chairman, Derek Calrow, says that if only they had known what I was going to say in the House last evening the attendance would have been at least double. Try explaining that to the Party hierarchy!

On 28th November silence reigns when I challenge colleagues at a meeting of the backbench Foreign & European Affairs committee to name but one policy emanating from the EU that we would not have opposed on principle if it had instead been initiated by the Labour Party in the Westminster Parliament. Crispin Blunt (Reigate) says GATT (General Agreement on Tariffs & Trade) which is a bit wide of the mark, but that's it – there are no other bids! There appears, at last, to be a recognition that I may have a point when I say (again!) that the EU policies are Collectivist and that they are therefore more akin to Communism than Conservatism. In the chair, David, now Lord Howell, appears not to take exception to what I have to say but then again perhaps I shouldn't be too surprised at that because in my experience David has always been a bit of a mugwumper.

Aside from considerations of the EU for a moment, there is a meeting at the Carlton Club on 29th to decide whether to admit ladies to full membership. The main point to emerge from the meeting as far as I am concerned is that there are a substantial number of members who realise that they are getting swept up in the Party's drive to be 'inclusive' – this is code for 'feminism' and all the other PC 'isms' – and the point is well made that the Carlton Club, although a Conservative club, is not an extension of Conservative Central Office (CCO). An American member says that he has flown over from the States purposely to try to ensure that the Carlton doesn't suffer the same fate as his club back home. He says that after his Washington club admitted women the bar takings went down, meat went off the menu, salad nicoise went on and the club folded! In the event the motion to admit women as full members does not achieve the necessary majority and a further motion to conduct a postal ballot of members on the same issue is also defeated.

As November draws to a close there is mounting speculation regarding

Michael Portillo. When I broach this subject with the Chairman of the '22 Committee, expressing the opinion that MP ought to be fired, Archie is unusually forthcoming and tells me that he is on his way to see the Leader to tell him that he has got to be prepared to put the proverbial pistol to the head of anyone who isn't willing to play in the team and, if necessary, pull the trigger. 'There are too many people around here playing different games' says Archie. The following morning's 'Daily Telegraph' reports that Hague has said that, in reference to MP, "I am determined that he will be the next Chancellor", so what d'you know! I only know that when I visit my nonagenarian father at the weekend he is absolutely fizzing about the fact that MP has hardly been off his TV screen for days.

On 5th December, the day I go to Turkey with a Parliamentary delegation to tell them that 'if Allah is merciful you will not have to join the EU', the news is that Ian Taylor has survived the de-selection battle in his Esher constituency with, I hasten to add, the active support of prominent 'eurosceptics' such as Bill Cash, David Davis and Richard Shepherd! The Conservative Party is, as they say, a broad church – we even embrace those who support communist policies – but a house divided cannot stand and I am having no second thoughts about my decision to leave whilst I still have the health and strength to continue the battle from a different perspective.

In this regard I am delighted when, on 12th December, the Management Committee of the Freedom Association unanimously and enthusiastically votes me in as Hon. Chairman, subject only to the approval of the Council meeting in a fortnight's time. Teresa Gorman is voted in as Director and Norris McWhirter becomes our new Hon. President. The following day Teresa and I meet in the Millbank Room where between us we consume one solitary Christmas lunch – I eat the starter, she has the main course and we have two spoons to attack the Christmas pud! To gain publicity for our mooted TFA Press Conference in January Teresa suggests that we shall both have to resign the Party Whip – I don't demur but realise that if we do this we will have well and truly burnt our boats.

At a drinks party thrown by the Parliamentary Christian Wives on 12th December I bump into Party Chairman, Michael Ancram. On the question of Parliamentary candidates he says that no obstacles are put in the way of retreads (former MPs seeking new seats) and least of all in the way of local candidates, although on one or two occasions CCO have been able, he says, to reveal features about local candidates that were unknown to their respective constituencies. He thinks it quite reasonable to send messages in support of colleagues facing de-selection notwithstanding the fact that constituency Associations are supposed to be autonomous. When I change the subject to talk about the continued haemorrhage of conservative minded voters to the UK Independence Party he appears fairly indifferent and simply says that if it all goes badly for the Party then people like himself will pay the price – but what about the country I ask myself, what price is the country paying as a consequence of there not being a truly conservative party for people to vote for? I get the impression that there may be questions that Michael would like to ask me but suspect that he lacks the courage to do so.

I am cheered when on 13th Andy Stewart, the former Member for Sherwood, tells me that whereas he and others used to think that I was a bit off the beam regarding my views on agriculture policy 'we can now see that you were right'. Less encouraging is hearing Wm. Hague going out of his way at the '22 Committee to praise the speech that Francis Maude had made in Berlin in June. This I regard as a deliberate poke in the eye with an exceedingly sharp stick, once again demonstrating that the Conservative Party's infatuation with the EU is far from ended. More in hope than anger I fire off yet another letter to the Chief Whip, this time referring to the Leader's remarks to the '22 which I regard as being unfortunate to say the least.

I wake on Friday 15th December to hear the BBC News and the 'Today' programme reporting on EU fishing quotas for the forthcoming year. Just after 07.00 I remonstrate with the Duty Editor at 'Today' saying that the British public are entitled to hear the other side of the story which is that reduced quotas inevitably mean greater quantities of discards i.e. perfectly wholesome fresh fish being dumped back dead into the sea to rot on the seabed. As I might have guessed an undertaking to get back to me is totally ignored but knowing that he is scheduled to meet Mark Damazer, the Assistant Director at BBC News, that very morning, to complain about BBC bias, I relay this and other similar experiences to Lord Pearson.

Leaving politics aside for a while, on 18th I go to the 25th wedding anniversary of my old Shrewsbury School history master. There are several other Old Salopians at the party but as far as I know Michael Heseltine has not been invited – indeed it would be strange if he was, given 'Rusty' Wood's aversion to MH's virulent europhilia. Amongst the assembled company is another former Shrewsbury master, Laurence Le Quesne, whose opinion of me at school was that I was the sort of lad who would go off to South America and start a revolution – why go so far I ask myself, we need one right here!

The following day I hold a further meeting with Teresa who has thankfully gone off the idea of us resigning the Party Whip for the purpose of drawing attention to our new involvement with the Freedom Association. We agree that a better way forward is for us to get one of the popular newspapers on side. I undertake to talk to Trevor Kavanagh, the Political Editor at the 'Sun' and if all else fails Teresa will approach her friend Andrew Alexander at the 'Daily Mail'. In the meantime Teresa has told me the tale about Sir Peter Emery (Devon East) once offering to share his taxi with her 'if only you will give up your silly ideas on Europe'. Overhearing what Sir Peter has said the taxi driver promptly says 'and if she agrees to that you can both get out and walk'!

On 19th December it's home for Christmas to find a list of 143 names hopeful of succeeding me as the MP for quite the loveliest constituency in the realm. The catch, according to Woody, is that the Chairman and the two Vice Chairmen have been summoned to CCO – doubtless to be told what is expected of them in this increasingly Stalinist Party.

2001

1

" Going off to run the Freedom Association "

Notwithstanding the fact that I shall not be in Parliament for very much longer I am a driven man and therefore cannot help continuing to fight every inch of the way in my determination to get my colleagues pointing in the right direction in terms of our country's freedom and independence.

My meeting with Iain Duncan-Smith on 15th January does little to shed any light on why the Conservative Party is in the state it's in, although what transpires at a breakfast of the ERG the following morning is perhaps a useful indicator. At that breakfast it is mooted that we should engage the services of a researcher. David Heathcoat-Amory, speaking in favour of this proposition, says that we need, for example, much more information on the CFP which he describes as being 'extremely complicated'. I respond by saying that 'once you understand it, it really is quite simple'. David insists that we need much more information and as I move towards the door, to catch former fisheries spokesman Patrick Nicholls as he is leaving the room, say, 'oh if it's fishing we're talking about I'll put David straight'. David takes exception to that remark and after the breakfast tells me never to do that to him again in front of colleagues! Not unreasonably I tell him that having followed the fortunes of the fishing industry for six years or more I don't think that there are many questions that I cannot answer. I suggest that we might arrange to meet to discuss these matters but very much doubt that he will make any effort to pursue this suggestion. David's preferred option, like so many of my dithering colleagues, is to kick the issue into the long grass – give it to a researcher to investigate and just hope that the time for action will be forever postponed. Interestingly, David H-A is one of only three Shadow Cabinet members out of 21 who has not readily agreed to meet me on a one-to-one basis to listen to what I have previously described as my Aldridge agenda. With the rare exception of Ann Widdecombe and Michael Ancram all the others have not questioned a single word of what I have had to say to them, nor have any of them had anything to say for themselves when, in my peroration, I have tried to provoke them by saying 'I am a Conservative, why are you, as a fellow Conservative, supporting collectivist policies'?

My attention is now turning to what Teresa and I can do to rejuvenate the Freedom Association. One of TFA's longest-standing members, Gerald Howarth, collars me to express concerns. He is worried because something that Teresa has said to him indicates that we are intent upon turning the Association into a single issue pressure group. I assure Gerald that under my chairmanship TFA will remain broadly based and he appears to be somewhat mollified when I suggest that we convene a meeting of all MPs currently sitting on the Association's Council.

The following day, 17th January, I lunch with Trevor Kavanagh who is sympathetic to the cause but when I ask him how we go about getting the front page responds by saying that many people ask him that question! He says that frankly the fact that two retiring MPs are going off to run the Freedom Association is not that big a story. Turning to more general matters Trevor says that in spite of being opposed to the Single Currency the 'Sun' will support Labour. He says that he believes that calling to leave the EU would frighten the horses and that faced with that decision the people would most likely vote to stick with what they've got - a classic case of holding on to nurse for fear of something worse! He rates the Opposition very poorly and hasn't got a good word to say about Francis Maude - indolent, laid-back, has done nothing and whatever he's tried to do has been a failure!

Another journalist with whom I am in touch is Christopher Booker who comes to the House so that I can tell him all about what I intend to be doing in future. Christopher seems genuinely pleased with what I have to say and there and then volunteers himself and Richard North as our research team!

Next day Teresa and I enjoy a convivial lunch at the Carlton Club with Federation of Small Businesses spokesmen Brian Prime and Donald Martin. They applaud our decision to take a more active role in the work of TFA and with 150,000 subscribing members their own organisation could clearly be a very important ally.

On 22nd I finally manage to speak to 'Daily Telegraph' editor Charles Moore who says that he will put one of his Lobby Correspondents on to me. True to his word, there is a message to contact Ben Brogan waiting for me when I get to the House. This leads to a very encouraging interview with Ben a couple of days later when he seems confident that we should get some 'column inches' out of 'changing the guard at TFA'. In the event our news item is eclipsed by the announcement at lunchtime that very same day that Peter Mandelson will be announcing his resignation as Northern Ireland Secretary at Question Time.

Speaking to Peter Hitchens, author of 'The Abolition of Britain', on 23rd January, he expresses the opinion inter alia that the Conservative Party is finished – 'until it apologises for some of the terrible things that it has done, not just under Major but under Thatcher too, people will not vote for it'. My own opinion is not so very different and I have already decided that when my membership of the Party expires next Sunday I will not renew it.

The sequel to this particular declaration of independence is delayed until 4th April when the Chief Whip hands me a copy of the Party rules stating that MPs should be members of the Party and would I therefore kindly renew my subscription. I am reluctant to do this but after speaking to Party Chairman, Michael Ancram, I agree to come quietly. That evening Ancram seeks me out in the Members Dining Room and invites me to join him in the Chess Room to agree 'a form of words' for the Press - the panic being occasioned by one Tom Baldwin of the 'Times' newspaper who is, they say, threatening to make a story out of my not any longer being a member of the Party. A 'form of words' is agreed but walking home later that night I am aghast at what I have done. As a consequence of trying to be characteristically reasonable and helpful I have gone back on my own principles and so it is that after a sleepless night I am up early the following morning to draft a letter to the Chief saying that, in succumbing to his plea last evening, I made a mistake and that I shall not, after all, be renewing my Party membership. On my way to the House on 5th April I deliver a copy of this letter to CCO in Smith Square before handing the original in at the Chief Whip's office at about 11.40. I then go into the Chamber for Agriculture Questions at the end of which James Cran comes looking for me and spends the next 45 minutes trying to talk me into withdrawing my letter. His best argument is that when he himself resigned from being Northern Ireland Secretary Patrick Mayhew's PPS in the August of 1997 the Press didn't actually use that story until the eve of the Party conference in October. Recalling how I had myself been door-stepped by the Press for comment as I arrived at my Bournemouth Hotel I can see that he has a point. James goes on to argue that refusal to withdraw my letter would be immensely damaging to the Leader, to which I counter by saying that I really don't see why I should be the one to give in when the 'left' in the Party - by which I mean Hezza, Clarke, Patten et al - are continually getting away with murder. I tell James that whilst most colleagues finding themselves in a similar situation would resolve the difficulty by trading their principle for a 'gong' or some other bauble, as a matter of principle I will not do that!

On 25th January the Freedom Association Council elect me, nem con, to succeed Norris McWhirter as Chairman. Gerald Howarth speaks at some length about how TFA must not do anything that might embarrass the Conservative Party this side of a General Election. This particular record is wearing a bit thin and one wonders how he and others think that one can possibly make omelettes without breaking eggs!

That same day Ted Heath attends the Fisheries debate in the Chamber to fulminate about the contents of an article by Christopher Booker published in the 'Sunday Telegraph' on 14th. In his article, under the heading 'How Heath betrayed our fishermen', Christopher had stated that "one of the murkiest episodes in the history of Britain's involvement with the European Union was Edward Heath's surrender of the richest fishing waters in the world as the price of UK entry into the Common Market." Heath's apologia, as recorded by Hansard, is comical. "Why would I have done what Christopher Booker suggests? I was born by the sea; I lived by the sea for 60 years; I swam in the sea; and I fished locally. One year, I won the local fishing championship. I fished for six hours, between 10 and 4 o'clock, and caught 146 lb 12 oz of the best cod." So that's alright then!

At the invitation of Lord (Malcolm) Pearson on 29th January I attend a lunch in the terrace pavilion of the House of Lords. It is immediately apparent that some of the assembled company still believe that the Conservative Party is on their side although Kim Bolt of US 'Republicans Abroad' tactfully explains how difficult it is going to be for the new Bush administration to do other than agree with the British Labour Government in the absence of any clearly stated opposing views.

Later in the day I am interviewed by the BBC for the edition of the 'Today' programme which is to be broadcast on Thursday. Is this the breakthrough that I – and Malcolm Pearson through his ongoing dialogue with the BBC – have been hoping for? The interviewer is especially keen to hear me say that the situation in which 46% of those contacted by a recent Mori poll want out of the EU altogether and yet not one single MP with the exception of myself was prepared to articulate that opinion, was unreal and unsustainable. The interviewer, one Gordon Carera who is new at the BBC, describes my interview as 'very powerful' which means they probably won't use it! Come the day and I waste three whole hours listening to the Beeb's half-hearted attempt at having a debate about the prospect of Britain leaving the EU. The programme, as broadcast, comprises 5 blocs viz: Conrad Black and Chris Patten; Charles Moore, Anthony Howard and Mark Damazer (BBC Head of Current Affairs); myself, Robin Cook, Dennis McShane and Nick Sparrow (ICM Polls); Commissioners Bolkestein and Kinnock, Edward McMillan-Scott and Nigel Farage (UKIP); Tim Congdon, Niall Ferguson and Raymond Blanc (Chef at 'Les Quatre Saisons', Oxford). My supposedly 'very powerful' contribution is reduced to two anodyne sentences but subsequently Malcolm Pearson says not to worry too much about the detail because the main thing is that at least some coverage has at last been given to the prospect of exiting the EU.

The following day I call upon Iain Milne and Keith Carson at their offices in the appropriately named Hope House in Great Peter Street where we talk about yesterday's lunch which Iain had also attended. During the course of our discussions I venture the opinion that whilst the Conservative Party has the potential to deliver our aspirations regarding the EU there is simply too much evidence pointing in the opposite direction viz: sending messages of support for Ken Clarke, David Curry and Ian Taylor to the Rushcliffe, Ripon & Skipton and Esher constituencies where these three rabid Europhiles have been threatened with de-selection: saying 'In Europe but not run by Europe' and that 'we will never leave the EU' and that, as evidenced by Hague's performance at the 'Save the Pound' rally in Birmingham, the Leader is only willing or permitted to go so far. Over a cup of coffee Iain reveals that he resigned from his position at the European Journal when Bill Cash gave instructions that under no circumstances were staff at the Journal to assist the 'Whipless Eight' and that neither must they mention the 'Whipless' in any European Journal publication. How absolutely fascinating that this telling truth should emerge only now, six years after the event!

On the last day of January, as I am walking to a conference at 1,Great George Street, I fall into step with Michael Spicer who is interested to know how we are going to play this evening's meeting of the '92 Group. On our first day back after the Christmas recess Michael had intimated to me that he was no longer interested in the chairmanship of the '92 as he had set his sights instead upon becoming chairman of the '22. To make this become a reality calls for some nifty footwork because the biggest obstacle to Michael's election will almost certainly come from any one of our '92 colleagues who might just fancy their own chances. The trick is to ensure that as far as possible the 'right' of the Party rallies behind one preferred candidate. At our meeting this evening the guest speaker is Wm. Hague and I tell Michael that the plan is for me, as Secretary of the group, to keep the Leader talking in the bar whilst chairman John Townend puts an urgent motion to the meeting that we should support only one candidate for the chairmanship of the '22 in the next Parliament. This is carried nem con and subsequently we elect Gerald Howarth and Laurence Robertson, both TFA Council members, as Chairman and Secretary respectively. They, together with Eric Forth, Andrew Hunter, Julian Lewis, Marion Roe and Michael Spicer himself as Steering Committee members should ensure that, when the time comes, Michael emerges as the 'right wing's' preferred candidate.

Also meeting in the same building in Great George Street is the 'Konrad Adenauer Foundation' which is sponsoring a meeting in conjunction with the 'Social Market Foundation'. By the time that I get there it is all over bar the shouting but a man on the door suggests that I take away a copy of the publication that they have just been launching. As if proof were needed, this document demonstrates that the British Conservative Party is no more opposed to European unification than any of the other Parties.

In the excitement of the day I forget to attend the weekly meeting of the '22 but, in any case, it all now seems so irrelevant. We know the problems well enough but the Party is bereft of ideas about how to resolve them!

At the now annual Congress for Democracy on 2nd February I stand up to make a contribution to the debate but as soon as I state my name there is spontaneous applause. I can only assume that those responsible for it must have read my 23rd December speech to the House of Commons.

In my remarks I instance the total negation of democracy within the EU regarding, for example, Agriculture policy; the impossibility of repatriating powers in the light of the 'enhanced co-operation' agreed at Nice and my conclusion, after listening to Commissioner Bolkestein on 27th June, that the only sensible thing to do is to pull out. Curiously, Malcolm Pearson subsequently counsels caution about saying 'OUT'. In the same debate Daniel Hannan makes an excellent fist of illustrating what he terms 'the seven deadly sins of the EU' but is put on the spot when a questioner queries whether his views are consistent with membership of the Conservative Party!

At the weekend Christopher Booker, writing in the 'Sunday Telegraph', features the BBC's less than satisfactory attempt to debate the prospect of the UK leaving the EU, as broadcast on the 'Today' programme last Thursday, and the 'Mail on Sunday' runs with a story about Wm. Hague blocking an attempt by Margaret Thatcher to speak out in favour of Britain leaving the EU.

On the 1st February, in a deliberate attempt to tease the Party hierarchy, I entertain former Tory MP and Government Whip, Roger Knapman, to lunch in Portcullis House. Roger is now the Leader of the UK Independence Party and invites me to attend his Party's National Executive Council (NEC) meeting on Monday 5th February – an invitation which I decline because TFA is strictly non-partisan and not least because it is Norris McWhirter's opinion that UKIP has more to gain than we have. Ironically, the Hon. Treasurer, Nigel Axelrad, and at least one other member of the Association Management Committee take the opposite view.

There is further mischief afoot when, on 6th February, with the help of my old friend John Farbon, we stage a fringe meeting at the National Farmers Union (NFU) Annual General Meeting in the Hilton Hotel on Park Lane. I have previously briefed James Gladstone as to what we are up to and also spoken at length to David Brown, the 'Daily Telegraph' agriculture correspondent. Jamie Gladstone is interviewed on the 'Today' programme at about 06.55 but this will prove to be the only publicity that we shall achieve, other than coverage in local newspapers. At the Hilton itself our attempts to interest NFU delegates in coming to listen to reasons why the farming industry would be better off out of the CAP are somewhat thwarted when David Prole, who has been handing out leaflets on our behalf in the foyer, is thrown off the premises! When I bump into David Brown in the gents toilet he is full of apologies for there being nothing about our meeting in either today's or yesterday's 'Telegraph' but goes on to say that he will get something in tomorrow's! In the event there are only about 25 people in the audience for our fringe meeting which, admittedly, includes a goodly number of 'Gill Groupies'. After the meeting it transpires that the farmer who had asked me how I could say what I said and still remain a member of the Conservative Party is in fact a UKIP Parliamentary candidate but answering his question was not difficult because I was simply able to tell him that in anticipation of that sort of questioning I had allowed my membership of the Party to lapse 10 days ago.

That afternoon Michael Fabricant (Lichfield), speaking in the House, begs to move "That leave be given to bring in a Bill to establish a Parliamentary Commission to investigate and report regularly to Parliament, at intervals determined by Parliament, on the costs and benefits of the United Kingdom's membership of the European Union". Just like all previous attempts to persuade Governments, whether Labour or Conservative, to carry out a cost/benefit analysis, Michael's valiant effort is destined to run into the sand. What to any self-respecting commercial organisation would be second nature is anathema to the political elite, simply because they know full-well what the outcome would almost inevitably be.

That evening Michael Howard joins John Whittingdale, Michael Spicer, Archie Hamilton, A. N. Other and myself at table in the MDR just as I am in the middle of recounting my tale about the meeting with Bolkestein. Michael is more than a little amused to be reminded of what he, as a former Home Secretary, had said to the Commissioner on that occasion. Later still that evening I hear Andrew Mackay, Shadow Secretary of State for Northern Ireland, say at the Despatch Box that 'I still believe that Britain's future is within the European Community', thus confirming what I had suspected when I joined he and Julie at dinner a fortnight ago. From what he said on that occasion I had concluded that he doesn't understand that the EU is socialism writ large and him saying that his own position is nearer to mine than Ken Clarke's is somewhat at odds with what I have just heard him say in the Chamber.

Next day, in the Tea Room, the conversation turns towards my future as Chairman of TFA. The aforementioned Andrew Mackay says that I will be able to run the Association from my house in Aberdovey in the mornings and play golf in the afternoons. On the contrary I say, 'we will be harrying Members like yourself who stand at the Despatch Box saying that our future is in the EU'! When I bump into Andrew 24 hours later he is clearly quite put out by this rather sharp remark but that still doesn't alter the facts of the matter which couldn't be clearer.

Earlier in the day, having personally booked a room for the purpose, I attend a meeting of Peers of the Realm organised by Ashley Mote. The object of the exercise is to petition the Queen as allowed under the terms of Magna Carta which permits a gathering of 25 Peers to depute three of their number to seek an audience of the Sovereign. The meeting gets off to a shaky start when Lord Mountgarret draws attention to the fact that there are less than 25 Peers present, one of whom declares himself to be a Scottish Peer and therefore disqualified from signing the petition. The day is saved by my constituent Lord Hamilton of Dalzell, brother of '22 Committee Chairman Archie Hamilton, who urges his colleagues to sign on the basis that if it is subsequently found to be ultra vires no harm will have been done. At that, a member of the audience promptly draws attention to the fact that the BBC, who are also in attendance, did not film that particularly patriotic contribution to our proceedings - now there's a surprise!

In the evening Bill Cash finds me in the Commons Library and wants to bend my ear about what Christopher Booker said about him in last Sunday's 'Telegraph'. "I'm not an alleged euro sceptic am I?", says Bill, to which I feel bound to say that if he's got any complaint about what Booker has written then he'd best sort it out with Booker himself because I certainly don't write the articles. Bill then changes tack and says that he thinks that it is a bit off for me to talk about leaving the EU when I'm not seeking re-election! Whenever are my colleagues going to stop playing charades and instead start saying what they mean and mean what they say? Such is the seriousness of the nation's plight that the time for playing games is long since passed.

On Friday 9th February I feel obliged to fire off a letter to the Chairman of the BBC Board of Governors regarding a report that the Liberal Democrat PPC for the Ludlow Constituency is scheduled to appear on BBC2 on Sunday in a programme about all the trials and tribulations facing the future of Kidderminster hospital. Surely this is a job for the elected representatives who have been up to their neck in this controversy, not some Johnny come lately who just happens to accord with the Beeb's political prejudices.

On 13th February I have a fascinating meeting with Kim Bolt in her capacity as representative of 'US Republicans Abroad'. She tells me that the Conservative Party is telling her people in the USA that its European policy is Renegotiation and, in some areas, Repatriation. She can't explain why the Party is not saying the same thing back in Britain. She reckons that Conrad Black (owner of the 'Daily Telegraph') has his own agenda which does not include Britain leaving the EU and that he is responsible for Maude and Portillo being in the Shadow Cabinet! Kim goes on to say that Republicans cannot understand why Hague and the Conservatives in general haven't made any overtures towards Washington to learn from the Republicans' success. She wholeheartedly agrees when I say that the British Conservative Party has been infiltrated by those who are most definitely not conservatives. We conclude by agreeing that she will try to get Jesse Helms, Chairman of the US Foreign Affairs Committee, to put some steel into Wm. Hague's backbone. After our meeting I wonder whether I haven't been a bit too melodramatic in suggesting that instead of being a sure ally of the USA there is a danger of the UK becoming less reliable as a direct consequence of our involvement in the collectivist EU.

At the invitation of John Hipwood, lobby correspondent for the Midland News Association, on 15th I am guest at a lunch in the Press Gallery where the Guest Speaker is Romano Prodi, President of the European Commission. There is a story in this for John because whilst I am being introduced Prodi cannot avoid noticing the controversial £ badge in my lapel but the much better story comes after Prodi has spoken. One of the 'reptiles' asks him what democratic legitimacy he has. Prodi replies by saying that twice he has been to the European Parliament and twice he has been endorsed by them! So that's OK then – it certainly beats tramping up and down peoples' garden paths canvassing their votes!

The following day there is a disappointing turnout at a debate sponsored by the Worcestershire Branch of the FSB in the County Hall. The small number of those present who favour membership of the single currency (11) is the same at the end of the debate as at the beginning but thankfully all is not lost because some of the 'don't knows' are persuaded to swell the numbers opposed to the Euro to 28. Hardly the big deal but not untypical of the way in which public opinion is now moving.

As February draws to an end Iain Duncan-Smith asks me what I am going to be doing with myself when I am no longer in Parliament. I tell him about my new challenge with the Freedom Association and how I should like him to address one of our 'fringe meetings' at the Conservative Party Conference in Blackpool in October. Without a moment's hesitation Iain accepts the invitation and rather ominously says that he will do it – whether he's in Shadow Government or not!

On the first day of the new month I am somewhat surprised when Tom Cox (Labour, Tooting) tells me that he has read the speech that I made in the House yesterday about abattoirs. He says how right I have been and what a pity Government haven't taken more notice. In terms of taking notice I tell Tom that not even my own side want to do that! The problem with being right in politics is that inevitably many more people are shown to be just plain wrong – this is definitely not the way to win and influence friends! A fortnight later, at a memorial service for the life of the late Harmar Nicholls, a former colleague, Michael Neubert (ex Romford), tells me that once out of Parliament one has no influence at all. My response to Michael is that these days one doesn't have much influence even when one is in Parliament!

An opinion poll for the ERG reveals that the public are not much interested in the European issue. My own view is that this revelation is a damning indictment of the failure of the Conservative Party to make it an issue. Whilst the speech which Wm. Hague has made at the weekend is a welcome development he is probably starting too late for it to be of any real benefit in the pending General Election. The notion that because the public are apparently not interested in the European question we therefore need not do anything about it is entirely spurious. Quite apart from the fact that, in my book, politicians have a duty to draw attention to dangerous developments, the argument that the public are not interested in certain matters has never to my knowledge deterred governments from legislating in precisely those same areas – far from it, as the Statute Book well and truly testifies!

On 6th March I table a 10 Minute Rule Bill, "European Union (Implications of Withdrawal) (No. 2)", which is scheduled to be presented on 27th. The following week, when asked, Dennis Skinner says that he won't be a sponsor of my Bill because as a matter of principle he never puts his name to cross-Party motions. In the course of a long chat he tells me that he cannot understand why it is that the 'Campaign Group' of Labour Members agree with him on everything else but not on the matter of the Single Currency. That is a fascinating question – it is as though, at the mention of the single currency, Members on both sides of the House take leave of their senses.

On 8th March Malcolm Pearson seeks my advice about taking part in a TV programme in the run-up to the General Election on the question of coming out of the EU. There is a danger of frightening the horses but on the other hand, as on a rifle range, one has to aim high to hit the target.

A very po-faced George Young (Hampshire NW) tackles me about the invitation that I have accepted to speak in his constituency at a public meeting in Andover organised by the UK Independence Party. The fact of the matter is that in my new role as Chairman of the Freedom Association I am prepared to speak anywhere, not as a member of a political party but as spokesman for a strictly non-partisan political pressure group. George, being of a Europhile disposition, possibly fears that I will urge his constituents to vote UKIP but I shall do no such thing.

2001

2

" Alone in Westminster Hall "

Attending my first meeting of the Congress for Democracy Agenda Committee, in my capacity as Chairman of TFA, I suggest that monies allocated to a 'NO' campaign in the event of a referendum on the single currency should be directed towards a PR company charged with winning the vote. The following day, 15th March, I spend half an hour with Congress Chairman Michael Spicer saying how important it is to engage a really top-flight PR company to run the 'No to Single Currency' campaign. Simply sharing out whatever money is available amongst the myriad of small organisations opposed to EMU will, on the one hand, be very contentious and, on the other hand, unlikely to achieve the result we're looking for. I urge Michael to approach 'Business for Sterling' et al and tell them that this is what must happen. Michael is a great conciliator but in this scenario he must approach them with a firm proposition – seeking everybody's opinion will be simply disastrous!

I have initiated a debate about fish stocks and on 20th March have the novel experience of finding myself alone in Westminster Hall to take issue with Fisheries Minister, Elliot Morley. Yet again I argue that the CFP is the root cause of the fishing industry's many problems and once again the hapless Minister is forced to defend the indefensible. During the course of his speech he says, in reference to the CFP, that "its overwhelming priority is conservation"! With literally thousands of tons of perfectly saleable fresh fish being thrown back dead into the sea every week of the year both I and the Minister know that this is tommy-rot. By dint of our treaty obligations Britain has to accept the iniquitous CFP, warts and all, and the political elite are terrified that if we start unpicking it that in itself might lead to an unravelling of the entire EU project.

In his remarks the Minister is kind enough to say that "although some of his hon. Friends initially showed an interest in fishing they soon disappeared from the scene, but the hon. Gentleman has been consistent in his attendance at fishery debates and his involvement in the arguments. I respect him for that even though, as he stated, I do not agree with him." As far as my Conservative colleagues are concerned the reality of the situation is that because there is neither the prospect of achieving any worthwhile amendment to the CFP, because that would require the unanimous agreement of all EU member states, nor any reward for even trying, as this would be at odds with the 'ever closer union' that all three main political parties are committed to, fisheries has become a virtual 'no-go area', especially for those with unfulfilled ambitions.

If nothing else, the fisheries debate, just like the agriculture debate, where in both instances the Westminster Parliament is virtually powerless, serves to bolster my decision not to seek re-election. A couple of days ago I had bumped into Pam Powell, widow of Enoch, at Matins in St Margaret's, Westminster. When I say to Pam that she probably thinks I am being wimpish about not standing again she says 'not at all, you're doing the right thing'.

After the fisheries debate I hold a further highly satisfactory meeting with Kim Bolt at which she reels off a long list of people and organisations that she thinks I ought to meet in Washington. There can be little doubt that forging a strong trans-Atlantic link would give TFA much better 'street cred'.

On 27th March, although not called to speak in the Chamber until 1740, I beg to move "That leave be given to bring in a Bill to establish a Committee of Enquiry into the implications of a withdrawal by the United Kingdom from the European Union". I am pleased with the way my presentation of this 10 Minute Rule Bill goes and extremely encouraged by the number of chums who turn up in support. Afterwards, Crispin Blunt (Reigate) and Nigel Farage (UKIP, MEP) ask for copies of my speech because they are both appearing on the 'Despatch Box' programme at midnight when, apparently, my Bill will be the talking point. Although my Bill attracts no Press attention it is some consolation when subsequent reports indicate that many people have seen it on various TV channels. A couple of days later I bump into Michael Kallenbach, Parliamentary correspondent for the 'Daily Telegraph', who says how pleased he is to meet me and how he and so many of his colleagues hold me in high regard. When I ask him why therefore I never get reported in the 'Telegraph' he asks for specific instances, the most obvious answer to which is my 10 Minute Rule Bill on Tuesday.

In the meantime John Townend has been getting himself into hot water and I wake on Wednesday 28th March to hear John defending himself on the 'Today' programme and also to learn that he has been censured by Wm. Hague. I am not best pleased that my colleague and friend is being treated like this and whilst defending John's views on immigration to journalists the following day my injudicious choice of analogy to describe the immigrant situation ensures that I too get swept up in the Press feeding frenzy. The next day I am reported in the 'Times', the 'Telegraph', the 'Independent', the 'Guardian', the 'Mirror' and I don't know what else besides, as the liberal journalists/editors do a hatchet job on me for having dared, in support of John Townend, to express an opinion on asylum seekers. Where were all the Press when I initiated debates on Asylum Seekers in Strasbourg and Westminster Hall? Closer to home the 'Birmingham Post' on Saturday simply regurgitates all the inaccuracies of Friday's dailies. All that I had told their lobby correspondent, Jonathan Walker, they have totally ignored. When I get the 'Shropshire Star' that evening I am relieved to see that John Hipwood's report is much more responsible and less sensational.

On Saturday morning, having already spoken to John Townend, I contact James Cran who tells me that there is more to the JT affair than meets the eye – Whips know everything! According to James, a few weeks ago at the German Embassy, JT had been so riled by what their Trade Commissioner had said about how things were going to be in the EU in future that John had shouted 'Sieg Heil' and walked out! The Ambassador, Herr Ploetz, had registered a complaint about JT's behaviour with Wm. Hague and that is why, when John's controversial comments about diluting our Anglo-Saxon culture became public, the Leader felt he had to slap him down – for fear that the German Embassy incident might also becoame public knowledge.

James seems reasonably relaxed when I explain my own involvement in all of this and thinks that taking a colleague's part when no one else is prepared to do so is a decent thing to have done. Only later do I discover that James was frantically trying to contact me yesterday, but even that would have been too late to save my bacon.

The regular weekly meeting of the '22 Committee later that day is addressed by Wm. Hague but, notwithstanding that we are now anticipating that Blair will announce the Dissolution of Parliament next Monday, I am unable to detect any real enthusiasm for what the Leader has to say.

Later that evening Richard Body and I address a meeting of the 'Anti-Common Market League' where I am again asked how I can claim that TFA is non-partisan whilst I, as its Chairman, am a member of the Conservative Party. In response to this question I simply point out that I allowed my membership of the Party to lapse on 28th January and think no more about it until the telephone starts ringing next day with calls, in quick succession, from the 'Mirror', 'Guardian' and 'Independent' all wanting to know about my resignation from the Conservative Party. It appears that somebody at last night's meeting has told the 'Mirror' what I said about allowing my Party membership to lapse. There's further fall-out from this when, on Sunday, George West, Chairman of the 'Campaign for an Independent Britain' (CIB) telephones to say that one speaker has already pulled out of next Saturday's CIB meeting and another is threatening to do so if I am on the platform. I am happy to tell George that I've no wish to make things difficult for him and if it helps I will stand down – a minor victory for those who oppose freedom of speech!

A long-standing member of CIB is my constituent Clem Shaw who has recently died. I have been asked to deliver the eulogy at his funeral on 3rd April and afterwards am sought out by Clem's first ever girl friend who tells me that her East Devon constituency sent a message to the LCCA during all the troubles at the time of Maastricht, urging them to deselect me. She tells me that at the time, their MP, Sir Peter Emery, denied having any hand in it! This I find hard to believe.

That same day I continue to live dangerously by doing a live interview with BBC Radio 5 on the vexed question of asylum seekers - having to watch my Ps and Qs most carefully! The following day I do further interviews on the same topic for local radio stations. The interviewer for Radio Beds,

Bucks & Hertfordshire is bullying and hectoring so I have to be doubly careful not to fall into the holes he persistently keeps digging for me.

After all the excitement of the past few days I am astonished when Sister Janes tells me that my blood pressure is on the low side of normal – it most certainly doesn't feel like it!

In the Members Tea Room on 4th April I pull Bruce Grocott's leg about his elevation to the House of Lords. As the Member for Telford, Bruce is my constituency neighbour and is Tony Blair's PPS. One thing leads to another and Bruce tells me that Norman Tebbit once said that the most dangerous sort of politician is a backbencher without ambition – I wonder who Bruce could possibly have in mind!

On 10th April I am just putting the finishing touches to my speech for this afternoon's Easter Adjournment debate when Hague's PPS, John Whittingdale, rings to ask me if I would be prepared to meet William later in the day. We agree a time of 15.30 in the Leader's office in the House. William completely disarms me by not pushing the idea that I should renew my Party membership although there is a veiled threat – totally impracticable of course – that I could have the Whip withdrawn, although 'we wouldn't want to do that to someone at the end of such a long involvement, would we'! At this point I interject to say that the whole problem as far as I am concerned stems from the fact that the Party continues to condone 'collectivist' i.e. 'communist', policies and I'm not a communist – far from it I say, I'm implacably opposed to communism. I go on to tell him that I've got a surprising new ally in the person of the Prime Minister, no less, who agrees with me regarding the CAP! William is anxious to establish that I won't be speaking out against the Party during the General Election campaign and then proceeds to spell out the 'deal'. In return for my undertaking to make no comment about my lapsed membership and not to speak against the Party – which as far as I am concerned is not on the cards anyway – he will draw a veil over the matter of the lapsed membership. Only later will I come to realise how much WH wanted this deal and how foolish I was to accept it with such alacrity – even wishing him the very best of luck at the polls but then again, why should I worry – he certainly won't need any help from me to go down big time for all the reasons that I have tried so hard to persuade him to see sense on these past four years.

Wednesday 11th April and I wake to hear Big Ben striking 04.30 and the dawning realisation that I blew it yesterday. Why, oh why, didn't I tell William that I would give him my answer in the morning instead of being so eager to accept the 'deal' - such as it was. Only now can I see how truly anxious William was that I should remain silent throughout the forthcoming election campaign. When all the evidence is pointing in the opposite direction why do I still want to believe that William is an honourable man as far as the European question is concerned? Answer: because the alternative, another Labour government, is even worse and with the best will in the world there isn't any other non-socialist Party capable of winning a seat in Parliament, let alone forming a government. The question is, does Wm. Hague really want to win or is he the political equivalent of football's Bruce Grobelaar? We may never know! (Bruce Grobelaar was a First Division footballer who was charged with deliberately throwing matches by letting the ball past him when, as goalkeeper, he could have saved it.)

At dinner in the MDR, on St George's Day, our first day back after the Easter recess, John Redwood ventures the opinion that there is a problem at the top because William doesn't consult the Shadow Cabinet, as evidenced by the fact that nobody was told that he had, on behalf of the whole Party, signed the Council for Racial Equality's 'race compact', hence the panning that the Party got in the Press and Media last week. Next day, by sheer coincidence, JR and I find ourselves together again, this time in the Tea Room where he tells Andrew Tyrie (Chichester) and I how he tried to put Margaret Thatcher off the idea of the Community Charge – the ill-fated 'Poll Tax' – but all to no avail. From what he says I can only conclude that Tyrie is an unreconstructed 'europhile' but given that he is a former Treasury civil servant that hardly comes as a surprise. Viewed from the 'ivory towers' of Whitehall 'ever closer union' undoubtedly has far greater appeal than it does for the likes of, say, the average member of the FSB.

At European Standing Committee 'A' on 25th the business is to consider the establishment of the 'European Aviation Safety Agency'. It all sounds like 'Motherhood & Apple Pie' until I recognise it for what it really is – yet another instance of EU 'collectivisation'. On the strength of that I force a Division which results in 5 votes for the motion and 1 against – of my Conservative colleagues there is no sign! To be fair, Shadow Aviation & Shipping Minister Robert Syms (Poole) does attend the Committee and makes a contribution to the debate, but, not being an appointed member of the committee, is not permitted to vote. When I bump into Robert the following day I can't help giving him the benefit of my views on EU collectivisation and try to explain that once you 'get it' the rest falls into place. The menace of collectivism is the theme that I continue to push in the Tea Room on Friday 27th when my victims are Graham Brady (Altringham & Sale) and Nick St Aubyn (Guildford).

The sole purpose for my being in the House on this particular Friday is in the forlorn hope that the preceding Private Members Bills about 'High Hedges' and 'Human Fertilisation & Embryology (Deceased Fathers)' will have run their course and that the Speaker will then call me to present my 'European Union (Implications of Withdrawal) (No. 2) Bill'. No such luck – as is so often the case on these Fridays, time runs out because the debate on the first Bill has been deliberately prolonged so as to 'talk out' the second one. In point of fact, with only 40 Members present the House on this occasion is barely quorate.

In the meantime I have received a 'phone call from John Townend who has clearly got his wires crossed as he thinks he's through to James Cran. He then asks me to give him James's number which I have to put the 'phone down to find. When we resume our conversation I have to tell John to stand still because he keeps breaking up. He says he's not walking about because he's in his car and he's just going into a tunnel. I then ask him where he is to which he replies, 'just outside Strasbourg' – and here's me thinking he's calling from his home in Westminster Gardens! Notwithstanding that James has told him to shut up about immigration and asylum seekers John cannot resist breaking cover the following day to give the pot another stir! The sequel to this is that whilst listening to the news bulletin on Classic FM at 18.00 on the 28th I hear Shadow Agriculture Minister Tim Yeo say that John Townend's views are 'repugnant' and that 'many in the Conservative Party will be very pleased when he is no longer a Conservative MP'. I am mildly surprised that the BBC doesn't also run with this story but whilst Yeo is the lead story on the 11 o'clock ITN news there is not a mention of him on the 10 o'clock News.

In high dudgeon about Yeo's outbursts on both radio and TV I speak in turn, on Sunday morning, to Townend, Cran and Peter Luff and, later in the day, to Deputy Chief Whip Patrick McLoughlin, not only about Yeo but also about Lord (John) Taylor who has gratuitously, perhaps because of his ethnicity, joined the fray.

On Monday 30th I get to the House just in time for the meeting of the 'Forward Look' Committee where I bide my time waiting for an opportunity to raise the matter of the Townend affair. When Tom King says the Government have failed to deliver on every count I follow him by saying that there is nothing to beat BUT that I am seriously worried about the effects that this weekend's events may have upon Conservative prospects. I go on to instance the unsatisfactory nature of a Shadow Cabinet Minister slagging off a backbencher in public, the correspondence that I have had with Lord Taylor and, not least, how my own position as Chairman of TFA has been compromised by not being able to respond to an unprecedented number of requests to go on radio and TV in defence of Freedom of Speech. Douglas Hogg follows me saying that much as he dislikes John Townend (mean spirited!) he defends his right to Free Speech. He then says that, conversely, he 'likes Chris Gill' who is quite right to raise this important point of principle and that there are enormous dangers in trying to muzzle free speech. Francis Maude then says something so memorable that I instantly forget what it is and then the Chief Whip launches into a long explanation before the meeting finally closes.

After the meeting I am besieged, first of all by John Whittingdale who says that it is thought that John Taylor may be trying to do another Shaun Woodward (i.e. defect to Labour), then by Douglas Hogg who says that I'm the best person to silence John Townend and then by the Chief who is clearly concerned to pacify me. He and I walk downstairs together and inter alia I tell him that unlike John Townend and I, Tim Yeo is bound by the 'collective responsibility' of Shadow Cabinet. Unfortunately the Chief is hotching to go to a meeting with the Speaker and so I am prevented from pursuing my theme any further.

Over dinner that evening I tell the Deputy Chief Whip, Patrick McLoughlin, how the Townend affair started. John's wife Jennifer has previously told me that the whole thing kicked off when Greg Knight, formerly the Member for Derby North, Deputy Chief Whip in the last Government and now PPC for John's seat, having listened to John's speech at his East Yorkshire CCA Annual Meeting thought it so good that he urged John to issue it as a Press Release. It soon becomes apparent that the current

Deputy Chief Whip is not particularly keen to pursue this topic of conversation – I wonder why!

Come May Day and John Townend is regretting having given in to the Leader. He had sought my advice at about 13.00 yesterday but subsequently buckled under pressure at his meeting with Hague shortly afterwards. Gerald Howarth, who has succeeded John as Chairman of the '92 Group, is fulminating about what is going on but doesn't have time to stop and discuss the matter and, for my part, I am getting more and more requests to do media interviews which, out of a sense of residual loyalty, I am turning down. I later learn that Laurence Robertson did the 'Newsnight' slot last evening and has subsequently been given an ultimatum by the Chief and James Cran to either sign a letter of apology or be slung out of the Party, the consequence of which, of course, would be that he would be prevented from seeking re-election as a Conservative in his Tewkesbury seat, or anywhere else for that matter. Laurence subsequently tells Wm. Hague and the Chief what he thinks about their style of leadership!

The Party is making heavy weather over this storm in a tea cup but this is neither the first time nor will it be the last when the Party leadership hangs colleagues out to dry because of something that they have said, instead of defending their right to say it. If the Party disagrees with what one has said then surely it would be better to invoke the spirit of Rousseau – I disagree with what you say but will defend to the last your right to say it – rather than humiliate colleagues and disappoint supporters alike by repeatedly caving in to the PC brigade.

On 2nd May, during the course of a long and interesting conversation with Paul Sykes, he tells me that he is finished with the Conservatives and will henceforth be helping the UK Independence Party to put candidates up in every constituency! Paul, like myself, has tried his damnedest to try to persuade the Conservative Party to return to the 'path of righteousness' and is now clearly totally exasperated by the experience – and who can blame him!

At tea-time I chat to Charles Wardle (Bexhill & Battle) who has recently lost the Party Whip for allegedly saying that he would support an Independent in his constituency rather than the Conservative PPC. Charles sounds me out about UKIP, of which I know little, and, in particular, about UKIP MEP, Nigel Farage, of whom I know less. Charles tells me that he is meeting Farage on Friday. Reading between the lines I guess that Charles has just realised that Al Fayed, who has reputedly offered him a job at £120,000 a year, isn't going to be much interested in him if he no longer has a seat in Parliament.

At Archie Hamilton's retirement party that evening I try to bolster Laurence Robertson's morale after his bruising encounter with the Whips and his having had to eat humble pie after supporting John Townend.

As far as I am concerned that is not the end of the Townend affair. After a Statement in the House on 3rd May, about the Foot & Mouth epidemic, I collar Shadow Agriculture Minister Tim Yeo and the following rather intemperate exchange ensues.

Gill: Hello Tim, I saw you on TV and heard you on radio saying that John Townend's views were repugnant and that many in the Conservative Party will be relieved when he is no longer a Conservative MP.

Yeo: What I actually said was that there were very many in the Party who wouldn't miss him.

Gill: I don't think you should have said that.

Yeo: It's what many people think.

Gill: That isn't the point. As a Shadow Cabinet Minister you should not have been speaking like that about a colleague.

Yeo: I don't see why not.

Gill: Because you are bound by the collective responsibility of the Shadow Cabinet. What if I, as Chairman of TFA, had gone on every TV and radio station that invited me, sounding off about Free Speech.

Yeo: I'm glad you didn't. Thank you for showing such restraint.

Gill: Don't you think that you, as a Shadow Cabinet Minister should also have shown restraint?

Yeo: It needed to be said.

Gill: In what capacity did you say it – in your own capacity or as a Party spokesman?

Yeo: Mind your own business.

Gill: It is my business

Yeo: It's none of your business.

Gill: Has anyone spoken to you about this.

Yeo: It's nothing to do with you.

Gill: It's a Party matter and I want to know.

Yeo: If you wish to complain you should do it through the official channels.

Gill: (as Yeo makes for the exit) If you won't answer the question I shall assume that you spoke on behalf of the Party.

No answer came the stern reply!

My Parliamentary 'swan song', on 8th May, is a debate that I have initiated in Westminster Hall on the subject of 'Best Value (Local Government)'. The Government Minister who responds to my speech says that she "found it very interesting to listen to the points made by the hon. Member for Ludlow, although I did not agree with a word that he said". As a Labourite she would say that wouldn't she, but that in no way detracts from the fact that I had the best of the argument. Personally I am content that my last debate is about Local Government because that is where I came in, so to speak, all those years ago, as a very young councillor on the 'all-purpose' Wolverhampton County Borough Council. What a pity it is that more of my Parliamentary colleagues haven't cut their teeth in local government before aspiring to run the country but when, at the beginning of this Parliament, I suggested that local authority experience should be de rigueur for PPC s the idea went down like the proverbial lead balloon!

The following day Malcolm Pearson takes me to tea in the Peers Dining Room where we run headlong into Norman Tebbit. Like spontaneous combustion, the two of them are soon joshing about forming a new Conservative Party once the General Election is out of the way! There is nothing conclusive arising from my meeting with Malcolm other than a suggestion that if he wants to publicise the findings of his media monitoring campaign, TFA's 'Freedom Today' would be pleased to run the story. Without prompting, Malcolm tells me that his father-in-law, Robert Fellows, was the Queen's former Secretary. Whether or not this explains Malcolm's reluctance to ask questions in the Lords about Her Majesty's constitutional position in the aftermath of the European Treaties I shall never know.

Today, Thursday 10th May, is the last day of this Parliament and I am pleased to be able to have a final crack at Gordon Brown at Treasury question time. My question to the Chancellor is "In advocating the single currency, will the Chancellor make sure to remind the British people that every time we have been on fixed exchange rates, unemployment has increased astronomically?" Needless to say, Brown sidesteps answering the actual question but concludes his reply by saying "The Conservative Party must make up its mind in this campaign. Is it against a single currency in principle, and therefore for ever, or against it only for one Parliament?" I couldn't have put it better myself!

At the end of the last vote at 17.51 Nick Winterton invites me to his office in Portcullis House for an end of term drink. There, somewhat to my surprise, I find the Chairman of the '22 Committee, Archie Hamilton, together with Eric Forth, Edward Leigh, Gerald Howarth and the 'Young Pretender', David Davis – not a 'wet' to be seen! Enjoying Nick's excellent champagne and the fascinating gossip makes me late for my rendezvous with James and Penny Cran at the Rochester Brasserie where we unwind at the end of what I can only describe as a far less than satisfactory Parliament.

At 08.10 on 17th May I listen to Wm. Hague being quietly barbecued about his inconsistencies by John Humphries on the 'Today' programme. This interview only serves to convince me that, in terms of winning the Election, we haven't a prayer but I suppose that I've known that all along because of William's failure to come down firmly on one side of the argument or the other or, failing that, at least stick to some sort of fundamental principle!

And so as I head for 'the blue remembered hills' of Shropshire I am happy to let my friend and colleague, Teresa Gorman have the last word. Teresa has told her husband Jim that if the Press call he is to say "Teresa don't do politics no more"!

Postscript

As I settle down to write the Postscript to this sorry tale of woe from long ago, there is a cutting in front of me from yesterday's newspaper (30th May 2012).

Under the headline 'Only extremists want a referendum over Europe, Clarke insists', it is reported that former Tory Party leadership contender Ken Clarke has expressed the opinion that a referendum on Britain's relationship with the European Union would be "silly" and of interest to only a few extreme nationalistic politicians.

Because each of the three old political Parties is apparently wedded to the concept of 'ever closer union' within the EU it could be said that it is a matter of almost supreme indifference to the old Europhile dinosaurs within the Conservative Party as to which Party actually forms the Government – win or lose, their ambition to see our country's freedom and independence subsumed into the EU is progressively pursued.

Perhaps things might have been different if Wm. Hague had heeded my advice all those years ago. How well I remember telling William that it would be better to lose Ken Clarke than lose the General Election, but, as readers will have gathered, far from hounding such people out of the Party as they had hounded me in the previous Parliament, CCO, during the Hague years, was only too keen to direct support to beleaguered colleagues facing de-selection in their own constituencies – provided they were of a Europhile disposition!

It is a matter of opinion as to whether the Conservative Party's fortunes would have improved if at any time during the past two decades it had adopted a different stance on the question of our country's relationship with the EU but what cannot be gainsaid is that its electoral performance, with the half-baked policies that it did adopt, has been nothing short of catastrophic - even failing to achieve an outright majority in 2010 when it faced an open goal with only the least popular Labour Government ever known to beat.

Wm. Hague is remembered for his 'silly little mantra' about 'being in Europe but not run by Europe'. More significantly he also once said "come with me and I will give you back your country" a slogan with so much more resonance but which, for mysterious reasons, he appears to have been forced to abandon.

A consistent thread running through these memoirs is the repeated refusal of the Europhiles , whether in Government, Opposition, the Broadcasting Corporation, Big Business or the professions, to expose their prejudices to public examination. My own efforts, as recorded in these memoirs, to get members of the Shadow Government to discuss these issues on a one-to one basis, or at least to justify their stance, all ran into the sand. The logical conclusion that I draw from these experiences is that these people will not join the debate simply because they haven't got a leg to stand on – instead they resort to calling their opponents 'cranks and gadflies' (Tory Leader, Michael Howard), 'fruitcakes and loonies' (Tory Leader, Dave Cameron), 'swivel-eyed' (Greg Barker, Tory Minister) and, most recent of all, 'extremist' (Kenneth Clarke, Justice Minister).

After 13 years in Opposition the hope was that the Conservative Party would have rejuvenated itself but, like Marie Antoinette, it appears to have learnt nothing and forgotten nothing. After two years in Government it is apparent that the Tories are bent on 'conserving' absolutely nothing – neither our national Culture (although, to be fair, they no longer appear to be quite so committed to multiculturalism as they once were), nor such things as our Armed Forces, the supremacy of Parliament, the primacy of British law, the inviolability of the British constitution and certainly not the birthright of every free-born Briton to be governed by laws made in their own Parliament by those that they themselves elect. To this seemingly endless catalogue of things that the modern Conservative Party has failed to conserve we must now apparently add the sanctity of marriage, the unspoilt beauty of the British countryside and, not least, the value of the proverbial 'pound in your pocket' as the National Debt sky-rockets from £800 billions in 2010 to a forecast £1.5 trillions by 2015.

At what point in time the Conservative Party ceased to be a truly 'conservative' Party is a matter which might engage the attention of future historians but, as viewed from my perspective, it has for some long time now been 'conservative' but in name alone – a sad demise for what once was arguably the world's most successful political Party, but a spectacularly successful coup for the 'collectivist' infiltration which has left it paralysed.

Appendix A

Letter to Rt Hon Lord Jenkins of Hillhead OM, Chairman of the Independent Commission on the Voting System – 22 July 1998.

My Lord

Following the meeting in the Grand Committee Room on the 30th June when the members of the Independent Commission on the Voting System listened to the views of Parliamentarians I felt that I should write to you explaining more clearly the point I put to you from the floor.

On 28th November 1994 the Conservative Party whip was withdrawn from me because I failed to respond to a 3-line whip to vote more money to the European Community.

Had I been in Parliament by dint of a Party list system there is no doubt that my political career would have ended there and then. Indeed by throwing me out of the Parliamentary Party the Conservative government almost certainly hoped that that would be the last that was heard of me in any case!

What they clearly had not bargained for was the fact that I (and the 7 other colleagues who suffered the same fate) were sustained by our own constituents and by the thousands of voices that were raised in our support in other parts of the UK and beyond, saying that we were right and that, in effect, the Government was wrong.

In the event, after an interlude of approximately 5 months, the Party Whip was unconditionally restored. In other words, the Government accepted that the voice of the so called 'rebels' was more in tune with public opinion that theirs, but more to the point in terms of the representation of the people, the people had been able to make their voice heard by dint of the fact that British Parliamentarians, under the present arrangements, are able to make a stand on matters of principle in a way that other Parliamentarians in other Parliaments, elected by list systems, are not.

The moral of the tale is, of course, that whatever its perceived deficiencies, the British system of representative democracy works. It is a two way street but it can only remain a two way street for as long as the Members of Parliament are ultimately answerable directly to their constituents and, in the final analysis, dependent upon them and they alone for the public office they hold. It ceases to be a two street, in which the interests of Constituents, Country and party are weighed and balanced by (and subject to the judgement of) the tribunes of the popel, when men and women are candidates at elections entirely as a consequence of decisions made by the Party bosses as to whose name does not appear on the Party list.

As a general principle you might like to bear in mind that Democracy only truly exists in the circumstances in which the electorate has the power to get rid of either unsatisfactory representatives (ie individual MPs) or even whole governments, if that is their desire. That most certainly was their desire on 1st May last year and I have no quarrel with that.

On the other hand under PR systems the danger is that inevitably patronage transfers from the People to the Political Parties and in those circumstances the power of the people (ie the electorate) to rid themselves of unpopular politisians or entire governments is forfeited.

In conclusion I would simply stat that my views are conditioned by the realities of experience, a very traumatic experience at that, and I trust that you and your colleagues on the Commission will recognise that they are worthy of more consideration than those based purely upon theory and assertion.

Yours sincerely
Christopher Gill MP

Appendix B

Letter to Mr D.J.R. Hill, Secretary, Royal Commission on the Reform of the House of Lords – 25 June 1999.

Dear Mr Hill

Thank you for your letter of 19th April 1999 inviting me to make a submission to the Royal Commission on the Reform of the House of Lords.

In arriving at a lasting solution regarding the future of the House of Lords it might be sensible to try to deal not only with the immediate problems caused by the abolition of the hereditary Peers but also long-standing difficulties and anomalies evident in the present constitutional arrangements.

The 'West Lothian Question' is probably the most obvious anachronism in the present system but by no means the only one.

The 'Barnett Formula' which ensures a greater expenditure of public money per capita in Scotland and Wales than in England is another.

With the advent of the Scottish Parliament and the Welsh Assembly, both of the above features of the present arrangements will be exacerbated. In consequence there are the stirrings of a popular movement for an English Parliament which represents a new but equally serious consideration.

Devolution and the latent demand for an English Parliament represent a burgeoning threat to the integrity of the United Kingdom which thus becomes yet another problem to be taken into the reckoning.

Rather than deal with the single issue of restructuring the Upper House simply to reflect the demise of the hereditary peers would it not be more sensible to take a broader view and see how the opportunity created by Lords reform could be used to resolve the problems outlined above?

The creation of a united Kingdom federal Parliament sitting on the red benches and an English Parliament sitting on the green benches would, at a stroke, eliminate four very real and readily identifiable problems.

The duties and responsibilities of the federal Parliament would be essentially those appertaining to Defence, Foreign Affairs, Law & Order and Treasury with all other functions devolved to the English and Scottish Parliaments and the Welsh and North Ireland assemblies.

Whilst admittedly this proposal envisages a unicameral systems, it has to be recognised that the precedent for this has already been well and truly established by Scottish and Welsh devolution.

What is more important is that this proposal eliminates any possibility of turf wars between two elected chambers and also because the federal Parliament would be elected by universal suffrage, removes the prospect of an upper chamber filled either partially or entirely with placemen. The question of competing claims for democratic legitimacy as between two Houses of Parliament would, in those circumstances, simply not arise.

A federal Parliament comprising members returned by Unitary Authorities and Counties would bind the United Kingdom together at a time when its historical cohesiveness is under threat as never before, solve the West Lothian Question; end the inequity of the Barnett Formula; satisfy the English dimension and represent an intelligible and practicable solution to an otherwise intractable problem.

It goes without saying that elections to the UK federal Parliament must be by the first past the post system so as to ensure that as far as is humanly possible, ultimate power rests with the people and is not handed over to the political parties.

I do not intend to expand upon this latter point which was fully explored in my letter to the Commission on the Voting System dated 22nd July 1998

Yours sincerely
Christopher Gill MP

Appendix C

Notes for a Speech to the Streetly Branch of the Aldridge Brownhills CCA on 22/10/99.

In 1997 Tony Blair masqueraded as a Tory.

Two years later he publicly attacks the 'forces of Conservatism'.

To repeat the words of our Leader, Wm. Hague, Tony Blair is a fraud.

Tony Blair never was, never is and never will be a Conservative .... Tony Blair is a Revolutionary!

In the name of 'Modernisation' he is overturning and disorienteering practically every institution in the land

- the House of Lords
- the Voting system
- the Supremacy of the Westminster Parliament
- the integrity of the United Kingdom

and is complicit in a whole raft of equally radical changes that I shall refer to presently.

What is my evidence for saying that our Prime Minister is a Revolutionary?

- 20 out of his 23 Cabinet Ministers are members of the Fabian Society
- this article published in the 'Spectator'
- his policies and his performance.......... by their deeds shall you know them!

I appreciate that it takes a big leap in the imagination but if just for one moment you could accept that Blair really is a Leninist then a whole lot of otherwise puzzling or inexplicable policies and decisions begin to make sense.

Firstly, the attack on 'the forces of conservatism' is explicable – quote Anatole Golytskin, a Russian dissident writing 10 years ago.

That quote from Golytskin's book called 'The Perestroika Deception' should help to explain that the Leninist meaning of Perestroika is not 'restructuring' as assumed in the West but 're-formation' (as in a military or other formal organisation) or, as the French say, 'reculer pour le mieux sauter'...i.e. recoil so as to be able to jump higher!

Secondly, with the active connivance of Tony Blair, both at home and abroad, parallel or duplicate institutions are being established.

Have just returned from a meeting of the Council of Europe ..... have seen at first-hand what is going on over there.

Since 1949, under the auspices of the Council of Europe, human rights have been the province of the European Commission on Human Rights.

Now the EU plans to establish its own powers in that very same area.

Also since 1949, the defence of Western Europe has been vested in NATO.

Now EU proposes to assume responsibility in these matters and, with immediate effect, intends to take over 'Crisis Management' as a prelude to, I believe, establishing total dominance in Defence.

As we all know, since 1st January this year, the EU has instituted an alternative to National Currencies ...... and .... coming down the track are its proposals to institute an alternative system of Criminal Justice.

There is a precedent for all these things .... Soviet Russia!

Under Lenin, alternative forms of government were established ...... they were called Soviets!

There was of course a Supreme Soviet, based in Moscow .... just as today there is a Supreme Soviet based in Brussels, representing an alternative system of government ......

An alternative to NATO in terms of Defence ....

An alternative to the Council of Europe in terms of Human Rights ....

An alternative to national Jurisprudence in terms of Criminal Law ....

And an alternative to national currencies and Parliamentary accountability ....

In other words, an alternative to Democracy!

But we mustn't delude ourselves that this process is confined to matters connected with the EU – it is not!

It's happening here too ..... right under our noses!

Take, for example, the alternative Governments in Scotland and Wales, currently frustrating the will of Parliament on such a mundane matter as the restriction on the sale of beef on the bone!

Take also the prospect of English Regional Assemblies creating their own challenges to the national Parliament ....

And even closer to home, the creation of non-statutory Community and District Forums challenging the position of democratically elected local Councillors.

The question we should all be asking ourselves is who will serve on all these alternative bodies and who is most likely to have the majority.

People will perhaps discount what I have said because it smacks of a conspiracy theory.

To them I would simply say this ....

There is another conspiracy and it's taking place right here in the West Midlands.

Scores of manufacturers making washers and springs, castings and fastenings etc. are engaged in a conspiracy .... and that conspiracy is to build cars and tractors and four-wheel drives in Coventry, in Oxford, in Longbridge and in Solihull ....

just as Tony Blair is engaged in a conspiracy to build the Socialist millennium!

He's dumped the baggage, the impedimenta of the past .... clause 4 and all that .... but the destination remains the same – the Socialist Utopia!

In the whole of Europe today there is only one political Party with the belief and the capacity to challenge and to expose and ultimately to defeat this socialist conspiracy and that Party is the British Conservative Party, under the leadership of William Hague!

He's nailed his colours to the mast and, for the sake of our country, we'd best do the same.

God bless you all!

Appendix D

GENERAL ELECTION RESULTS 1987 – 2010							
Date of Election	11/6/87	9/4/92	1/5/97	7/6/01	5/5/05	6/5/10
Total No. Of Seats	650	651	659	659	646	650
Total Votes Cast	32,530,204	33,614,074	31,286,284	26,368,204	27,148,510	29,687,604
Labour seats	229	271	418	413	355	258
Labour votes	10,029,270	11,560,484	13,518,167	10,724,953	9,552,436	8,606,517
Labour %	30.83	34.4	43.21	40.67	35.19	28.99
Conservative seats	376	336	165	166	198	306
Conservative votes	13,760,935	14,093,007	9,600,943	8,357,615	8,784,715	10,703,654
Conservative %	42.3	41.9	30.69	31.7	32.36	36.05
Lib/Dem seats	22	20	46	52	62	57
Lib/Dem votes	7,341,651	5,999,606	5,242,947	4,814,321	5,985,454	6,836,248
Lib/Dem %	22.57	17.8	16.76	18.26	22.05	23.03
Others seats	23	24	30	28	31	29

Index

Bretwalda Books Ltd